Russia and the North

Russia and the North

Edited by
Elana Wilson Rowe

UNIVERSITY OF OTTAWA PRESS
Ottawa

The University of Ottawa Press acknowledges with gratitude the support extended
to its publishing list by Heritage Canada through its Book Publishing Industry
Development Program, by the Canada Council for the Arts, by the Canadian
Federation for the Humanities and Social Sciences through its Aid to Scholarly
Publications Program, by the Social Sciences and Humanities Research Council,
and by the University of Ottawa.

We also gratefully acknowledge
the Norwegian Institute of International Affairs (NUPI)
whose financial support has contributed to the publication of this book.

LIBRARY AND ARCHIVES CANADA
CATALOGUING IN PUBLICATION

Russia and the North / edited by Elana Wilson Rowe.

Includes bibliographical references and index.
ISBN 978-0-7766-0700-9

1. Russia, Northern—Politics and government. 2. Russia,
Northern—Economic conditions. 3. Russia, Northern—Environmental
conditions. 4. Russia, Northern—Social conditions. 5. Russia (Federation)—
Politics and government—1991-. 6. Russia (Federation)—Foreign relations.
7. Russia (Federation)—Military policy. I. Wilson Rowe, Elana, 1980-

JZ1616.R86 2009   320.947'090511   C2009-902895-6

Published by the University of Ottawa Press, 2009
542 King Edward Avenue
Ottawa, Ontario K1N 6N5
www.press.uottawa.ca

uOttawa

Contents

List of Contributors vii

List of Abbreviations xi

Introduction 1
Policy Aims and Political Realities in the Russian North
ELANA WILSON ROWE

Chapter One 17
Troublemaking and Risk-Taking:
The North in Russian Military Activities
PAVEL K. BAEV

Chapter Two 35
Cross-Border Cooperation in the North:
The Case of Northwest Russia
GEIR HØNNELAND

Chapter Three 53
Climate Change in the Russian North:
Threats Real and Potential
CRAIG ZUMBRUNNEN

Chapter Four 87
Recent Developments in the Russian Fisheries Sector
ANNE-KRISTIN JØRGENSEN

Chapter Five 107
Northern Offshore Oil and Gas Resources:
Policy Challenges and Approaches
ARILD MOE and ELANA WILSON ROWE

Chapter Six 129
Growth Poles and Ghost Towns in the Russian Far North
TIMOTHY HELENIAK

Chapter Seven 165
Indigenous Rights in the Russian North
INDRA ØVERLAND

Chapter Eight 187
Oil and Gas Development in Russia and
Northern Indigenous Peoples
ANNA A. SIRINA

Afterword 203
The Intersection of Northern and National Policies
ELANA WILSON ROWE

Index 211

List of Contributors

PAVEL K. BAEV is a research professor at the International Peace Research Institute, Oslo (PRIO); he is also affiliated with the Centre for the Study of Civil War at PRIO. After graduating from Moscow State University (M.A. in political geography, 1979), he worked in a research institute in the USSR Defense Ministry and then in the Institute of Europe, Moscow, before joining PRIO in October 1992. From 1995 to 2001 he was the editor of PRIO's quarterly journal, *Security Dialogue*. His research interests include the transformation of the Russian military, the dimension of energy within Russian-European relations and the post-Soviet conflicts in the Caucasus and the greater Caspian area. His latest book, *Russian Energy Policy and Military Power*, was published by Routledge, London, in 2008.

TIMOTHY HELENIAK is a faculty research associate in the Department of Geography at the University of Maryland. He has researched and written extensively on migration, regional development and demographic trends in Russia and the other countries of the former Soviet Union. He is currently working on a National Science Foundation grant, conducting research on migration and regional development in Siberia and the Russian Far North. He previously worked at the World Bank and the US Census Bureau, and was an adjunct professor at Georgetown University. During the 2001–2002 academic year, he was a research fellow at the Kennan Institute.

GEIR HØNNELAND holds a Ph.D. in political science from the University of Oslo and is the research director of the Fridtjof Nansen

Institute, Norway. He has published a number of articles and books on Russian environmental politics and international relations in the European North, among them *Russia and the West: Environmental Co-operation and Conflict* (Routledge, 2003); *Implementing International Environmental Agreements in Russia* (Manchester University Press, 2003) and *Russian Fisheries Management* (Brill, 2004). He has also co-edited *Tackling Space: Federal Politics and the Russian North* (University Press of America, 2006) and *International Cooperation and Arctic Governance* (Routledge, 2006).

ANNE-KRISTIN JØRGENSEN is a political scientist and a research fellow at the Fridtjof Nansen Institute, Norway. She has worked previously as the Counsellor for Fisheries at the Norwegian embassy in Moscow (2002–2006) and as an inspector for the Norwegian Coast Guard (1988–1995). She specializes in the management of natural resources, fisheries management in particular, and environmental issues in Northwestern Russia. Among her publications on these topics are *Implementing International Environmental Agreements in Russia* (Manchester University Press, 2003), and *Integration vs. Autonomy: Civil-Military Relations on the Kola Peninsula* (Ashgate, 1999).

ARILD MOE is presently the deputy director and a senior research fellow at the Fridtjof Nansen Institute, Norway. He has a cand.polit. degree from the University of Oslo with political science, Russian language and public law. His research interests include the Russian energy sector, in particular the oil and gas industry; the regional dimension in the Russian petroleum sector; offshore activities in the Barents Sea; Russian climate politics and oil companies and corporate social responsibility. He has also studied Arctic policy issues.

INDRA ØVERLAND has a Ph.D. from the Scott Polar Research Institute at the University of Cambridge, UK. He has worked on a broad range of issues related to energy, aid and indigenous peoples, focusing on the post-Soviet Arctic, the South Caucasus and Central Asia. He has extensive experience as a practitioner at the Norwegian Ministry of Local Government and Regional Development, the Norwegian Refugee Council and the Nordic Research Board, and is currently head of the Energy Programme at the Norwegian Institute of International Affairs.

ANNA A. SIRINA is a senior researcher at the Institute of Ethnology and Anthropology, Russian Academy of Sciences, Department of Siberian Studies. She holds a Ph.D. from the IEA RAS. Her main research interests are in cultural/social anthropology, cultural geography and the history of Russian anthropology. She has published a monograph and numerous articles, both in Russian and in English. Her main research interests are in cultural/social anthropology, cultural geography and the history of Siberian anthropology. In 2008 she was a guest editor of a special issue of the journal *Ethnografichesoe Obozrenie*, entitled "Ecology, Oil and Culture: An Anthropology of the Mining Industry".

ELANA WILSON ROWE is a senior research fellow at the Department for Russian and Eurasian Studies at the Norwegian Institute of International Affairs. She holds a Ph.D. from the Scott Polar Research Institute at the University of Cambridge, UK. She has worked on a broad range of issues relating to circumpolar and Russian politics, including climate change policy and the knowledge politics of international multilateral contexts. She is the co-editor of *The Multilateral Dimension in Russian Foreign Policy* (Routledge, 2009).

CRAIG ZUMBRUNNEN is a professor of geography at the University of Washington and a faculty member of the Jackson School of International Studies' Russian East European and Central Asian Studies program and Middle East Studies program. From 2000 to 2004 he served as co-director of the University of Washington's Program on the Environment and is a core faculty member of the University of Washington's interdisciplinary program in urban ecology. He received a Ph.D. in geography (1973) from the University of California at Berkeley and was a member of the geography department at Ohio State University from 1972 to 1977, before joining the geography department at the University of Washington. Since 1968 he has primarily focused on interdisciplinary research and field experience in the former Soviet Union, dealing with urban, natural resource management, energy, climate change and environmental pollution problems. His recent research has focused on combining his long-term interest in environmental problems in the former Soviet Union with international interdisciplinary team-based and problem-based research in urban ecology, sustainable development and information technology.

List of Abbreviations

AMEC	Arctic Military Environmental Cooperation
BCM	billion cubic metres
BEAC	Barents Euro-Arctic Council
BEAR	Barents Euro-Arctic Region
CDM	Clean Development Mechanism (Kyoto Protocol)
CFE	Conventional Forces in Europe
EEZ	Exclusive Economic Zone
EIA	environmental impact assessments
ESPO	Eastern Siberia-Pacific Ocean (pipeline)
EU	European Union
FDI	foreign direct investment
FSU	former Soviet Union
GCM	General Circulation Model
GHGs	greenhouse gases
ICES	International Council for the Exploration of the Sea
IET	international emissions trading
ILO	International Labour Organization
IPCC	Intergovernmental Panel on Climate Change
IPY	International Polar Year
JI	Joint Implementation (Kyoto Protocol)
LNG	liquefied natural gas
NATO	North Atlantic Treaty Organization
PSA	production-sharing agreement
RAIPON	Russian Association of Indigenous Peoples of the North

SSBN	ballistic missile submarine
TAC	total allowable catch
UN	United Nations
UNCLOS	UN Convention on the Law of the Sea
UNFCCC	United Nations Framework Convention on Climate Change and the Kyoto Protocol
VNIRO	Russian Federal Research Institute of Fisheries and Oceanography
WTO	World Trade Organization

Introduction

Policy Aims and Political Realities in the Russian North

Elana Wilson Rowe

T he chapters in this book examine key aspects of Russia's policy towards the North, both within its own borders and internationally. Focusing on the North is by no means a peripheral pursuit when it comes to Russian politics. The North (and so-called areas equivalent to the North) as it is defined today encompasses more than sixty percent of Russian territory and extends from a land border with Norway to a sea border with the United States (Strel'tsov 2007). Although only sparsely populated, with 11.5 million inhabitants counted in the 2002 census and even lower estimates given in 2008 (10.6 million), the North accounts for twenty percent of Russia's gross domestic product and twenty-two percent of all Russian exports (Ministry of Finance 2008). Russia also has a central role to play in the international politics of the North, being the largest Arctic state geographically and an important regional and global actor in energy markets that are increasingly looking northwards.

Russian engagement in the North, both domestically and internationally, plays out against a regional background of change. In contrast to the northern militarization that characterized the Cold War, the immediate post-Soviet years saw high levels of cooperation in the North on environmental, social and military issues. Today, the classic geopolitical interests of Arctic states are once again at the forefront as climate change and a growing demand for energy raise levels of concern and interest. The Kremlin's approach to northern politics evidences, as discussed in greater detail in the concluding chapter of this book, what I describe as a tension between the 'open' and the 'closed' North. In other words, northern policies often encompass both more outward oriented inclinations, exemplified by cross-border cooperation, as well as a tendency towards increasing securitization of northern issues and northern territory and defense of 'national northern interests.'

Unlike some other Arctic states (such as Canada and Norway), Russia does not have a unified strategy identifying broad economic and political aims and challenges for the North. Rather, Russia's northern policy is dispersed across a variety of fields, from domestic migration politics to energy policy. The aim of this book is to pick up on these threads of northern policy and to illustrate how the centralized, relatively economically strong and politically assertive Russia of today defines and addresses northern spaces, peoples, opportunities and challenges.

This introductory chapter identifies more broadly the central features, intervening variables and motivations shaping Russia's current 'northern policy,' which are examined in greater detail in the subsequent chapters. This chapter outlines historical and present approaches to the Russian North as a domestic space, examines some features of international cooperation in the North and then describes how Russia frames issues driving political attention to the North, namely northern military presence, climate change, hydrocarbons and disputed national claims at sea. The chapter concludes with an outline of the book.

Domestic Policy towards the Russian North

Historically, the question of the open versus the closed North is irrelevant—the North during the Soviet period was without a doubt a closed nationalized space. Long a homeland to a multitude of indigenous peoples, northern resources played an important part in the Soviet planned economy, and mastering/developing the North (*osvoenie severa*) played a corresponding role in Soviet ideology. The Soviet focus on the North positioned the Arctic firmly as a factor in both Russian national identity and conceptions of security and sovereignty (see Baev, this book; Blakkisrud 2006). This emphasis on the North, however, resulted in Russia inheriting from the Soviet Union an overpopulated North ill-suited to the logic of a market economy. Russian northern policy during the transitional 1990s could be described as haphazard and focused primarily on emergency measures to respond to economic and social crises in the region. Some areas (Chukotka, for example) experienced supply shortages equalling a humanitarian crisis, necessitating the involvement of organizations like the Red Cross.

Northern issues in the immediate post-Soviet years found a home in the State Committee on Northern Issues (Goskomsever). This committee, however, was not a stable one and in the seven years of its existence (1992–2000) it was disbanded and re-established six times. After 2000 the Ministry of Economic Development and Trade took on a central role in coordinating northern policy. The dissolution of the specific northern committee reflected the signals sent by Vladimir Putin that northern issues were to be handled via 'regular' channels not specific to the North (Blakkisrud 2006).

Although both the federal and regional governments continue to struggle with the chronic supply shortages that characterized the Yeltsin era ("Sever Vsegda Krainniy" 2005), the contours of a more clearly discernible Russian policy on the North emerged under then president Putin (2000–2008). As Blakkisrud (2006) argues in his comprehensive study of Russia's post-Soviet northern policy, this approach was initially based on principles of market economics with an eye towards ensuring that the North became a profitable part of the Russian state. A distinction was drawn between the 'profitable North' and the 'unprofitable North.' The profitable North—areas rich in hydrocarbons and minerals—should be further developed. Regions that can today be considered part of the profitable North are those with existing, developing or potential oil and gas output. Yamal-Nenets and Khanty-Mansi Autonomous Okrugs stand out as key producers, while Nenets Autonomous Okrug, Tomsk Oblast, the Komi Republic, the Sakha Republic, Irkutsk Oblast and the Evenk Autonomous Okrug are emerging as important players as well (Kryukov and Moe 2006). It is in these regions, as the final two chapters of this book attest, where the relationship between resource extraction companies, the state and indigenous peoples becomes increasingly complicated.

Meanwhile, the unprofitable North—areas dependent on federal support and without prospects for viable economic activity—is to be scaled down and the nonindigenous population are being encouraged to resettle. At present, one hundred small communities in Komi, Buryatia, Sakha, Magadan, Chukotka and the Nenets Autonomous Okrug are slated for closure (see Heleniak, this book). Despite gradually improving living conditions in the North as a whole, certain areas and populations continue to face environmental and social challenges. As

Gennady Oleynik, a representative to the Federation Council of the Russian Federation from Khanty-Mansiiysk Autonomous Okrug, ironically pointed out, the North attracted one-fifth of all foreign investment and paid forty-seven percent of all taxes collected by the Russian state in 2006, while life expectancy stagnates at ten years below the Russian average (Goble 2008; Federal'noe Sobranie 2007).

In thinking about policy change in the North, it is also essential to take into consideration the effects of Putin's recentralization of power on northern regions. The early days of the post-Soviet period were marked by a pronounced decentralization, with many formerly centrally held competencies being devolved to regional governments. Boris Yeltsin's federal treaty (March 1992) and the new Constitution (1993) stated that any competency not listed specifically as either a federal or a joint federal-regional competency fell within the mandate of regional government. During this period, resource-rich regional governments were able to exert increasing control over natural resource management, extraction and taxes (Blakkisrud and Hønneland 2006). Technically, subsoil development was considered a shared federal-regional competency, with the federal government leading with new initiatives and the regional government enjoying more involvement in proposal development and implementation. However, most regional governments took a more progressive role, many establishing their own oil and gas concerns and taking an active and influential interest in the negotiation of licences and monitoring of projects (Kryukov and Moe 2006).

Decentralization was replaced with recentralization after the change of presidency in 1999–2000. Putin's goal was to strengthen the executive vertical and to ensure that regional profits flowed into federal coffers and that federal policy was implemented. By 2004 the State Duma passed a revised law on subsoil resources that effectively returned mineral/subsurface resource management to the federal government. Consequently, one can say that this vast territory and all its resources are now governed from Moscow rather than Magadan or Murmansk.

At the same time as the Russian federal government has been working primarily to treat the North via 'normal channels' in Moscow, the importance of the North as a natural resource base has increased. From being on the brink of bankruptcy in 1998, Russia's economic recovery has been driven primarily by (and remains highly dependent on) high oil and gas prices. Many of the natural resources, which accounted for eighty percent of all Russian exports in 2007 (Denisov 2008; "Russia's Economy: Smoke and Mirrors" 2008), are to be found in the North. The region is once again a crucial factor in Russian economic development and was an important aspect of the political stance as an 'energy superpower' that emerged as central to Putin's presidency. While policy thinking on these important natural resources remains to an extent unconsolidated (see Moe and Wilson Rowe, this book), the resources of the Russian North and the Russian North itself have doubtless regained strategic importance.

There are recent signs that suggest that this strategic importance of the North is once again resulting in efforts to develop a regional holistic policy approach. In a recent press release from the Ministry of Finance, a new "governmental concept for support of the economic and social development of the Northern regions" is outlined (2008). The goal of this concept, which is included within the "Maritime Doctrines of the Russian Federation towards 2020", is to comprehensively examine Russian governmental interests and policy in the North and to outline programs to ensure state security and sustainable development in the North. Issues presently drawing Russian attention northwards, as cited in this press release, include sustainable development, the protection of borders (especially delineating boundaries of the Russian continental shelf), environmental protection, infrastructure, scientific questions, security issues and natural resources.

The International North

Since the end of the Cold War, the governments and peoples of the Arctic have increasingly engaged in a range of cooperative activities designed to address issues of shared concern and to raise the profile of the Arctic as a political and geographical region. The subsequent proliferation of activities aimed at promoting stable and ongoing cooperation in the High North has to do with the Arctic being a relatively secure source of nonrenewable resources (oil, gas and minerals), an awareness of the heightened impact of global environmental problems on the Arctic environment (such as global warming and transboundary pollutants) and the increased politicization of Arctic indigenous peoples (Keskitalo 2004; Stokke and Hønneland 2007; Tennberg 2000; Young 1992).

This focus on the North has led to the creation of several new international organizations and endeavours in the 1990s, such as the Arctic Council, the Barents Euro-Arctic Region and the Council of Baltic Sea States. Russian participation in the Arctic Council, for example, was sporadic during the economic downturn and political transition that marked the 1990s (Wilson Rowe 2009). Today, with a stronger economy and a more seasoned post-Soviet civil service, Russian participation is more consistent. In terms of the Barents cooperation, Hønneland (this book) notes that the results are mixed. While one can point to success on the level of people-to-people exchange and health initiatives, little progress has been made in terms of developing and implementing a shared and enduring political and economic agenda in the European North. Progress within the Barents cooperation, perhaps especially on more important political and economic issues, is hampered by Russian suspicion that the multilateral forum, as well as other forms of cross-border cooperation, has been an avenue for Norwegian and other Nordic counterparts to pursue their interests at the expense of a 'weakened' post-Soviet Russia.

Overall, Russia is not an active agenda setter in these forums and Russian involvement in and objectives for the forums remains overwhelmingly oriented towards the safest zones of low political cooperation. One example of the often rather successful 'low politics' cooperation that can be achieved with Russian partners on nonstrategic issues in the North is that of access to the Russian Arctic under the auspices of the International Polar Year (IPY) that ran from 2006 to 2008. At an October 2005 Senior Arctic Official meeting within the high-level intergovernmental meetings that characterize the Arctic Council, a Swedish representative expressed concern over the high tariffs charged by Russia for icebreaker services in the Northern Sea route, even for endeavours involving scientific research for IPY. By the closing ministerial in October 2006, the Russian explorer and Duma representative Artur Chilingarov could report in his statement that icebreaker fees would be reduced by fifty percent for IPY research activities (Wilson Rowe 2009).

Russian representatives to these forums abstemiously avoid issues that may seem to be of greater strategic (security, foreign policy, economic) importance. Problematically for Arctic cooperation, it seems that environmental problems, once the mainstay of much of this cooperation, are now being reclassified as strategic and are therefore less open for cross-border cooperation now than in the 1990s (Wilson Rowe 2009).

Other reasons for the rather low-key Russian engagement overall may be that these Arctic multilateral settings are not seen as prestigious forums in which Russian national interest should be pursued, and that Russians are skeptical about the possibility of achieving desirable outcomes in any multilateral setting (Wilson Rowe and Torjesen, 2009).

While multilateral forums seem to serve a purpose in dealing with issues that manage to stay on the low political agenda, the North is confronted with a number of issues increasingly perceived of as cutting to the heart of central state interests of sovereignty, security and access to natural resource wealth. That northern multilateral forums have been more or less explicitly constructed to exclude such politically problematic issues (Wilson and Øverland 2007) raises the question of in which type of forum and in what manner Russia and other northern states will pursue their newly 'regeopoliticized' northern interests.

Northern Concerns

Globally, the strategic significance assigned to the North by a number of circumpolar states has once again grown, in part because the region is argued to hold twenty-five percent of the world's undiscovered petroleum reserves and because climate change is rendering the northern icescape less predictable in the short term and more open in the long term. Such changes in sea ice are bringing unresolved questions of national jurisdiction to the fore. As Borgerson (2008) argues in an article that points to a number of important challenges facing governance of the North (although arguably overplaying the Russian threat), "the Arctic region is not governed by any comprehensive multilateral norms and regulations because it was never expected to become a navigable waterway or a site for large-scale commercial development." The 1982 UN Convention on the Law of the Sea (UNCLOS) is the most relevant regime for resolving maritime boundary disputes and allocating responsibility in the North, but even this regime applies only partially to the complex Arctic basin picture (see Baev, this book, for more detail).

Military Presence

Russia's growing attention to the geopolitics of the Arctic has been occasionally accompanied by a rhetoric of and, to some extent, actual increase of northern military presence to "protect Russian national interests" in hydrocarbons, shipping, fisheries and territorial claims (see, for example, Kramnik 2008). It is, however, worth noting that these plans remain, on the whole, very vague. In his overall assessment of Russia's military capacity, with a particular focus on the North, Baev (this book) argues along the same lines that "the all too apparent weaknesses in Russia's strategic posture make it senseless to consider relaunching a military brinkmanship in the North, in which Moscow would hardly be able to impress its potential competitors". At the same time, Baev notes that the resumption of Russian Arctic military activity does pose a threat of accidents and raises safety issues, as the Northern (naval) fleet is "called upon to demonstrate its usefulness in every possible way", with an emphasis on solo Russian military heroics rather than international security cooperation.

Climate Change

While the consequences of global climate change contribute to an increasingly uncertain geopolitical picture in the North, which is of concern to many states, it remains unclear how embedded international consensus understandings of climate change are in Russian policy-making circles. As ZumBrunnen notes in his chapter in this book, Russia ratified the Kyoto Protocol to the United Nations Framework Convention on Climate Change—a partially global mechanism designed to address climate change via setting limits to greenhouse gas emissions—in November 2004. The decision to ratify was based primarily on the consideration of economic benefits that could flow from ratification as, due to a marked decrease in industrial production during the dissolution of the Soviet Union, Russia's greenhouse gas outputs declined significantly. This placed Russia favourably in relation to the potentially economically beneficial carbon trading mechanism of the Kyoto Protocol. Since then, Russian politicians and policy-makers have expressed doubts about the causes and impacts of climate change.

Arctic Oil and Gas

The increased geopolitical tension in the Arctic also has to do with a growing reference to the region as one of the keys to future global energy security. While the actual amount of Arctic petroleum remains speculative, with little actual exploration, the US Geological Survey estimates that twenty-five percent of the world's remaining undiscovered petroleum resources may be located in the Arctic. Rising global demand for oil and gas, in tandem with the related phenomenon of climate change, render the Arctic an important feature of future oil and gas production. Already today the Arctic produces about one-tenth of the world's crude oil and a quarter of its gas. Of this, eighty percent of the oil and ninety-nine percent of the gas come from Russia (AMAP 2008).

The tension between the tendencies of international cooperation and national control is clearly manifest in debates around the development of Russia's northern hydrocarbons. Since 2005 there has been growing attention paid to the question of how to promote private investment (both Russian and foreign), while maintaining control over Russian natural resource assets defined as 'strategic.' The evolving regime, although to a large extent still marked by unconsolidated policy-thinking (see Moe and Wilson Rowe, this book), limits investment in certain strategic fields (including the entire offshore) to companies with a minimum of fifty-one percent Russian ownership, with the Russian side ideally represented by the state-controlled companies Gazprom or Rosneft (Perovic and Orrtung 2007).

Maritime Claims

In terms of shoring up national claims about northern maritime rights, several circumpolar states have reinforced their northern presence via military means and scientific research. The August 2007 planting of a Russian flag on the seabed at the North Pole is a vivid example of such attempts to stake out—if only symbolically—such a claim. The Russian expedition consisted of a nuclear icebreaker and a research ship. Upon reaching the North Pole, these vessels sent two submersibles to the seabed to take soil samples, meant to support Russia's claims about the boundaries of its continental shelf to UNCLOS, and to plant a Russian flag (which was in many ways a gesture towards domestic, rather than international, audiences as Baev attests in this book).

Russia had previously submitted a petition to the UN Commission on the Limits of the Continental Shelf in 2002, which was put on hold due to insufficient scientific evidence. In the Soviet period, a huge sector covering about one-third of the Arctic Ocean was designated as Soviet territorial waters. Russia's claim today to UNCLOS is similar in geographic proportions and advanced on the assertion that the Mendeleev and Lomonosov underwater ridges are a continuation of the continental shelf. The Arctic 2007 expedition team aimed to confirm Russian claims to over one million square kilometres of the Arctic shelf, which may contain nine to ten billion cubic metres of hydrocarbons according to Russian estimates (ITAR-TASS 2007). This is important as, according to UNCLOS, a country's economic zone at sea may be extended only if the boundaries of the continental shelf go beyond the standard two-hundred-mile economic zone.

This symbolically resonant scientific expedition certainly highlights the role that science has played and continues to play in evidencing state presence and sovereignty in the North (Bravo and Sörlin 2002). As expedition leader (and politician) Artur Chilingarov stated plainly. "It is no secret that polar countries are trying to make the Arctic an international resource. We, however, must make it plain to the global community that we will not give up our interests in the Arctic" ("Arctic Spring Fever" 2008). At the political level, both then President Putin and Foreign Minister Sergei Lavrov lauded the effort and claims made for Russia. However, both assiduously emphasized that all such claims had to be settled in the appropriate international settings. These statements, plus the fact that the expedition team was actually international (involving one Swede and one Australian as team members), says much about the complex intertwining of nationalism and internationalism in the Russian North.

Structure of the Book

The beginning chapters of the book examine foreign and security policy in the Russian North. In Chapter One, Pavel Baev outlines how the North figures into Russian security policy and examines the northern implications of Russia's recent emphasis on rebuilding the military complex, including the plans and programs for modernizing Long Range Aviation and the Northern Fleet. In Chapter Two, issues of bilateral cooperation (Norwegian-Russian cooperation in fisheries, environmental protection and nuclear safety) and Arctic regionalization (with a particular focus on the Barents Euro-Arctic Cooperation) are taken up by Geir Hønneland. In Chapter Three, the question of climate change is explored, with both its potential domestic and international policy challenges outlined. Craig ZumBrunnen summarizes overall climate change impacts on Russia, highlights ways in which climate change is already affecting the human and physical landscapes of the Russian North and Far East and outlines Russian positions on the international level, especially in relationship to the Kyoto Protocol.

Later on in the book, natural resource policy-making around two features of the northern political economy—hydrocarbons and fish—are examined. In Chapter Four, Anne-Kristin Jørgensen examines the performance of the Russian fisheries in the post-Soviet period, detailing challenges and conflicts, as well as the most recent cycle of reforms designed to ensure that the fisheries sector will be economically viable in a market structure. This chapter identifies a kind of tug-of-war between traditionalists and modernizers over this important northern economic sector and highlights an important caveat—that even the most high-priority political initiatives can die a bureaucratic death. In Chapter Five, Arild Moe and Elana Wilson Rowe place northern offshore petroleum development in the context of overall Russian energy priorities and examine how the tension between strategic and market concerns plays out in relation to offshore oil and gas development.

Next, the book looks at the social politics of the domestic North in an examination of both demographic and indigenous rights policies and practices. Timothy Heleniak, in Chapter Six, analyzes changes in population and migration patterns in the Russian North, using data from the 1989 and 2002 censuses, and outlines the structure and perceived effectiveness of federal policy responses, including new approaches to labour management. Heleniak characterizes post-Soviet northern demographic change as shrivelling, with some key areas of population growth appearing along with areas (especially in the Far East) of steep demographic decline. Consequently, he argues that one must think of the North as a constellation of many different geographic spaces— rather than a single block—as there are clearly different demographic destinies for various different parts.

Indra Øverland, in Chapter Seven, presents an overview of the rights of Russia's northern indigenous peoples (who have historically inhabited more than half of the territory of today's Russia) and compares the legislative regime to international standards, pointing to both points of convergence and divergence. While important in and of themselves, the extent to which indigenous peoples' rights are protected has much to say about "Russia's transition from a 19th-century empire to a 21st-century state, a transition that is particularly complex because of the intervening decades under Communist rule" (Øverland, this book). In Chapter Eight, the final chapter of this book, Anna Sirina takes the question of indigenous peoples' rights within Russia one step further with a study of how these rights are implemented in practice, particularly when weighted against the economically and politically significant oil and gas sector. This study is developed via both a broad overview, as well as an in-depth case study of the interface between indigenous rights and livelihoods and the development of the Eastern Siberia-Pacific Ocean Pipeline project.

Finally, the book closes with a brief afterword that places the key findings about northern policy brought out in the preceding chapters in the context of broader Russian national and international politics and ambitions.

NOTES

1. The definition of 'the North' continues to change, with statistics on the North sometimes encompassing only those Northern territories falling fully within the Arctic, such as the Russian Ministry of Finance's recent report citing that the northern population was only one million persons, of which 136,000 were indigenous (Ministry of Finance 2008).

2. Norway's northern strategy is articulated in a document, "Regjeringens nordområdestrategi", produced by the Ministry of Foreign Affairs [http://www.regjeringen.no/Upload/SMK/Vedlegg/Rapporter/302927-nstrategi06.pdf]. Canada's northern strategy is at present still under development, although plans are to release it shortly [http://www.northernstrategy.ca/].

3. At the same time, the North certainly remains undeveloped in relationship to other parts of Russia. For example, the amount of roads in the North is ten to fifteen times lower than the Russian average. It is also worth noting the geographic variation the North encompasses. Out of all the roads in the North, the majority are in the European Arctic (where that number is still eight times lower than the rest of Russia). See Strel'tsov (2007) for more detail.

4. See the Federal'noe Sobranie's v 2006 godu (2007) for an in-depth comparison of the economies of various Russian northern districts.

5. The North in the context of such broader political trends is a topic that is returned to in the afterword of this book.

6. 'High politics' is usually defined as involving questions of war and peace, foreign affairs, defense and domestic security, while 'low politics' concerns social and financial issues (Trenin and Lo 2005).

7. For example, in a 2005 press conference, Putin's economic advisor Andrei Illarionov stated that the "theory of global warming is not borne out by scientific data and is, strictly speaking, charlatanism" ("Johnson's Russia List 9169," available online at [http://www.cdi.org/russia/johnson/9169-18.cfm] [consulted 15 May 2006]). More recently at a conference on the Kyoto Protocol, Sergei Mironov, the pro-Kremlin speaker in the federation council, argued that carbon emissions did not affect the climate and, if anything, resulted in global cooling (*Moscow Times*, 28 May 2007).

REFERENCES

AMAP (Arctic Monitoring and Assessment Programme). 2008. "Oil and Gas Assessment 2007." [http://www.amap.no/oga/] [consulted 1 July 2008].

"Arctic Spring Fever." 28 April 2008. RIA Novosti.

Blakkisrud, Helge. 2006. "What's to Be Done with the North?" In *In Tackling Space: Federal Politics and the Russian North*, ed. Helge Blakkisrud and Geir Hønneland. Lanham, MD: University Press of America.

Blakkisrud, Helge, and Geir Hønneland. 2006. "The Russian North—An Introduction." In *Tackling Space: Federal Politics and the Russian North*, ed. Helge Blakkisrud and Geir Hønneland. Lanham, MD: University Press of America.

Borgerson, Scott. March/April 2008. "Arctic Meltdown: The Economic and Security Implications of Global Warming." *Foreign Affairs*, 63–77.

Bravo, Michael, and Sverker Sörlin. 2002. "Narrative and Practice—An Introduction." In *Narrating the Arctic: A Cultural History of Nordic Scientific Practices*, ed. Michael Bravo and Sverker Sörlin. Canton, MA: Science History Publications.

Denisov, Andrey. 29 February 2008. "Russia's Economic Minister Nabiullina Interviewed on Policy Issues." *Vremya Novostei*.

Federal'noe Sobranie Rossiiskoi Federatzii: Apparat Komiteta Soveta Federatzii po delam severa I molochislennikh narodov. May 2007. "Informatzionno-Analiticheskaya Spravka o sotzial'no-ekonomicheskom polojenii sub'ektov Rosskiiskoi Federatzii polnos'yu ili chastichno otnecennikh k severniym raionam v 2006 godu" (2006 informational-analytical guide to the social-economic situation of federal subjects fully or partly belonging to the northern regions). [http://www.severcom.ru/analytics] [consulted 1 July 2008].

Goble, Paul. 22 January 2008. "Russian North Deserves Better Treatment and More Respect." Window on Eurasia Blogspot. [http://windowoneurasia.blogspot.com/2008/01/window-on-eurasia-russian-north.html] [consulted 1 March 2008].

ITAR-TASS. 30 October 2007. "Russia to Apply for Arctic Shelf Development by Year End."

Keskitalo, ECH. 2004. *Negotiating the Arctic: The Construction of an International Region*. New York: Routledge.

Kramnik, Ilya. 14 May 2008. "Reaching out in the Arctic: RIA Novosti Military Commentator." *RIA Novosti*.

Kryukov, Valeriy, and Arild Moe. 2006. "Hydrocarbon Resources and Northern Development." In *Tackling Space: Federal Politics and the Russian North*, ed. Helge Blakkisrud and Geir Hønneland. Lanham, MD: University Press of America.

Perovic, J., and R. Orrtung. 2007. "Russia's Energy Policy: Should Europe Worry?" *Russia Analytical Digest* 18: 2–7.

"Russia's Economy: Smoke and Mirrors." 1–7 March 2008. *The Economist*.

Russian Federation. Ministry of Finance. 2008. "Ofitzial'naya informatziya k sasedaniyu Pravitel'stva Rossiiskoi Federatzii 2 aprel'ya 2008" (Press release: Official information for the meeting of the government of the Russian Federation). [http://www1.minfin.ru/ru/official/index.phpid4=6040] [consulted 1 May 2008].

"Sever Vsegda Krainniy" (The North is always on the edge). December 2005. Gazeta.ru. [http://www.gazeta.ru/comments/2005/08/12_e_353572.shtml?print] [consulted 1 January 2006].

Stokke, Olav, and Geir Hønneland, eds. 2007. *International Cooperation and Arctic Governance: Regime Effectiveness and Northern Region Building*. London: Routledge.

Strel'tsov, Y. 2007. Federal'noe Sobranoe Rossiskoy Federatzii: Apparat Komiteta Soveta Federatzii po delam severa i molochislennikh narodov. "O sostayanii seti avtomobil'nikh dorog v rainoakh v svete realizatzii zadach, postavlennikh v Poslanii Prezidenta Rossiiskoi Federatzii Federal'nomy Sobraniyu Rossiiskoi Federatzii na 2007 god (informatzionno-analiticheskaya zapiska)" (Federation Council of the Russian Federation: Committee on Northern Issues and Indigenous Peoples. On the condition of the automobile road network in the regions in light of realization of the tasks set by the administration of the president of the Russian Federation for the Federation Council of the Russian Federation for 2007). [http://www.severcom.ru/analytics] [consulted 1 July 2008].

Tennberg, Monica. 2000. *Arctic Environmental Cooperation: A Study in Governmentality*. Aldershot, UK: Ashgate.

Trenin, Dmitry, and Bobo Lo. *The Landscape of Russian Foreign Policy Decision-Making*. Moscow: Carnegie Moscow Centre.

Wilson, Elana, and Indra Øverland. 2007. "Indigenous Issues." In *International Cooperation and Arctic Governance: Regime Effectiveness and Northern Region Building*, ed. Olav Schram Stokke and Geir Honneland. London: Routledge.

Wilson Rowe, E. 2009. "Russian Regional Multilateralism: The Case of the Arctic Council." In *The Multilateral Dimension of Russian Foreign Policy*, ed. Elana Wilson Rowe and Stina Torjesen. London: Routledge.

Wilson Rowe, E., and S. Torjesen. 2009. "Key Features of Russian Multilateralism." In *The Multilateral Dimension of Russian Foreign Policy*, ed. Elana Wilson Rowe and Stina Torjesen. London: Routledge.

Young, Oran. 1992. *Arctic Politics: Conflict and Cooperation in the Circumpolar North*. London: University of New England Press.

Chapter One

Troublemaking and Risk-Taking: The North in Russian Military Activities

Pavel K. Baev

Introduction

The second half of 2007 registered an unprecedented upsurge of international attention to an area that had long drifted into a political limbo and was only briefly lifted from it in the early 1990s with the launch of the Barents Initiative.[1] The main drivers of this gain in priority have been climate change (perhaps the hottest political issue of that year) and the steady climb in oil prices. The immediate trigger, however, was provided by a Russian expedition that managed to plant the national flag on the seabed, close to the geographic North Pole. Russia is also chiefly responsible for the distinct security twist of the international debates that came out in the recent European Union report co-authored by Solava and Ferrero-Waldner (2008: 8): "The increased accessibility of the enormous hydrocarbon resources in the Arctic region is changing the geo-strategic dynamics of the region with potential consequences for international stability and European security interests."

The history of Russia's exploration of the Arctic, rich and heroic as it is, does not figure significantly in the current political discourse, which aims mostly at reversing the 'retreats' of the 1990s and disproving the perception of abandoned periphery. It is, nevertheless, useful to reflect upon the historically prominent military dimension in Russia's 'conquest' of the High North. Most expeditions in the 18th to 19th centuries were organized by the admiralty with geopolitical rather than commercial interests in mind, and the sale of Alaska in 1867, which is now typically resented as discarding a key asset, was determined primarily by the shock of discovering the scale of Russia's political isolation and military vulnerability in the Crimean War. It was World War I that demonstrated the value of ice-free ports on the Kola Peninsula for maintaining a secure line of communication to the Entente allies, but the British intervention in the Archangel region also informed Moscow about military risks on this flank. The newly born Soviet Union managed to assert its sovereignty over Wrangel Island by terminating the Canadian attempt at establishing a settlement, but since the mid-1930s, the pattern of developing the northern areas acquired a tragic and grim character as the camps of the Gulag 'archipelago' became the main centres of activity (see Heleniak, this book, for more on Arctic settlement patterns).

World War II reconfirmed the vital importance of the Arctic lines of maritime communications and provided a strong impetus for strengthening the Soviet Northern Fleet. A whole new level of militarization, however, was reached with the start of the nuclear era, as the High North was turned into the main theatre of strategic confrontation between the United States and the Soviet Union. According to the Soviet Union's vision and planning, the development of Arctic regions, besides building on the legacy of Stalin's camps, was strictly subordinated to its military-strategic aims, and it was only the end of the Cold War that instantly destroyed that rationale, leaving the massive infrastructure to decay and rot.

Today's 'securitization' of a complex agenda that includes mostly entries requiring international cooperation (like exploration and navigation, environment protection and tourism) is caused primarily by deadlocked border disputes and overlapping territorial/maritime claims. While traditionally these 'conflicts' have been a matter of low-profile diplomatic bickering, Moscow's new penchant for aggressive foreign policy rhetoric, manifested particularly by President Vladimir Putin's Munich speech, has given them new intensity.[2] Rhetoric in itself would have perhaps made only a temporary impression, and indeed the reconfiguration of political leadership in Russia in spring 2008 has brought a noticeable softening of tone, including Putin's unimpressive performance at the April 2008 NATO (North Atlantic Treaty Organization) summit in Bucharest.[3] The significant increase in Russia's military activities in the North, however, could be an altogether different matter. Taking this as a working assumption, this chapter aims at assessing the impact of these activities and outlining the near-term prospects of building military capabilities by the largest (in geographic terms) Arctic power. It starts with a brief evaluation of the security dimension in Russian geopolitical perspectives on the Arctic, then examines the current status and the programs for modernization of the Long-Range Aviation and the Northern Fleet, and concludes with an appraisal of the interplay between energy and security developments in the North.

Moscow's Northern Geopolitics and the Drift to a 'Cold War-Lite'

The question about whether a new Cold War between Russia and NATO has already started has been raised in the Western media so many times since Putin's Munich *démarche* that neither a straightforward nor a more elaborate negative answer appears sufficient to provide a convincing reassurance.[4] Indeed, the stream of official statements from Moscow about the 'direct threat to national security' coming from NATO enlargement and from the US strategic assets to be deployed in Poland and the Czech Republic has barely slackened since May 2008, and it does imply the return to strategic confrontation. The unspecified accusations—recycled from one of Putin's speeches to another that have now been picked up by Dmitri Medvedev—against those who are irritated by Russia's "rising from its knees" and so try to tear from it some "juicy morsels", are eagerly elaborated by 'patriotic thinkers,' all the way to the proposition for building a 'Fortress Russia.'[5]

There is certainly plenty of inconsistency in these anti-NATO and anti-US invectives. In expressing his disappointments and reservations, former President Putin was always careful to keep the essential channels of cooperation open, while his hand-picked successor, Medvedev, has so far stayed clear of any controversies (Baev 2008b). What is important to emphasize here, however, is the geographic spread of the revived perceptions of 'encirclement' that now stretch from the US Manas air base in Kyrgyzstan to the Baltic states, where a squadron of fighters from one of the NATO states is regularly 'visiting.' In this 'arc,' the premonitions about the failure of the coalition operation in Afghanistan overlap with fantasies about the 'Great Game' in the Caspian area, and the spiralling tensions with Georgia resonate with Ukrainian squabbles and quarrels with the Baltic states. The North, however, is essentially absent from this picture of real and imagined threats and opportunities. This lack of strategic attention remains striking even when explanations regarding the reactive nature of Russia's policies and Finland's pronounced reluctance to contemplate an application to NATO are lined up together.

The sharp disagreements around the Conventional Forces in Europe (CFE) treaty (1990–1999), from which Russia has unilaterally withdrawn since December 2007, provide one illustration of this phenomenon.[6] Putin's objections, spelled out in his 2007 address to the Federal Assembly and reiterated at the Bucharest summit, are centred on the fact that NATO countries have not ratified the treaty and that the Baltic trio has refused to accede to it after joining the alliance. The real problem, which is only slightly covered by these arguments, is that Russia has increased its forces in the North Caucasus Military District beyond the "flank limits" (or "territorial ceilings") as stipulated by the revised version of the CFE; hence the portentous rejection of these "colonial provisions" (Litovkin 2007). What is peculiar about this apparently irresolvable dispute is that Moscow has raised no objections against the flank limits in the northern flank, where it is technically at great disadvantage vis-à-vis NATO, and has shown no intention of strengthening its downgraded grouping of forces in the Leningrad Military District.[7]

This relatively benign northern perspective was altered in the summer of 2007, not so much by the flag-planting expedition as by the resumption of flights by the strategic bombers of the 37th Air Army over the Arctic.[8] As described below, that 'breakthrough' did not really amount to much and was driven by an entirely unstrategic rationale, yet portrayed as a means to secure Russia's maritime interests. It is significant, nevertheless, that even in adopting the 'realist' paradigm that predicted brutal competition for the 'no man's shelf' and for access to resources, Moscow has stuck to a strictly legally correct and diplomatically impeccable approach.[9] There have been no attempts to 'securitize' the maritime border disputes with Norway in the Barents Sea and with the US in the Chukchi Sea; the main focus of Russia's policy has been the claim for extending its control over the continental shelf beyond the two hundred nautical miles as stipulated by the Law of the Sea Convention, which it ratified in February 1997. This claim was first submitted to the UN (United Nations) Commission on the Limits of the Continental Shelf in late 2001 (without any brouhaha), but it was turned down due to insufficient scientific data. Russia has been duly collecting the missing data since then, preparing to resubmit the claim, which is yet to be done as of spring 2009.[10] The risky experiment that entailed launching two submersibles at the North Pole did not yield any valuable scientific results, but its colossal 'patriotic' resonance has in fact seriously compromised the integrity of Russian research and made the approval of the claim very problematic.

The 1.2 million km² of Arctic shelf that Russia wants to add to its vast inventory are not claimed by any other country (except the very pinnacle of the North Pole), so in principle its application is not that controversial, but the 'securitization' of the maritime agenda definitely works against the normal legal resolution of the issue. Moscow may appear to have undermined its own position, which in itself is not that unusual, but in this case, the northern campaign quite probably serves other more current political purposes than just winning the essentially unusable underwater territories. The patriotic propaganda, combining stories of 'heroic' exploration with the advertising of military muscle-building, is aimed at creating a positive message pertaining to the very core of the still vague Russian national identity, very much along the same lines as Stalin's 'conquest of the North' (*pokorenie severa*) campaign in the late 1930s.[11] Russia's emphasis on military activities serves the additional purpose of providing a boost to the top brass, thus securing their noninterference in the delicate process of reformatting the presidential power, a process that continues at the time of this writing (Litovkin 2008; Baev 2008c).

Strategic Aviation Gives It Its Best Shot

The main instrument for demonstrating Russia's renewed attention to, and restored military capabilities in, the northern theatre has been, rather improbably, the Long-Range Aviation—traditionally the weakest leg in the strategic triad. Unlike other strategic forces, the 37th Air Army managed to muddle through the lean years of the 1990s without heavy losses; it even managed to increase its assets by securing the return of bombers from Kazakhstan and Ukraine (eight modern Tu-160 were returned in 1999). President Putin did not pay much attention to this force until August 2005, when he took a long flight on a Tu-160 bomber and observed the launch of long-range cruise missiles, which apparently convinced him of the high demonstrative value, if not operational efficiency, of the Strategic Aviation. The funding of this army was substantially increased and, unlike the other strategic forces, it was earmarked for maintenance and training. Meanwhile, funds for development and production of new weapon systems were channelled through different agencies, so there were no funding cuts due to pressing needs after unsuccessful tests. In fact, only one Tu-160 bomber has been, after many delays, assembled at the Kazan air factory (mostly from parts produced back in the 1980s) and delivered in April 2008 to the 121st Guards Heavy Bomber Regiment based in Engels, Saratov Oblast.[12] There are only sixteen of these planes in the fleet of eighty bombers, the rest being the Tu-95MS (*Bear* H), produced in the 1970s and 1980s, based on the design from the early 1960s.

The much improved maintenance of the planes and training of the crews provided President Putin with an opportunity to announce with great fanfare that regular flights would resume outside Russian airspace (flights that had been discontinued in 1991). He probably overplayed this opportunity when he chose to use strong words to describe the training flights ("These patrols are strategic in nature"), which made it necessary for the command of the Long-Range Aviation to clarify that the bombers would carry no nuclear weapons and, in fact, no weapons at all (Golts 2007). Nevertheless, the flights that have been performed about once a month since then have attracted much international attention, particularly when a pair of Tu-160s made an approach towards Noordwijk, the Netherlands, where NATO defense ministers were holding a meeting on 25 October 2007.

The flights have been conducted in both Pacific and Atlantic directions (and sometimes over the Black Sea as well); the significant difference between them being that Russia's access to the former from the Ukrainka air base (Khabarovsk krai) is wide open, while the latter can only be reached via Arctic airspace. That has created a new challenging task for the air forces of the Northern European states; for that matter, the British RAF (Royal Air Force) conducted twenty-one intercepts of Russian bombers from July 2007 to April 2008 ("RAF 'Intercepted Russian Planes'" 2008).[13] The Russian bombers have been careful to avoid violations of national airspace (one incident in Japanese airspace was registered in February 2008) and do not make hard targets for intercepting, particularly as far as the slow-moving *Bears* are concerned. While the Russian High Command often emphasizes the importance of these flights for securing national interests in the Arctic, the bombers have no value in naval operations, since their standard armament, long-range cruise missiles, could be used only against stationary targets on land.[14]

The real risk in these 'patrols' comes from the high probability of technical failure, particularly during complicated maneuvers like refuelling. As of early 2009, there have been no serious accidents since September 2003, when Tu-160 exploded in the air with the loss of all of its crew, yet the pressure of long-range flights inevitably takes its toll.[15] The reactivation of several air bases in the Far North (Anadyr, Monchegorsk, Olenya, Tiksi, Vorkuta), while strategically important, constitutes another source of risk, as they could provide only the most basic services. History can supply a meaningful warning in this respect as Stalin's penchant for strategic flights over the Arctic was cut short by the tragic disappearance of his favourite flying ace, Sigizmund Levanevsky, and the crew of five in the brand new DB-A in August 1937.[16]

The Navy Keeps Up Pretenses

While the Long-Range Aviation has grabbed much attention since the summer of 2007 with its periodic appearances, the main permanent factor in the securitization of the Arctic agenda is still the Northern Fleet. It has held pivotal importance in the Soviet Navy since 1956, when the first diesel submarine with ballistic missiles entered service. At the peak of its strength in the mid-1980s, it included some 170 submarines (of which forty-five were strategic nuclear cruisers armed with ballistic missiles, SSBN [ballistic missile submarine]) and fifty major surface combatants that were supposed to form an impregnable bastion in the Barents Sea.[17]

The post-Soviet period has seen a dramatic decline of the Northern Fleet, which currently has some thirty submarines (of which nine are SSBNs) and twenty major surface combatants in various state of disrepair. It was not in any way involved in the celebrated flag-planting expedition in 2007 (the explorers complained that US spy planes were following its progress), but its underwater cartography is crucial for preparing the claim for expanding the territorial shelf. Securing Russia's maritime interests is one of the key arguments used by the navy command in demanding more funds and resources. However, this proposition does not correspond to the firmly set priority of modernizing the strategic arsenal of the navy, first of all the SSBN squadrons that are deployed with the Northern and Pacific fleets.[18]

The beginning of Putin's era was marked by a horrible tragedy in the Northern Fleet that claimed the brand new nuclear submarine *Kursk* and all of its crew. This tragedy made the commander-in-chief aware of the accumulated problems in the navy and added to their resolution. This commitment was formalized in the Naval Doctrine approved in mid-2001, but its ambitious guidelines were entirely detached from the budget and operational realities (Baev 2002). Putin was scandalized by the double failure to launch missiles at the Northern Fleet presidential exercises in February 2004 ("Missile Failures Mar Putin's Show" 2004), and he ordered that the fleet concentrate its efforts and resources on the construction of *Yuri Dolgoruky*, the pilot new-generation SSBN, perhaps imagining the launch of this leviathan as one of the high points marking the end of his presidency. This was not to happen as the *Bulava*, the new ballistic missile that became Putin's pet project, has shown poor results in tests and is not expected to be ready before 2012. So, the submarine in the years to come would remain accountable under the arms control agreements (since the launch tubes are operational) but unarmed (since no other missile fits its tubes).[19]

This setback, while politically embarrassing, is not catastrophic for the navy, as it still has six *Delta*-IV submarines that are one after another undergoing overhauls and have been re-armed with the *Sineva* missiles (the SSBN *Tula* of the Northern Fleet is the first one with a full complement of these missiles). At the same time, as the six *Delta*-III submarines have to be decommissioned in the next few years, a serious reduction in the strength of the naval deterrent appears unavoidable, and the Pacific Fleet might find itself without a single strategic submarine. For that matter, the number of strategic submarine patrols in 2007 was down to three from five in 2006 (Norris and Kristensen 2008). Overall, the strategic element of the navy demands and consumes a lion's share of funding, with very little to show for it.

At the same time, the conventional naval forces are struggling with underfunding and logistical shortages and are often called upon to 'show the flag,' since the demonstrations by the strategic submarines are far from impressive. Hence, the order to the flagship of the Northern Fleet aircraft carrier *Admiral Kuznetsov* to depart for Atlantic exercises in early December 2007, which was a bad season for training but the right moment to gain some political dividends (Aleksandrov 2008). The training 'cruise' was very successful. After extensive repairs, Kuznetsov and the nuclear cruiser Petr Veliky made another long cruise in autumn 2008 but the continuation of this pattern is barely possible due to the shortage of basic infrastructure, including docking and repair facilities, always the Achilles heel of the Northern Fleet.

The shipbuilding programs that have been scaled down towards smaller ships, like the *Steregushchy* corvettes, are reporting delays and overspending, which shows that wishful Gorshkov-school thinking evolves into a totally surrealistic perspective painted in the official statements about the plans for deploying five to six aircraft carriers in the Northern and Pacific Fleets.[20] Visiting Murmansk on his campaign trail in January 2008, Medvedev explained that the Navy had no ships to support the fishermen who were frequently "harassed" by the Norwegian Coast Guard. The situation was unlikely to improve anytime soon, although already in April 2008, Admiral Vysotsky promised to provide "psychological support" to fishermen in the Spitzbergen area (Farizova 2008; "Navy Will Provide" 2008). Overall, the growing political pressure on the Northern Fleet to demonstrate its usefulness in every possible way, from providing strategic deterrence, to punishing pirates off the shores of Somalia, increases the risk of accidents as many of its assets are pushed beyond the limits of safety.

Military 'Protection' for the Arctic Hydrocarbon Bonanza

The proposition that the Arctic sea shelf contains enormous reserves of oil and gas is often taken as an axiom in the fast-evolving geopolitics of the North. This energy-abundance theme is strongly present in the identity-building propaganda that is driving (rather than merely embellishing) Russia's new policy towards the Far North. Pragmatism comes more like an afterthought in the urge to prove that Russia is able to advance its 'natural rights' and through this process discover what it really is about. Fantastic estimates of untapped resources spill over from media commentary into official statements, and the rare sober voices that argue that the Mendeleev and Lomonosov underwater ridges do not look geologically promising as a potential hydrocarbon province are not able to make much of an impression.[21] The inflated assessments of natural riches in the contested parts of the Arctic shelf lead directly to the conclusion that Russia has to assert its claims forcefully and be prepared to defend its possessions by military means.

The logic of such reasoning might appear to be not exactly straight, but it finds authoritative confirmation in the discourse adopted by Russia's supreme authority. President Putin (2008), in his farewell address to the State Council, dismissed Western criticism of the curtailing of democracy in Russia as a "veneer of clamorous rhetoric" and then elaborated on the deeper sources of that hostility:

> A fierce battle for resources is unfolding, and the whiff of gas or oil is behind many conflicts, foreign policy actions and diplomatic demarches. In this context, it is understandable that the world should be showing growing interest in Russia and in Eurasia in general. God was generous in giving us natural resources. The result is that we are running up against repeats of the old 'deterrence' policy more and more often. But what this usually boils down to, essentially, are attempts to impose unfair competition on us and secure access to our resources.

The top brass have few doubts in interpreting these 'realist' (but in real terms—truly delusional) guidelines as orders for expanding military activities of every kind, from ballistic missile launches to counter-terrorist exercises, expecting that besides the always uncharitable funding from the state budget they would receive donations from rich sponsors. However, the state-owned companies that are legally certified to work on the Arctic shelf (i.e., Gazprom and Rosneft) are in no rush to engage in this hard work and show no interest in any protection from the armed forces, relying on their own perfectly legitimate paramilitary structures (Rodin and Moshkin 2007).

Outlining the prospects for exploring and developing the shelf at a special meeting of the Sea Collegium, chaired by Vice Prime Minister Sergei Ivanov, Rosneft's CEO Sergei Bogdanchikov took a long-term view towards the year 2050 and produced figures for necessary investments that exceeded by the order of magnitude not only the net capital of his company, loaded by heavy debt, but the possible capacity of the state budget under the most favourable scenario.[22] In fact, investments in even the better explored offshore fields, such as Prirazlomnoe in the eastern part of the Barents Sea, have been trimmed down year after year, so in mid-to-long-term expert assessments, the share of offshore in gross oil production would not increase to more than seven to ten percent from the current 2.7 percent (Skorlygina 2008).

When the discussions are translated from grand plans to practicalities, it typically and rather embarrassingly turns out that the vessels and equipment necessary for conducting the exploratory drilling have been rented out to Norwegian companies and cannot be returned before 2010 (Podobedova 2008). This simulation of active development of the shelf resources hardly needs any military 'protection', so it is only in theory that the armed forces could have provided help in transport, maintenance and communication. In reality, the logistics of the Northern Fleet, including the search-and-rescue service, are in such a dismal state that it would remain a receiver rather than a provider of help for years to come.

The only offshore projects in Russia that are indeed on track are those where foreign partners play a key role, Sakhalin-1 and -2 in the Far East being the main examples, with all of the controversy around the latter one, and Shtokman in the Barents Sea making a promising start (as demonstrated by Moe and Wilson Rowe in this book). As Gazprom's plan for developing the 'green' Yamal fields is drifting towards the outer border of mid-term future, Shtokman shapes up as Russia's best bet for overcoming the so-called gas crunch—a very probable prospect when the rise in internal demand would force a reduction of export. The Shtokman project has perhaps had more than its fair share of bureaucratic and corporate troubles, and military activities in the Kola Peninsula (which is by far the most militarized and nuclearized area in the Arctic) definitely present a serious additional problem for its practical implementation.

For Total and StatoilHydro (as well as for other possible international partners), interactions with the Russian military, with their obsession with secrecy and rather cavalier attitude to nuclear risks, fall firmly into the avoid-at-any-costs category. At the same time, the Northern Fleet has a remarkably positive experience in cooperating with several Western partners, including the United States, in implementing a wide range of projects aimed at safe storage of nuclear waste, utilization of decommissioned submarines and assessment of the environmental damage from military activity (including, for instance, examination of the K-159 nuclear submarine that sank in August 2003 near the mouth of the Kola Bay).[23] This experience could be expanded, as the development of Shtokman would give a boost to economic activity in the Murmansk Oblast, but for now Russia's military leadership prefers not to notice the very real benefits and yet instead entertains unrealistic but 'heroic' ambitions for ruling the Arctic seas.

Conclusion

In the Russian tradition, development of the Far North goes hand in hand with its militarization. Currently, Moscow has reasons to assume that while it may be lagging behind in exploration and industrial technologies (that are available for sale or rent), it has an edge in its available military instruments. Constructing geopolitical schemes of a "Great Arctic Game", Moscow does not necessarily believe that "the region could erupt in an armed mad dash for its resources", assuming that its military superiority is recognized by its northern neighbours.[24] The hydrocarbon greed, entirely understandable in a country that is so dependent on exporting raw materials, certainly plays a big role in shaping Russia's Arctic ambitions, but the essence of this evolving policy is not in getting there first with development projects but in establishing a claim that would effectively prevent anybody else from applying their superior technology to the increasingly accessible shelf. Military means, even if not very modern and more than slightly rotten, are quite instrumental in supporting that ambition. Their exploitation, however, requires a relaxed definition of 'acceptable risk.' Russia may remain sincerely unconcerned about the consequences of climate change and environmental damage from its military activities, but the future of its energy depends upon expanding international cooperation. Cutting down on unilateralist 'patriotic' rhetoric is a necessary first step in establishing such cooperation, and further advances would require—as well as facilitate—deep cuts in the ageing arsenals. Thus, getting serious about doing energy business with the West would help Moscow to create good prospects for cooperative demilitarization.

NOTES

1. My research on the Russian military posture is supported by the Royal Norwegian Defense Ministry. This chapter draws on my recent paper (Baev 2007). On the early days of the Barents Initiative, see Stokke and Tunander (1994); on its current state of affairs, see Hønneland (this book).

2. One sober reflection on Putin's speech at the Munich security conference in February 2007 is Trenin (2007); for a typical Russian commentary, see Bykov and Vlasova (2007).

3. On the anticlimactic address at the Russia-NATO Council in Bucharest, see Golts (2008a).

4. A balanced perspective is developed by Arbatov (2007); a perceptive European view is Hassner (2008); my attempt at addressing this issue is in Baev (2008a).

5. On Putin's discourse, see Medvedev (2004); on the contours of a "new epoch of confrontation", see Karaganov (2007). One ambitious conceptualization of Russia's global role is *Proekt Rossiya* (2008).

6. Formally, Russia has 'suspended' its participation, but such a step is not envisaged by the treaty's provisions; see Tuzmukhammedov (2007).

7. A sharp description of recent military exercises in Karelia is in Holdsworth (2008).

8. This air army is often referred to as the Long-Range Aviation, while the special command in the Air Force that had this name was disbanded in 1998; see Lefebvre (2003).

9. Moderately alarmist Western assessments, for example that "Arctic nations are locked in a multitude of territorial disputes that were once considered academic but are morphing into flashpoints that may spark armed conflict" (Harrington 2008), are typically interpreted by Russian experts as signals of an inevitable clash of interests; see Tsyganok (2008).

10. In April 2008, the UN commission made its first ever ruling and approved Australia's claim on 2.5 million km^2 of continental shelf; see "Australia Extends Rights over Sea" (2008).

11. Mainstream commentators in Moscow now confidently assert that "Stalin saw further than most [of] his current noisy denouncers"; see Lizun (2007). One sharp criticism of contemporary pseudo-Stalinism is Kolesnikov (2007).

12. This delivery was originally planned for 2006. The current plan of producing one new aircraft every two years appears quite unrealistic; see the informed exchange on the blog run by Podvig (2008).

13. On the French decision to deploy a squadron of fighters to Iceland to intercept Russian bombers in the summer of 2008, see Vinocour (2008).

14. For that matter, the 'combat task' involving an overflight above the US aircraft carrier *Nimitz* in February 2008 did not make that much military sense, since the *Bear* H in question could not constitute any threat to the ship; see "Russian Air Force" (2008).

15. The repairs to the engines of the Tu-160s, which have long been discontinued in production, are a particularly complicated task; see Bondarenko (2007).

16. The tragedy signified a serious setback for the development of Soviet long-range aviation; for a well-researched overview, see McCannon (1998).

17. On 17 June 1962 the first Soviet SSBN K-3 (*November* class) surfaced at the North Pole and planted the Soviet flag on the ice; Communist Party of the Soviet Union General

Secretary Nikita Khrushchev personally greeted the submarine (which received for that achievement the name *Leninsky Komsomol*) at the pier in Severomorsk; (see "Soviet Submarine K-3 Leninsky Komsomol" 2008).

18. One typical example of the official doctrinal reasoning can be found in an article written by Admiral Vladimir Vysotsky (2008), who was appointed commander-in-chief of the Navy in September 2007 after two years of commanding the Northern Fleet.

19. The failed test launch of the *Bulava* in November 2007 was kept secret, and the naval staff had insisted that the project was on track to completion until the meeting of the Military-Industrial Commission in February 2008, which approved the new schedule; see Sergeev (2008).

20. One sober analysis of the current posture of the Russian Navy is Barabanov and Lukin (2008); for an optimistic picture of expanding shipbuilding since 2010, see "Commander of the Navy" (2008).

21. One example of such 'pessimism' is Milov (2007). It is perfectly understandable that researchers in such academic institutes as Shirshov Institute of Oceanology, who have only recently started to receive funding for their programs, are in no rush to disprove the sensationalist assessments, even if they are deeply skeptical about the politicization of the research; see Gorodnitsky (2007).

22. Bogdanchikov clarified with remarkable accuracy that his figures (amounting to Russia's GDP for 2007 multiplied by 2.5) should be increased by sixteen percent if Russia would gain additional shelf territories in the Arctic; see "Rosneft Hosts Maritime Board Meeting" (2007).

23. Carefully updated data on these programs can be found at the Bellona Foundation website; see, for instance, Digges (2008). The report on offshore oil and gas development in northwestern Russia prepared by Bellona is also very informative; see Lesikhina et al. (2007). One sharp reflection on the reluctance of the Russian military to reflect upon this cooperation is Golts (2008b).

24. Somewhat alarmist warnings in the commendable Borgerson (2008: 64) article are moderated by his appeal for a US leadership (which is hardly envisaged by Russia), which could only begin with the US Congress ratifying the UN Convention on the Law of the Sea (which Moscow would sincerely welcome).

References

Aleksandrov, Sergei. 15 February 2008. "The Demonstration of Military Feebleness." *Nezavisimoe voennoe obozrenie*. [http://nvo.ng.ru/armament/2008-02-15/4_vmf.html].

Arbatov, Aleksei. 2007. "Moscow and Munich: A New Framework for Russian Domestic and Foreign Policies." *Working Paper 3*, Moscow: Carnegie Center. [http://carnegie.ru/en/pubs/workpapers/76508.htm].

"Australia Extends Rights over Sea." 21 April 2008. BBC News. [http://news.bbc.co.uk/2/hi/asia-pacific/7358432.stm].

Baev, Pavel K. January 2008a. "Russia's Security Policy Grows Muscular: Should the West Be Worried?" *Briefing Paper 15*, Helsinki: UPI. [http://www.upi-fiia.fi/eng/publications/upi_briefing_papers/].

———. 10 June 2008b. "Medvedev Tries to Gain Trust in Europe and Respect in the CIS." *Eurasia Daily Monitor*. [http://jamestown.org/edm/article.php?article_id=2373136].

———. 31 March 2008c. "Putin Seeks to Reaffirm Control over Disgruntled *siloviki*." *Eurasia Daily Monitor*. [http://jamestown.org/edm/article.php?article_id=2372929].

———. October 2007. "Russia's Race for the Arctic and the New Geopolitics of the North Pole." *Occasional Paper*, Jamestown Foundation, Washington, DC. [http://www.jamestown.org/docs/Jamestown-BaevRussiaArctic.pdf].

———. 2002. "Russian Navy after the Kursk: Still Proud but with Poor Navigation." *PONARS Memo 215*, Washington, DC: CSIS. [http://www.csis.org/ruseura/ponars/pm/].

Barabanov, Mikhail, and Mikhail Lukin. 25 February 2008. "Where the Russian Navy Is Going." *Kommersant-Vlast*. [http://www.kommersant.ru/doc.aspx?DocsID=856120].

Bondarenko, Andrei. 21 December 2007. "Strategic Air Assets Are Grounded." *Nezavisimoe voennoe obozrenie*. [http://nvo.ng.ru/notes/2007-12-21/8_strategi.html].

Borgerson, Scott G. March/April 2008. "Arctic Meltdown: The Economic and Security Implications of Global Warming." *Foreign Affairs*, 63–77.

Bykov, Pavel, and Olga Vlasova. 19 February 2007. "Who Would Like It?" *Expert*. [http://expert.ru/printissues/expert/2007/07/rech_putina/].

"Climate Change and International Security." 14 March 2008. Paper from the High Commissioner and the European Commission to the European Council. [http://www.consilium.europa.eu/cms3_applications/applications/solana/index.asp?lang=EN&cmsid=246].

"Commander of the Navy Explained How His Force Will Strengthen Russia's Nuclear Potential." 5 April 2008. Newsru.com. [http://newsru.com/russia/04apr2008/glavkom.html].

Digges, Charles. 26 February 2008. "Norway and UK to Share £3.9 Million Burden of Dismantling Russian November Class Sub." Bellona Foundation. [http://www.bellona.org/articles/articles_2008/uknorway_subdismantling].

Farizova, Suzanna. 14 January 2008. "The Candidate Said 'Fish.'" *Kommersant.* [http://www.kommersant.ru/doc.aspx?DocsID=841800].

Golts, Aleksandr. 4 April 2008a. "Farewell to NATO." *Ezhednevny zhurnal.* [http://www.ej.ru/?a=note&id=7958].

———. 2 May 2008b. "Runny Nose Has Reached Andreeva Bay." *Ezhednevny zhurnal.* [http://www.ej.ru/?a=note&id=8025].

———. 23 August 2007. "Flying Very-Very Low." *Ezhednevny zhurnal.* [http://www.ej.ru/?a=note&id=7348].

Gorodnitsky, Aleksandr. 10 September 2007. "The Sea-Bottom Was in Our Hands." Interview with *Novaya gazeta.* [http://novayagazeta.ru/data/2007/69/25.html].

Harrington, Caitlin. 16 January 2008. "Eyeing Up the New Arctic." *Jane's Defence Weekly*, 22–27.

Hassner, Pierre. April 2008. "Russia's Transition to Autocracy." *Journal of Democracy*, 19: 2: 5–15.

Holdsworth, Nick. 8 February 2008. "All Burnt Out: How Putin's Red Army Lost Its Fire." *Daily Mail* (UK). [http://www.dailymail.co.uk/pages/live/articles/live/live.html?in_article_id=513132&in_page_id=1889].

Karaganov, Sergei. October-December 2007. "A New Epoch of Confrontation." *Russia in Global Affairs* 4. [http://eng.globalaffairs.ru/numbers/21/1148.html].

Kolesnikov, Andrei. 3 August 2007. "The Polar War Goes On." Grani.ru. [http://grani.ru/opinion/kolesnikov/m.125502.html].

Lefebvre, Stephane. 2003. "The Reform of the Russian Air Force." In *Russian Military Reform 1992–2002*, ed. Anne C. Aldis and Roger N. McDermott. London: Frank Cass, 141–160.

Lesikhina, Nina et al. 2007. "Offshore Oil and Gas Development in Northwest Russia: Consequences and Implications." *Bellona Report.* [http://www.bellona.org/reports/report/russian_arctic_shelf].

Litovkin, Viktor. 28 March 2008. "General Affront." *Nezavisimoe voennoe obozrenie.* [http://nvo.ng.ru/forces/2008-03-28/1_afront.html].

———. 21 June 2007. "Frozen CFE." *RIA-Novosti.* [http://www.rian.ru/authors/20070621/67564124.html].

Lizun, Vladimir. 2007. "Russia Returns to the Arctic." *Russian Federation Today*, 16. [http://www.russia-today.ru/2007/no_16/16_talks.htm].

McCannon, John. 1998. *Red Arctic: Polar Exploration and the Myth of the North in the Soviet Union, 1932–1939*. Oxford: Oxford University Press.

Medvedev, Sergei. November 2004. "Juicy Morsels: Putin's Beslan Address and the Construction of the New Russian Identity." *PONARS Memo 334*, Washington, DC: CSIS. [http://www.csis.org/ruseura/ponars/pm/].

Milov, Vladimir. 17 September 2007. "There Is No Oil or Gas in the Part of the Arctic that Russia Claims." *New Times*. [http://newtimes.ru/5/magazine/2007/issue032/art_0014.xml].

"Missile Failures Mar Putin's Show." 19 February 2004. CNN World News. [http://edition.cnn.com/2004/WORLD/europe/02/18/russia.accident/index.html].

"Navy Will Provide 'Psychological Support' to Russian Fishermen in the Spitzbergen Area." 18 April 2008. *RIA-Novosti*. [http://www.rian.ru/defense_safety/20080418/105393996.html].

Norris, Robert S., and Hans M. Kristensen. May/June 2008. "Russian Nuclear Forces, 2008." *Bulletin of the Atomic Scientists*, 64: 2: 54–57.

Podobedova, Lydmila. 29 April 2008. "Shelf Fraud." *RBC Daily*. [http://www.rbcdaily.ru/2008/04/29/tek/340087].

Proekt Rossiya (Project Russia). 2008. Moscow: Eksmo.

Putin, Vladimir. 8 February 2008. Speech given at the expanded meeting of the State Council on Russia's development strategy through to 2020. [http://president.kremlin.ru/eng/speeches/2008/02/08/1137_type82912type82913_159643.shtml].

"RAF 'Intercepted Russian Planes.'" 30 April 2008. BBC News. [http://news.bbc.co.uk/2/hi/uk_news/7376336.stm].

Rodin, Ivan, and Mikhail Moshkin. 2 March 2007. "Gazprom and Rosneft Take to Arms." *Nezavisimaya gazeta*. [http://www.ng.ru/politics/2007-03-02/3_transneft.html].

"Rosneft Hosts Maritime Board Meeting." 19 April 2007. Rosneft Press Release. [http://www.rosneft.com/news/today/18042008.html].

"Russia Added New Tu-160 to Its Bomber Force." 29 April 2008. Russian Strategic Nuclear Forces. [http://russianforces.org/blog/2008/04/russia_added_new_tu160_to_its.shtml].

"Russian Air Force: The Overflight above US Aircraft Carrier Was a Combat Task." 13 February 2008. Newsru.com. [http://newsru.com/russia/13feb2008/nimitz.html].

Sergeev, Oleg. 25 January 2008. "Bulava Is Not Added to the Arsenal." *Nezavisimoe voennoe obozrenie*. [http://nvo.ng.ru/forces/2008-01-25/1_bulava.html].

Skorlygina, Natalya. 21 April 2008. "Sergei Bogdanchikov Dived to the Golden Sea-Bottom." *Kommersant*. [http://www.kommersant.ru/doc.aspx?DocsID =885039].

"Soviet Submarine K-3 Leninsky Komsomol." 2008. Wikipedia. [http:// en.wikipedia.org/wiki/Soviet_submarine_K-3].

Stokke, Olav Schram, and Ola Tunander, eds. 1994. *The Barents Region: Cooperation in Arctic Europe*. London: SAGE.

Trenin, Dmitri. May 2007. "Russia's Strategic Choices." *Policy Brief 50*, Washington, DC: CEIP. [http://www.carnegieendowment.org/files/ pb50_trenin_final.pdf].

Tsyganok, Anatoly. 7 March 2008. "The White Silence Area Is the Future Hot Spot." *Nezavisimaya gazeta*. [http://nvo.ng.ru/concepts/2008-03-07/1_ arktika.html].

Tuzmukhammedov, Bahtiyar. 10 December 2007. "CFE Cannot Be Suspended." *Nezavisimaya gazeta*. [http://www.ng.ru/courier/2007-12-10/13_dovse .html].

Vinocour, John. 21 April 2008. "Europe's Unlikely Attempt to Renew a 'Partnership' with Russia." *International Herald Tribune*.

Vysotsky, Vladimir. 25 January 2008. "Ready for Combat and Cooperation: Possessing a Modern Navy Is a Historical Necessity for Russia." *Nezavisimoe voennoe obozrenie*. [http://nvo.ng.ru/concepts/2008-01-25/ 7_vmf].

Chapter Two

Cross-Border Cooperation in the North: The Case of Northwest Russia

Geir Hønneland

Introduction

The Kola Peninsula in the northwestern corner of the Russian Federation was one of the most heavily militarized regions of the world a couple of decades ago, and largely closed to foreigners. Still home to the Russian Northern Fleet, it is assumed that the influence of the military and other power institutions is more significant here than elsewhere in Russia, and that this would reduce the potential for international cooperation. However, the region has, since the end of the Cold War, been drawn into a network of international collaboration of a civilian nature with its Nordic neighbours. The Barents Euro-Arctic Region (BEAR) was established in 1993 between several Northern European states and regional administrative entities in Norway, Sweden, Finland and Russia.[1] Its aim is to encourage interaction across the old East-West divide in the European North, and the partnership involves collaborative projects in a number of sectors, ranging from trade and industry to student exchange and indigenous issues. In addition, various bilateral cooperation schemes have developed between Russia and the Nordic countries to solve particular problems or meet particular challenges in the North. Notably, the valuable fish resources of the adjacent Barents Sea are managed bilaterally by Norway and Russia, and various Western states have taken it upon themselves to help alleviate the environmental problems on the Kola Peninsula.

This chapter gives a brief overview of BEAR and the bilateral cooperation between Russia and Norway on fisheries management and environmental protection, including nuclear safety, in the Barents Sea region. The latter section also touches briefly upon multilateral initiatives for nuclear safety on the Kola Peninsula. International cooperation in the area is most extensive between Norway and Russia, and the selected cases cover the thematic areas where such cooperation is most far-reaching. Towards the end of the chapter the implications of political developments and changing priorities on the Russian side are discussed.[2]

The Barents Euro-Arctic Region

The idea of a Barents region was first presented by the Norwegian Minister of Foreign Affairs Thorvald Stoltenberg in April 1992. After consultations with Russia and the other Nordic states, BEAR was established by the Kirkenes Declaration of January 1993, in which Norway, Sweden, Finland and Russia determined to work together at both the regional and national levels. At the regional level, BEAR initially included the three northernmost counties of Norway, Norrbotten in Sweden, Lapland in Finland and Murmansk and Arkhangelsk Oblasts and the Republic of Karelia in Russia. BEAR's geographical scope has subsequently been extended. In 1997 Nenets Autonomous Okrug, located within Arkhangelsk Oblast, became a member in its own right. Västerbotten (Sweden), Oulu and Kainuu (Finland) and the Republic of Komi (Russia) have later been included. All of these regional entities are represented on the Regional Council of BEAR, along with a representative of the indigenous peoples of the region. The collaboration also has a national tier in the Barents Euro-Arctic Council (BEAC), where Denmark, Iceland and the European Commission are represented in addition to the four core states. The following countries have observer status in the BEAC: Canada, France, Germany, Italy, Japan, the Netherlands, Poland, the United Kingdom and the United States.

The overall objective of BEAR is to contribute to stability and prosperity in the area. More specifically, its formal goals are embodied in the concepts of normalization, stabilization and regionalization. The cooperation project aims at reducing the military tension (see Baev, this book, for more detail), the environmental threat and the East-West gap in standards of living in the region. Furthermore, the project is linked to the overall regionalization process underway in Europe, as well as in the Arctic, turning previously peripheral border areas into meeting places between states in a transnational network involving many-sided interaction.[3] Functional areas of special focus are environmental protection, regional infrastructure, economic cooperation, science and technology, culture, tourism, health care and the indigenous peoples of the region (especially the Saami, who are found in all four countries of the Barents region).

One of the most striking features of the changes that have taken place in the East-West relations of the European North since the end of the Cold War is the massive exchange of people across the borders, both on a temporary and permanent basis. The tourist flow between East and West has risen dramatically; political and business delegations frequently visit partners on the other side of the border; a range of exchange students stay in other countries of the region for longer or shorter periods and, finally, most towns on the Nordic side of the border now have Russian settlements of various sizes. Many Russians have married on the Nordic side and hence have received a permanent residence permit. Others have come through the numerous exchange programs under the auspices of BEAR and have subsequently acquired temporary residence and work permits on account of their special competence. This is "the Barents generation", young aspiring Russians with competence in Nordic languages and Western business and administration practice. Some wish to stay in the West; others plan to return home after some time. A common feature, however, seems to be a sense of belonging in a new multicultural European North—or the Barents region.[4]

As a political project, BEAR has experienced its ups and downs. While ambitions were high during its formative years, it soon turned out to be more difficult than anticipated to create viable large-scale business cooperation between Russia and the Nordic countries in the Barents region. One apparent success story after the other eventually ended in failure. In several famous cases, the Russians simply pressed their Western counterparts out when their joint company started to run a profit.[5] As a result, business cooperation was given lower priority in BEAR from the late 1990s, and so-called people-to-people cooperation became BEAR's new hallmark: student exchange, cultural projects and other ventures that involve human interaction between Russia and the Nordic countries. A separate Barents Health Program was established in 1999, focusing primarily on new and re-emerging communicable diseases, such as HIV/AIDS and tuberculosis. Both the people-to-people cooperation and the Barents Health Program have generally been

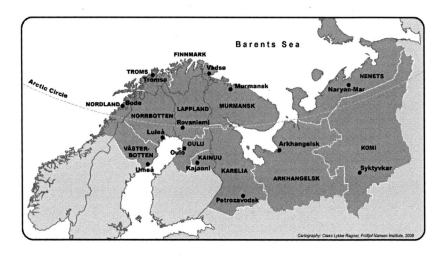

Figure 2.1. The Barents Euro-Arctic Region.
Source: The Fridtjof Nansen Institute.

judged as being successful, and small-scale business cooperation across the East-West border of BEAR is also developing.[6]

Bilateral Cooperation with Norway on Fisheries Management

The Barents Sea comprises those parts of the Arctic Ocean that lie between the North Cape on the Norwegian mainland, the South Cape of Spitsbergen Island in the Svalbard archipelago and the Russian archipelagos of Novaya Zemlya and Franz Josef Land (see figure 2.1). Traditionally, the fish and marine mammals of the Barents Sea have provided the basis for settlement along its shores, particularly in northern Norway and in the Arkhangelsk region of Russia. Since the Russian Revolution of 1917, the city of Murmansk on the Kola Peninsula has functioned as the nerve centre of the northwest Russian fishing industry. The Barents Sea contains a great abundance of fish stocks of a variety of species. The most important stock from a commercial point of view is the Northeast Atlantic cod, which is by far the largest cod stock in the entire northern Atlantic.

The UN (United Nations) Conference on the Law of the Sea (1975–1982) led to a transition from multilateral negotiations for the

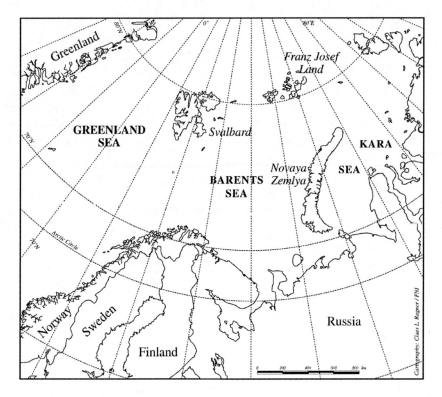

Figure 2.2. The Barents Sea.
Source: The Fridtjof Nansen Institute.

Barents Sea fisheries under the auspices of the Northeast Atlantic
Fisheries Commission to bilateral negotiations between coastal states
with sovereign rights to fish stocks. Norway and the Soviet Union
entered into several bilateral fishery cooperation agreements in the
mid-1970s. The Norwegian-Russian management regime for the
Barents Sea fish stocks defines objectives and practices for cooperative
management between the two states within the fields of research, regulations and compliance control.

Cooperation between Russian/Soviet and Norwegian scientists in
the mapping of Barents Sea fish resources dates back to the 1950s. It is
now institutionalized under the framework of the International Council
for the Exploration of the Sea (ICES). Quota settlement and technical regulation of fisheries are taken care of by the Joint Norwegian-

(Soviet/)Russian Fisheries Commission, which has met annually since 1976. The commission includes members of the two countries' fishery authorities, ministries of foreign affairs, marine scientists and representatives of fishers' organizations. Most importantly, it sets total allowable catches (TACs) for the three fish stocks that are defined as joint stocks of the two countries: cod, haddock and capelin. Cod and haddock are shared on a fifty-fifty basis, while the capelin quota is shared sixty-forty in Norway's favour. Finally, cooperation in compliance control was initiated in 1993, after the Norwegian Coast Guard revealed a considerable Russian overfishing following Russian vessels' new practice of delivering most of their catches in Norwegian ports instead of in Murmansk. Compliance control includes the exchange of catch data and inspectors, as well as the harmonization of various enforcement routines.

Three main periods can be distinguished in the thirty years since the bilateral management regime came into force: before and after the collapse of the Soviet Union, and before and after the turn of the millennium.[7] Until the early 1990s, discussions in the Joint Norwegian-Soviet Fisheries Commission mainly centred on the size of the TACs and whether the smallest permitted mesh size in nets and the minimum length of fish should be increased. As the Soviet northern fishing fleet was mostly engaged in distant-water fisheries (mainly outside Western Africa and South America) and hence not so dependent on the nearby fishing grounds of the Barents Sea, the Soviet contingent to the commission generally opted for the lower TAC recommendations given by ICES, while the Norwegian contingent in most years pressed quotas upwards. Norway, on the other hand, wanted to increase the lowest permitted size of fish and net mesh, but it failed to persuade the Soviets to introduce this regulation measure. The fish are generally smaller in the Soviet/Russian part of the Barents Sea, which explains the Soviet/ Russian unwillingness to increase the mesh size, as it would likely result in a smaller Russian catch.

The 1990s were characterized by a large-scale introduction of new, and coordination of existing, technical management measures (e.g., the joint introduction of satellite tracking and selection grids in trawls) and general agreement about the annual TAC levels. The Russians had now become more interested in the valuable cod stock—in Soviet times, they had been more concerned with quantities than global market prices (see Jørgensen, this book, for more detail)—and were more dependent on the Barents Sea fisheries as distant-water fishing was discontinued in the post-Soviet period. However, the Northeast Arctic cod stock was very healthy throughout the 1990s, so TACs could be set at comfortable levels without setting ICES's scientific recommendations aside. New problems emerged—both from a biological and an institutional point of view—when the cod stock began to reach crisis levels around the turn of the millennium.

The decline of the cod stock in the late 1990s coincided with international recognition of the precautionary principle, which says that lack of scientific certainty should not be used as a reason not to undertake management measures that could prevent degradation. It was adopted by ICES and the Joint Norwegian-Russian Fisheries Commission in the late 1990s. At the turn of the millennium, ICES recommended drastic reductions in the Barents Sea cod quota, but the commission annually established quotas far above these recommendations. The Russian contingent to the commission strongly opposed the need for implementing quota reductions. The Norwegian contingent generally supported the scientific recommendations, although opinions varied within the Norwegian fishing industry. While the Norwegians debated whether the established TACs were sustainable or not, the Russians seemed to view the issue as a battle between the two states, or rather, between Russia and the West. Both the Russian media and the Russian members of the Joint Norwegian-Russian Fisheries Commission accused Norway of having ulterior motives for supporting lower TACs, such as maintaining high world market prices for cod at a time when the country was starting artificial breeding of the species. Norway largely gave in to Russian demands to keep quotas high, since the alternative—no TAC agreement at all, and the effective dismantlement of the bilateral management regime—was far less attractive an option.

For 2001 the parties for the first time agreed upon a three-year quota. This gave them some breathing space and a buffer against sudden developments. Two years later, the commission devised a fresh set of decision and action rules for management of its side of the Northeast Arctic cod stock, aimed at ensuring biological viability and greater economic predictability for fishery-dependent communities in Norway and Russia. These action rules mandated, among other things, that average fish mortality should be kept below the precautionary limit over three-year periods and that TACs should not change more than ten percent from one year to another.

Russian overfishing after the breakup of the Soviet enforcement system was presumably brought to a halt by the measures introduced under

---

the enforcement cooperation scheme between Norway and Russia in 1993. However, while the exchange of catch and landing data between the two countries might be a necessary factor in eliminating catch under-reporting, it is hardly a sufficient one. Sanctioning mechanisms in Russia, and the sincerity of Russian officials' wishes to eliminate overfishing, are uncertain elements in this respect. Further, catches once again were delivered to transport vessels at sea from the late 1990s, as they were during Soviet days. While fresh fish in the intervening period was brought to Norwegian ports, fishing vessels now handed the fish over to transport vessels as frozen products for delivery to European countries (e.g., Denmark, the Netherlands, the United Kingdom, Portugal and Spain). As a result, the catch data exchange system of Norwegian and Russian enforcement authorities was no longer of much use.

Two specific questions emerged: how much fish was being transferred from vessel to vessel in the Barents Sea, and how much of these fish products were being delivered to third countries. Seen from the point of view of Norwegian fisheries management authorities, the Russians have not been particularly eager to help in either endeavour. Around 2002-2003 the Norwegian Directorate of Fisheries increased its efforts to estimate actual Russian catches in the Barents Sea. Based on the results, ICES estimated unreported catches of Northeast Arctic cod as follows: 90,000 tons in 2002; 115,000 tons in 2003; 117,000 tons in 2004 and 166,000 tons in 2005. This implies an annual overfishing in the range of twenty-five to forty percent of the TAC during the period. In other words, the Russians have, according to ICES, overfished their national quotas of Northeast Arctic cod (which are approximately fifty percent of the TAC) by some fifty to eighty percent annually. Russian fisheries management authorities admitted in the fall of 2006 to not knowing how much fish is actually transferred at sea and delivered to third countries, but they estimated Russian overfishing to be around twenty thousand to thirty thousand tons annually in recent years.

Bilateral Cooperation with Norway on Environmental Protection

The Joint Norwegian-Soviet Commission on Environmental Protection was established in 1988. One year earlier, the Soviet leader, Mikhail Gorbachev, had delivered his famous Murmansk speech, where he appealed to a "civilization" of the militarized High North in general, and international cooperation on environmental protection in particular. Pollution from the nickel smelter Pechenganikel on the Soviet side of the border had rendered visible damage to the environment, including the Norwegian side, so the top priority of the commission during its first years was to modernize the Pechenganikel combine in order to reduce sulphur dioxide emissions.

From the early 2000s, nuclear safety became a new priority as news reached the public that the Soviets had dumped radioactive waste in the Barents and Kara seas and that they were no longer able to take care of the increasing amounts of spent nuclear fuel and radioactive waste on the Kola Peninsula. Norway launched a plan of action on nuclear safety in northwestern Russia in 1995, and three years later a separate Joint Norwegian-Russian Commission on Nuclear Safety was established. Over the next decade, Norway spent around US$ 150 million on nuclear safety projects on the Kola Peninsula. The overriding goal of the plan of action was to protect health, the environment and business against radioactive contamination and pollution from chemical weapons. The activities under the plan of action were categorized into four prioritized areas: (i) safety measures at nuclear facilities; (ii) management, storage and disposal of radioactive waste and spent nuclear fuel; (iii) research and monitoring of radioactive pollution and (iv) arms-related environmental hazards. Priority was given to safety measures at the Kola nuclear power plant, investigations and evaluation of pollution in northern ocean areas and the construction of storage and effluent treatment facilities for radioactive waste and spent nuclear fuel.

At the same time, it was a main priority of the Norwegian government to draw other Western countries into a multilateral partnership to ensure nuclear safety in northwestern Russia. In 2002 the G8 countries pledged up to US$ 20 billion for the Global Partnership against the Spread of Weapons and Materials of Mass Destruction. Among the G8's priority concerns were the dismantlement of decommissioned nuclear submarines, particularly on the Kola Peninsula. The signing of the framework agreement for the Multilateral Nuclear Environmental Program in the Russian Federation in May 2003, covering, among other things, taxation and liability issues, further enhanced international nuclear remedial cooperation in the region. Another major multilateral cooperation structure, initiated by Norway in 1996, is the Arctic Military Environmental Cooperation between Norway, Russia, the United

Kingdom and the United States. The initiative is directed towards military-related environmental issues in the Arctic, primarily the decommissioning of nuclear submarines on the Kola Peninsula.

While nuclear safety became the environmental issue involving the big money, the Joint Norwegian-Russian Commission on Environmental Protection engaged in creating institutional cooperation between the two countries in areas such as pollution control, biodiversity and the protection of cultural heritage. Institutional cooperation became the hallmark of the commission around the mid-1990s. Emphasis was placed not only on solving pressing environmental problems but developing sustainable cooperation patterns between Norwegian and Russian environmental institutions. From the Norwegian side it was an explicit goal to assist building up a sound environmental bureaucracy in Russia, with a main focus on the transfer of competence. The single largest project was the Cleaner Production Program, which involved training engineers at Russian enterprises to save resources and reduce waste.

Since 2002-2003 protecting the marine environment of the Barents Sea has been the declared main objective of the commission.[8] Its initial main priority, the modernization of the Pechenganikel combine, has not materialized. Norway offered to contribute NOK 300 million (at the time, some US$ 50 million) in 1990, but after years of planning, the project was halted in 1997. A Finnish initiative was also stillborn. The Norwegian project was revived in 2001, when the Norwegian minister of the environment and the Russian minister of economy signed an agreement on a modernization project that would involve a ninety percent reduction in emissions of sulphur dioxide and heavy metals by 2006–2007. Reconstruction has not yet started, and again the outcome is uncertain. The owner of the now privatized smelter, Norilsk Nikel, has little incentive to make the necessary investment to make its production more environmentally friendly, and Russian environmental authorities cannot force the company to do so.

Russian Developments and Priorities

Moscow's priorities of the cooperation initiatives reviewed above have varied between the functional sectors and over time. BEAR has not been a top priority for the Russian foreign policy leadership. This is not to say that Russia has not supported the initiative, but that projects have mostly been financed by the Nordic side. Cooperation on environmental protection has clearly also been supported by Moscow, but developments have been hampered by the lowered status of the Russian environmental bureaucracy. After a 'green wave' in the later years of the Soviet Union, a series of setbacks followed. Within a few years, popular environmental concern had all but disappeared. Less than one decade after the establishment of the new federation, the environmental bureaucracy built up in the final years of Soviet rule had been effectively dismantled.

The first blow came in 1996, when the Ministry of Ecology and Natural Resources was downgraded to the State Committee for Environmental Protection. At the same time, the Ministry of Natural Resources was established on the basis of the old State Committee for Minerals and the State Committee for Water. The former was the most influential, built on the former Soviet Ministry of Geology, and the new ministry came to be dominated by geologists. It was assigned certain environmental protection functions, especially related to minerals and water regulation, but also more general policy-making.

The second blow came in 2000, when the State Committee for Environmental Protection, along with the State Committee for Forestry, was abolished and its remnants incorporated into the Ministry of Natural Resources. As many environmental problems are the result of the extraction of natural resources, a conflict of interest between the extraction and protection interests seemed more than likely. The geologists in the ministry soon took precedence over the ecologists. The general reorganization of Russia's federal bureaucracy in 2004 led to a fragmentation of the country's system for environmental protection.[9]

The Ministry of Natural Resources is still responsible for policy-making related to environmental protection, but monitoring is now taken care of by the Federal Service for Surveillance in Ecology and Resource Use (Rosprirodnadzor) and the Federal Service for Ecological, Technological and Nuclear Surveillance (Rostekhnadzor). The division of responsibility between the two services, the former subordinate to the Ministry of Natural Resources and the latter directly to the government, is still not quite clear. However, Rosprirodnadzor is responsible for nature protection (for instance, nature reserves and national parks) and the surveillance of production standards, while Rostekhnadzor controls pollution levels. In addition, there is the Federal Service for

Hydrometeorology and Environmental Monitoring (Rosgidromet), directly subordinate to the government.[10]

In the bilateral cooperation with Norway, the two reorganizations left gaps in the established cooperation routines. The years 2000 and 2004 are the only years when no meetings in the Joint Norwegian-Russian Commission on Environmental Protection took place. For long periods in both 2000 and 2004 the Norwegian contingent was simply not able to get in contact with its Russian counterpart. Since 2004, however, the Norwegians have found the Russian Ministry of Natural Resources to be a stable cooperation partner, and the Russian contingent has in recent years contributed significantly more to cooperative projects in financial terms than it did during the 1990s. At the same time, the administrative capacity of the Russian Ministry of Natural Resources to handle the bilateral cooperation is considerably smaller than that of the Norwegian Ministry of the Environment.[11]

The bilateral cooperation with Norway on fisheries management in the Barents Sea has clearly been given higher priority by Moscow than BEAR and environmental protection. The Joint Norwegian-Russian Fisheries Commission has met every year, with active participation from the Russian side. Nevertheless, there seems to be a sense in Russia that the Norwegians took advantage of the political turmoil and financial upheavals in Russia in the 1990s. Hence, there have been more problems with bilateral cooperation since the turn of the millennium than during the 1990s and even during the Cold War.

As mentioned above, the 1990s brought a range of new technical regulation measures to Barents Sea fisheries. The initiative largely came from the Norwegian side. The most prominent example was the introduction of selection grids in cod trawls. Clearly, this measure (intended to enhance the out-selection of small fish) reduced the catches and also represented an additional hassle to fishing operations. At the end of the 1990s, there was a growing acknowledgement in Russian fisheries circles that this regulatory measure was largely to the detriment of Russian fishers in the Barents Sea. The logic behind this was that Norway gave the larger share (around seventy-five percent) of its cod quota to coastal fishers fishing with gear other than trawl, while the entire Russian fleet consisted of ocean-going trawlers and was hence troubled by the new regulation.

As also described above, the cod stock was significantly reduced at around the same time, and ICES recommended sharp cuts in the annual quotas. Norway wanted to follow the advice from ICES, but many Russians started to question the impartiality of this international research organization. Many also pointed to the connection between increased Norwegian self-confidence—expressed through the arrest by the Norwegian Coast Guard of a Russian vessel in the disputed Fishery Protection Zone around Svalbard in 2001—and the chaos found in the Russian system for fisheries management during the 1990s. The Soviet Ministry of the Fishing Industry was downgraded to the State Committee for Fisheries when the Soviet Union was dissolved and the Russian Federation established. During the 1990s, the committee had to stave off interference from a range of other federal agencies, in particular the Ministry of Economic Development and Trade, the Ministry of Natural Resources, the Ministry of Agriculture and various "power agencies", i.e., uniformed services involved in maintaining state security. The Federal Border Service (subsumed into the FSB in 2003) took over responsibility for enforcement at sea in 1998. The Ministry of Agriculture managed to take over responsibility for fisheries management for shorter periods twice during the 1990s. The Ministry of Economic Development and Trade succeeded in introducing a system for the sale of fishing quotas by auction in 2000.[12] The general Russian sentiment at the time was that Norway was taking advantage of institutional chaos on the Russian side to introduce management measures that were largely to Norway's benefit.

Since around 2002–2003, a major concern from the Norwegian side, and also from ICES, has been overfishing by the Russians in the Barents Sea. As mentioned above, Norway has felt that the overfishing has not been taken seriously by the Russians. Adding to this, the Russian Federal Research Institute of Fisheries and Oceanography (VNIRO) in the mid-2000s presented an alternative model for assessing the fish stocks of the Barents Sea, indicating that there is two to three times more Northeast Atlantic cod than estimated by ICES.[13] So far, Russia has agreed that ICES assess the new model over the next several years. However, Russian skepticism of ICES is growing, and strong forces in the Russian fisheries administration have advocated withdrawal from this multilateral fisheries research organization.

In an interview by the author of this chapter at VNIRO in December 2007, the director of the institute started by stating that "it is horrible what is going on in the Barents Sea at the moment".[14] In a Norwegian setting, such a statement would clearly refer to the overfishing taking place according to ICES. However, the VNIRO director was actually referring to an alleged "underfishing" of the Northeast Atlantic cod stock, as annual quotas could be significantly higher if the new model had been applied for stock estimation. The representatives of VNIRO did nothing to conceal their suspicion that ICES is under the influence of Western intelligence services and intends to harm Russian economic interests. While Russia is still a member of ICES, representatives of the Russian delegation to the Joint Norwegian-Russian Fisheries Commission have repeatedly proposed that Norway and Russia take care of fisheries research in the Barents Sea on a bilateral basis instead of through a multilateral organization such as ICES.

The cooperation regimes reviewed here have to varying degrees been influenced by the general recentralization that has taken place in Russian politics since 2000, which is described in greater detail in the introductory chapter of this book. In fisheries management, the northwest Russian regions became quite influential during the 1990s, but have since lost most of their power. Regarding environmental protection, the picture is less clear. After the first reorganization in 2000, the environmental bureaucracy was generally weakened—without really influencing the centre-region relation itself in any significant way—but the 2004 reform actually strengthened the power of regional authorities in environmental protection. As a result of the reform, the Ministry of Natural Resources was no longer to be represented at the regional level. Instead, the new (and old) monitoring services were supposed to take care of environmental issues in the regions.

The lack of policy-making and implementing functions at the regional level has led many Russian regions to intensify their own environmental work.[15] For instance, in Murmansk Oblast a department for environmental protection was established in 2005 with the aim of coordinating the various monitoring services in the region and filling the gap left by the abolishment of the regional office of the Ministry of Natural Resources. New legislation introduced in 2004–2005 also enhanced the role of federal subjects in environmental protection. As far as BEAR is concerned, regional authorities have a greater role to play than federal authorities. While their formal authority in this transnational cooperation may not have been significantly changed, the general political developments that have occurred in Russia since 2000 have not increased their room to maneuver, to say the least.

Conclusion

The main cooperation schemes between Norway (and to some extent the other Nordic states) and Russia in the Barents Sea region vary in nature. The most general one is BEAR, which includes a range of issues but has in recent years mainly concentrated on people-to-people projects and health care issues, i.e., explicitly soft policy areas. Arguably, the most focused cooperative arrangement, and economically most important, is the Joint Norwegian-Russian Fisheries Commission, which sets annual quotas for some of the fish stocks of the Barents Sea. Such quotas have to be established each year to avoid anarchy in the fishing of some of the most abundant fish stocks in the world. In a middle position are the Joint Norwegian-Russian Commission for Environmental Protection and the Joint Norwegian-Russian Commission for Nuclear Safety. These commissions deal with issues that might pose a threat to health and the environment in northwest Russia, and possibly also on the Norwegian side of the border.

Not unexpectedly, Russia's priority is fisheries management. BEAR is largely left to the regional authorities (and as far as financing goes, to the Nordic states), which since the turn of the millennium have lost much of the power they had at the time when this regional collaboration was initiated. Cooperation with Norway on environmental protection is managed by federal authorities, but here the problem is that this policy area enjoys practically no priority in Russian politics, quite unlike the situation a decade ago (and even more so, two decades ago, when bilateral environmental cooperation between Norway and the Soviet Union was first established). The fishing industry involves big money, and here a number of Russian actors seek influence, ranging from private shipowners to various bodies of governance on both the regional and federal level. A general tendency since the early 1990s is that the Russian contingent to the commission is more eager than its Norwegian counterpart to press quotas upwards. Recently, Russian scientists have also introduced new models for assessing the size of fish stocks, indicating that there is much more cod in the Barents Sea than acknowledged by ICES. Russian skepticism of this multilateral research organization is mounting, and one major question for the future of Norwegian-Russian cooperation on fisheries management is whether Russia will continue to respect ICES's advice or lay pressure on Norway towards a further bilateralization of fisheries research.

In a larger time perspective, northwest Russia's relationship with the Nordic countries has, of course, fundamentally changed. Of the collaboration regimes discussed here, only the bilateral fisheries management system between Norway and Russia extends back to the Cold War. Until the late 1980s, institutionalized contact between the Soviet Union and the Nordic countries in the High North was minimal. The 1990s marked a period of dramatic increase in cross-border cooperation in the region, in line with general tendencies, such as the fall of the Iron Curtain and the 'Westernization' and decentralization of Russian politics. New challenges have emerged after the turn of the millennium. The political role of Russian federal politics has been reduced, which in turn has decreased the clout of international cooperative arrangements with a prominent role for the regional level, such as BEAR. More importantly, there is a new Russian awareness—often outright skepticism—of the political solutions proposed by the country's Western neighbours.

NOTES

1. A discussion of the BEAR collaboration at the time it was established is found in Stokke and Tunander (1994). Stokke and Hønneland (2007) discuss the achievements of the collaboration a decade later.

2. Methodologically, the chapter builds on personal interviews with Russian and Norwegian actors, primarily civil servants and scientists, for a number of different research projects undertaken by the author over the last decade. Key periods have been related to evaluations carried out on the BEAR collaboration in 2001, as well as on the bilateral cooperation schemes between Norway and Russia regarding nuclear safety in 2000, fisheries management in 2005–2006 and environmental protection in 2007. The majority of interviews on the Russian side took place in Murmansk, while some were carried out in Moscow and Arkhangelsk. All the interviews with Russians were carried out in Russian, i.e., without the aid of an interpreter.

3. For discussions of region-building in the European North, see Hønneland (1998), Neumann (1994) and Stokke and Hønneland (2007). For broader discussions about region-building in the Arctic, see Keskitalo (2003) and Tennberg (2000).

4. See Hønneland (1998; 2005) for a discussion of identity politics in BEAR.

5. See Hønneland (2005) for more detail.

6. For further discussions of BEAR achievements, see Hønneland (2003; 2005) and Stokke and Hønneland (2007). A thorough discussion of health cooperation between Russia and the Nordic states in the European North is found in Hønneland and Rowe (2004).

7. This distinction is applied in Hønneland (2006). The Barents Sea fisheries management regime is further discussed in Hønneland (2000; 2004a), Nakken (1998), Stokke (2001) and Stokke, Anderson and Mirovitskaya (1999) .

8. The work of the Joint Norwegian-Russian Commission on Environmental Protection is discussed in Hønneland and Rowe (2008).

9. The main aim of the reform was to downsize the federal bureaucracy, reduce duplication of work and create a more logical structure in the ministerial sector, particularly in the relationship between ministries and their subordinate bodies. The executive power was from now on to consist of three categories of federal bodies: policy-making ministries, implementing agencies and monitoring services.

10. See Oldfield (2005) for an overview of Russian environmental politics after the Cold War.

11. While the Norwegian Ministry of the Environment has one to two people working full time on its bilateral cooperation with Russia, the responsible civil servant in the Russian Ministry of Natural Resources has to handle bilateral cooperation with more than two dozen other states in addition to Norway.

12. See Hønneland (2004b) for an overview of Russian fisheries management after the Cold War.

13. It goes beyond the scope of this chapter to explain the difference between the traditional and the alternative models for assessing fish stocks. One major difference, however, is that the traditional models are based on random surveys carried out by marine scientists while the new Russian model is based on actual catch data reported by fishing vessels.

14. Interview conducted at VNIRO, 5 December 2007.

15. See Hønneland and Jørgensen (2005) for a discussion of the effects of the 2004 reorganization of the federal bureaucracy on environmental governance in Russia's northern regions.

References

Hønneland, G. 2006. *Kvotekamp og kyststatssolidaritet: Norsk-russisk fiskeriforvaltning gjennom 30 år*. Bergen, Norway: Fagbokforlaget. Published also in Russian in 2007 as *Bor'ba za kvoty i solidarnost' pribrezhnykh gosudarstv: 30-letnyaya istoriya rossiysko-norvezhskogo sotrudnichestva v oblasti upravlenia rybolovstvom*. Murmansk: PINRO Press.

———. 2005. *Barentsbrytninger: Norsk nordområdepolitikk etter den kalde krigen*. Kristiansand, Norway: Høyskoleforlaget.

———. 2004a "Fish Discourse: Norway, Russia and the Northeast Arctic Cod." *Human Organization* 63: 1: 68–77.

———. 2004b. *Russian Fisheries Management: The Precautionary Approach in Theory and Practice*. Boston: Martinus Nijhoff Publishers/Brill Academic Publishers.

———. 2003. *Russia and the West: Environmental Cooperation and Conflict*. New York: Routledge.

———. 2000. *Coercive and Discursive Compliance Mechanisms in the Management of Natural Resources: A Case Study from the Barents Sea Fisheries*. Boston: Springer.

———. 1998. "Identity Formation in the Barents Euro-Arctic Region." *Cooperation and Conflict* 33: 3: 277–299.

Hønneland, G., and J. H. Jørgensen. 2005. "Federal Environmental Governance and the Russian North." *Polar Geography* 29: 1: 27–42.

Hønneland, G., and L. Rowe. 2008. *Fra svarte skyer til helleristninger: Norsk-russisk miljøvernsamarabeid gjennom 20 år*. Trondheim, Norway: Tapir akademisk forlag.

———. 2004. *Health as International Politics: Combating Communicable Diseases in the Baltic Sea Region*. Burlington, VT: Ashgate.

Keskitalo, E. C. H. 2003. *Negotiating the Arctic: The Construction of an International Region*. New York: Routledge.

Nakken, O. 1998. "Past, Present and Future Exploitation and Management of Marine Resources in the Barents Sea and Adjacent Areas." *Fisheries Research* 37: 25–35.

Neumann, I. 1994. "A Region-Building Approach to Northern Europe." *Review of International Studies*, 20: 53–74.

Oldfield, J. 2005. *Russian Nature: Exploring the Environmental Consequences of Societal Change*. Burlington, VT: Ashgate.

Stokke, O. S. 2001. "Managing Fisheries in the Barents Sea Loophole: Interplay with the UN Fish Stocks Agreement." *Ocean Development and International Law* 32: 241–262.

Stokke, O. S., L. G. Anderson, and N. Mirovitskaya. 1999. "The Barents Sea Fisheries." In *The Effectiveness of International Environmental Regimes: Causal Connections and Behavioral Mechanisms*, ed. O. R. Young. Cambridge, MA: MIT Press.

Stokke, O. S., and G. Hønneland, eds. 2007. *International Cooperation and Arctic Governance: Regime Effectiveness and Northern Region Building*. New York: Routledge.

Stokke, O. S., and O. Tunander, eds. 1994. *The Barents Region: Cooperation in Arctic Europe*. London: SAGE.

Tennberg, M. 2000. *Arctic Environmental Cooperation: A Study in Governmentality*. Burlington, VT: Ashgate.

Chapter Three

Climate Change in the Russian North: Threats Real and Potential

Craig ZumBrunnen

"Of course you can see the effects of global warming. Sheet ice that normally covers the waters of the Barents Sea is quickly starting to shift and disappear. In recent years, you can't really see this permanent sea ice. It comes and goes. If the wind blows this way, it brings the ice to the coast. If it blows the other way, it floats away."

—Vera Letkova, meteorologist (Elder 2008).

"It's been a mild winter, lots of rivers are drying up. For us, it makes no difference—it'd be better if it were even warmer. But it bothers the reindeer."

—Ivan Kane, nomad reindeer herder NARYAN-MAR, Nenets Autonomous District (Elder 2008).

Introduction

Other individual chapters in this book focus on the Russian North from a wide range and number of perspectives and issues, such as international relations in both bilateral and multilateral settings; indigenous peoples; border issues; demography; migration; oil and gas extraction and changing northern administration and federalism. To varying degrees—no pun intended—this chapter either explicitly or implicitly casts a shadow or sheds some light on nearly all of these issues. As its title and the two beginning quotes suggest, however, it does so through an environmental lens of climate change and global warming.

This chapter begins with a brief introduction to global climate change and trends in greenhouse gases (GHGs) before turning to the trends and sources of Russian GHGs and the role of the Russian North. Next, Russia's GHG trends are situated within regional and global contexts. A number of the real and potential impacts of climate change in the Russian North are explored. Concomitantly, the potential systemic positive feedback impacts of global warming, forcing factors on global warming itself, are identified. The impacts, both positive and negative, of global warming on the Russian oil and gas extraction and distribution infrastructure are duly noted, as are the real and potential climate change impacts on other northern transportation and settlement infrastructures.

The recent history of Russian climate policy positions and Russia's ratification of the Kyoto Protocol are also cursively reviewed in this chapter. In this regard, such issues as the importance of Russia's ratification of the Kyoto Protocol, the nature and roles of Russia's Kyoto stakeholders, the Russian negotiating positions on the Kyoto mechanisms and the reasons behind Russia's ratification of the Kyoto Protocol are examined. Important Kyoto concepts and mechanisms are then explained, especially those of most relevance to Russia joining the protocol. Missing elements needed for full Russian compliance with Kyoto requirements are considered, as are the rationales for Russia's efforts to meet compliance. Finally, it is hypothesized that Russian political considerations will dominate over economic ones, and in turn, economic considerations will dominate over climate change considerations and policy for some time. In other words, it is very important to recognize the confounding highly interconnected multiple political-economic-climate-change implications of the fossil fuel energy sectors of the Russian North.

Empirical Assessment of Climate Change and Global Warming Trends

The empirical evidence from direct observations and environmental proxy data for global warming has become overwhelming and there is now very little scientific controversy that global temperatures are

---

increasing. Manning (2008), the director of the Intergovernmental Panel on Climate Change (IPCC) Working Group I Support Unit, lists the following thirteen observed patterns as being both real and unequivocally linked to global warming (the last nine in the list being also directly linked to sea level rise):

- surface temperatures increasing;
- tropospheric temperatures increasing;
- atmospheric water vapour content increasing;
- ocean heat content increasing;
- Greenland and Antarctic ice sheets losing mass;
- glaciers and snow cover decreasing;
- extent of Arctic sea ice decreasing;
- area of seasonally frozen ground decreasing;
- midlatitude wind patterns/storm tracks shifting poleward;
- more intense and longer droughts;
- frequency of events of heavy precipitation increasing;
- extreme temperatures increasing; and
- tropical cyclone intensity increasing.

Most of the negative temperature anomalies during the past century correlate with significant volcanic eruptions (see figure 3.1) that for short periods of time have significantly increased the earth's albedo (the reflection of solar radiation back into space). Recently, the pronounced cooling discontinuity beginning in 1945 has been revealed to be the apparent result of uncorrected instrumental biases in the sea surface temperature record (Thompson et al. 2008). Given the differences in heat capacity between land and sea surfaces, rates of evaporative cooling, transparency and water mixing, it should come as no surprise that the temperature anomalies over land surfaces have been more dynamic than changes in sea temperatures.

With ninety percent certainty, the latest IPCC assessment emphatically concludes that anthropogenic forcing is the major cause of the empirically well-documented patterns of global warming on the earth. Among of the strongest lines of evidence reported by the IPCC that support this conclusion are the differences between the two graphs in figure 3.1. The top graph represents overlays of global mean surface temperature anomalies from observations, numerous General Circulation Model (GCM) simulation scenarios that included both anthropogenic

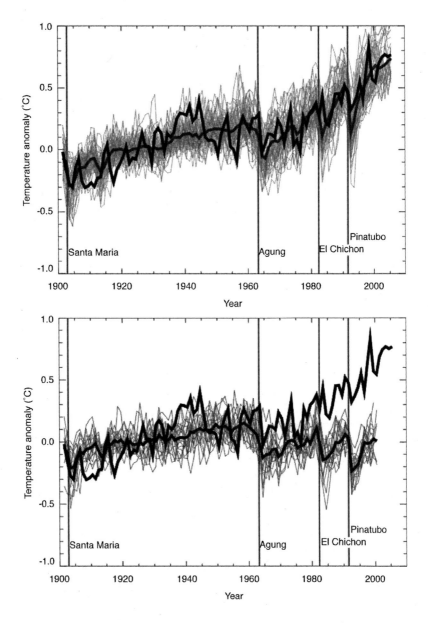

Figure 3.1. The Barents comparison between global means surface temperature anomalies from observations and AOGCM simulations forced with both anthropogenic and natural forcings (top graph) and natural forcings only (bottom graph), 1900–2000
Source: IPCC (2007).

and natural forcing and a composite or average of all the simulations that included both anthropogenic and natural forcing. The bottom graph overlays global mean surface temperature anomalies from observations, numerous GCM simulation scenarios that only include natural forcing and a composite or average of the simulations that include only natural forcing. Clearly, neither natural forcing alone (bottom graph) or anthropogenic forcing alone can replicate the measured observations, but models that include both natural and anthropogenic forcing (top graph) replicate the observations with a high level of agreement.

The two dominant anthropogenic forcing factors are the release of GHGs, primarily from the combustion of fossil fuels, and anthropogenic albedo changes generated by land use/land cover changes. The rather dramatic increases in global fossil-fuel-based carbon emissions since the 1950s have come from the burning of petroleum and natural gas (see figure 3.2). The dramatic downturn in carbon emissions following the economic collapses of East European and post–Soviet Union newly independent states is clearly visible in figure 3.2. On the other hand, the

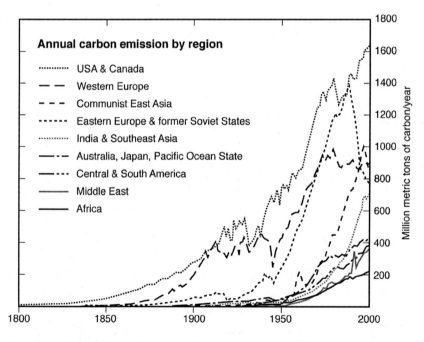

Figure 3.2. Regional trends in annual carbon emissions, 1800–2000.
Source: Marland, Boden and Andres (2007).

powerful role of the oceans as a net carbon dioxide sink will be increasingly weakened as global oceanic water temperatures rise, as carbon dioxide is inversely soluble with water temperature.

Russian Greenhouse Gas Emission Trends

More germane for this research is the dramatic decline in GHG emissions that followed the economic collapse of the former Soviet Union and East European countries during the 1990s. These declining carbon dioxide emissions trends, which are visible as a single track line in figure 3.2, are more clearly differentiated and discernable in table 3.1, with their lows underlined. Figure 3.3 reveals the relative decline both absolutely and proportionally in agricultural carbon dioxide discharges from 1990 to 2004, along with relative increases in the shares released by Russian industries and waste sectors. While the overall physical quantities of different GHGs decreased from 1990 to 2004, figure 3.4 reveals that their individual shares have been fairly stable. Because the Kyoto Protocol agreement regarding carbon dioxide emission reduction targets is based on 1990 emission levels, the dramatic decline in Russian industrial output in the early post-Soviet transition years became Russia's basis for becoming a major potential player in the Kyoto-based global carbon-offset trading markets. In 2003 the world's energy-related carbon dioxide emissions totalled 25.2 $GtCO_2$ (gigatons of carbon dioxide), with the United States, China and Russia accounting for twenty-three percent, fifteen percent and six percent, respectively. In just the last five years, recent estimates indicate that China now exceeds the United States for being the largest source of carbon dioxide emissions and could account for half of all carbon dioxide emissions by 2020 (Parker 2008).

Total Russian emissions reached a low in 1999 (see table 3.1) following the August 1998 Russian financial crash. There were no significant changes in the economic sector shares of Russian Federation GHG emissions (see figure 3.5), nor much change in the share of different GHGs in Russia's total discharge between 1990 and 2004 (see figure 3.6). The energy sector dominated during both time periods, contributing about eighty-one percent in terms of carbon dioxide equivalents. In both time periods, carbon dioxide was the overwhelming major GHG gas emitted (approximately seventy-seven to seventy-eight percent), followed by

Year	Total CO2	Gas Fuels	Liquid Fuels	Solid Fuels	Gas Flaring	Cement Production	Per Capita Emission	Bunker Rate Fuel*
1992	541,511	226,466	168,274	134,640	3,740	8,391	3.65	0
1993	494,142	217,281	143,272	123,856	2,947	6,786	3.34	0
1994	427,246	195,526	110,672	113,536	2,453	5,059	2.89	0
1995	410,370	194,628	99,767	108,308	2,704	4,964	2.78	7,857
1996	407,559	198,815	90,714	111,693	2,556	3,781	2.76	7,436
1997	402,240	194,597	100,541	100,982	2,489	3,631	2.73	7,303
1998	396,036	194,221	101,599	94,191	2,489	3,536	2.70	6,859
1999	394,887	196,469	94,826	97,308	2,422	3,862	2.71	7,090
2000	401,144	199,245	95,968	99,170i	2,354	4,406	2.73	7,454
2001	400,068	203,194	97,113	94,900	0	4,801	2.77	7,666
2002	397,964	203,398	94,670	94,770	0	5,127	2.76	7,954
2003	415,454	213,981	100,359	95,539	0	5,576	2.90	8,082
2004	415,951	216,517	95,241	92,427	5,551	6,215	2.89	8,201

* metric tons of carbon

Table 3.1. Russian Federation fossil fuel carbon dioxide emissions (in thousand metric tons of carbon), 1992–2004.
Source: Marland, Boden and Andres (2007).

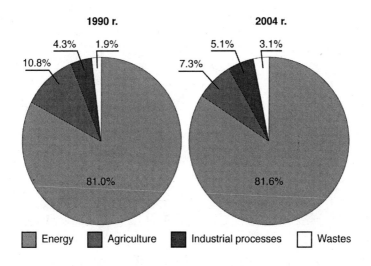

Figure 3.3. GHGs (in carbon dioxide equivalents) in the Russian Federation by sectors, 1990 and 2004.
Source: Russian Ministry of Economic Development and Trade (2006).

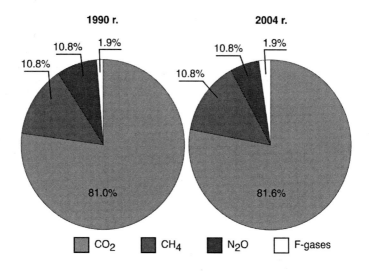

Figure 3.4. Share of different GHGs in total discharge in Russia (in carbon dioxide equivalents), 1990 and 2004.
Source: Russian Ministry of Economic Development and Trade (2006).

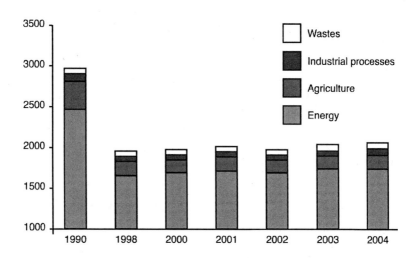

Figure 3.5. Dynamic discharge of GHGs, 1990, 1998 and 2000–2004, without consideration of land use, land use change and forestry.
Source: *4th National Communication in Compliance with Articles 4 & 12 of the Framework Convention of United Nations about Climate Change and Article 7 of the Kyoto Protocol* (2006).

RUSSIA AND THE NORTH

methane (approximately fourteen percent) and nitrous oxide (7.9 percent in 1990, down to 5.7 percent in 2004). This modest share decline for nitrous oxide is related to the decline in Russian agricultural activities. However, it is worth commenting on some of the different trends in the sources of GHG emissions from 1992 to 2004.

First, emissions from gas fuels slowly declined, reaching a low in 1998, and have been modestly increasing annually since then, being still slightly lower in 2004 than 1992. Thus, overall, the emissions from gas fuels have been fairly flat, which environmentally, is relatively positive, as the combustion of gas fuels produce much less carbon dioxide per unit of caloric energy than liquid or solid fossil fuels. Emissions from liquid fuels declined dramatically between 1992 and 1995, and then fluctuated up and down within a range of five percent annually, reaching a low in 2002. They are now on the increase with the booming Russian energy sector. Emissions from coal burning were over thirty percent lower in the nadir year of 2004, compared to 1992, reflecting the decreasing competitiveness of coal in the Russian industrial sector and the continuing shift to less carbon-intensive gas and liquid fuels. Several sources claim that the Russian data on releases of carbon dioxide from

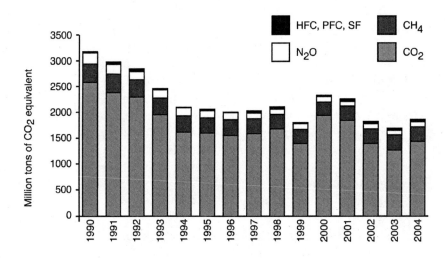

Figure 3.6. Contribution of different GHGs to the total anthropogenic emissions of the Russian Federation.
Source: *National Report of the Russian Federation on the Emission Commitments* (2007).

gas flaring in oil fields are poorly inventoried and data are completely absent for the years 2001–2004. As part of the requirements for being in compliance with Kyoto, Russia has again begun to report releases from gas flaring, which from a climate change perspective are troubling. As table 3.1 reveals, the gas flaring emissions for 2004 were approximately 235 percent higher than for those reported in 2000 and 148 percent higher than those reported in 1992. If anything, these data are all likely to under-report the actual releases, but the dramatic upturn cannot be questioned, and it is related to the lack of gas-capturing infrastructure in many of Russia's current oil producing fields.

Overall, the global cement industry contributes about five percent to global anthropogenic carbon dioxide emissions. Carbon dioxide is emitted from the calcination of limestone, the combustion of fuels in kilns and the power generation involved in cement production (Worrell et al. 2001: 303–329). In 2003 Russia's and America's contributions to global carbon emissions from the cement industry (2 percent and 4.6 percent, respectively) were trivial compared to China's 42.6 percent (Marland, Boden and Andres 2006). In 1998 emissions from the Russian cement industry had dropped to slightly under forty percent of their 1992 levels, but with the rebound of the construction industry in Russia, carbon emissions from cement production in 2004 returned to seventy-five percent of their 1992 level. Per capita emissions have modestly increased since their low in 1998, due to a combination of economic recovery and population decline. Finally, discharges from the combustion of bunker fuels were added to the emissions inventory in 1995 and have shown a steady increase since their estimated low in 1998.

In summary, all of the emission parameters are still lower today than in 1992, and more importantly, lower than the 1990 Kyoto base year for determining carbon allowances and carbon credits. However, all the emission parameters are now increasing. Thus, the question arises: How much carbon credit can Russia 'afford' to sell so as not to impinge on its own economic growth?

Climate Change in the Russian North: Real and Potential

The central objective of this section is to enumerate, elucidate and briefly comment on the major real and potential, largely human-induced, dynamic climate change and environmental change impacts.

With regard to climate change and global warming, the Russian North is of major significance, both for Russia and the entire planet. Another objective is to explore some cryosphere processes and their role in climate change in the Russian North. In fact, as we shall see, it is precisely in the Russian North and Far East where anthropogenic climate change is already having measurable impacts on the Russian Federation's physical and human environments. In other words, climate changes are occurring most dramatically and rapidly in the geographic regions where the majority of Russia's fossil fuel deposits are located. Accordingly, the trends of many of these climate changes portend significant challenges, as well as some new opportunities for Russian human and resource development during this century.

In the northern hemisphere, as a result of anthropogenic forcing, major changes in winds, temperatures and storm tracks are already being detected. Overall, the major changes currently being experienced and likely to intensify in the future are warmer and wetter winters across Northern Europe; increased annual precipitation (especially rainfall across Siberia); increased temperatures throughout all or nearly all of the Russian Federation; the probable complete melting of Arctic Sea ice during the summer; permafrost melting; northward and higher elevation movement of treelines; significant habitat destruction and northward and higher-elevation migration of flora and fauna ranges; major disruption of human urban, transportation, agricultural and energy industry infrastructure and potential major human-induced changes in climate-regulating feedback systems. These environmental changes are indeed troubling and unprecedented in regard to their number, geographical scope and rates of change.

According to the A1B 'business as usual' assumptions of the fourth IPCC assessment (IPCC 2007: 21), the mean projected global warming during the period from 1980–1999 to 2090–2099 will be 2.8 °C and much of the land area will warm by approximately 3.5 °C, while the cooling over some oceanic areas will be associated with the upwelling of cold deep ocean water. However, temperatures in many Arctic regions have already warmed as much as 4 °C over the last century, mostly in the past couple of decades, and the 'business as usual' scenario projects the Arctic to be warmer by ~7 °C by 2100 (see figures 3.7 and 3.8).

Additionally disquieting is the fact that GHG emissions so far this century are already outpacing the GHG emission assumptions used in the A1B 'business as usual' scenario. Statistical analyses of the various

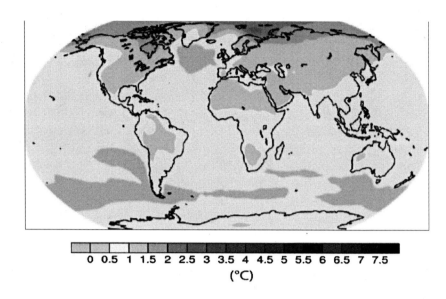

0 0.5 1 1.5 2 2.5 3 3.5 4 4.5 5 5.5 6 6.5 7 7.5
(°C)

Figure 3.7. Temperature changes in A1B 'Business as Usual' scenario for 2020-2029.
Source: IPCC (2007).

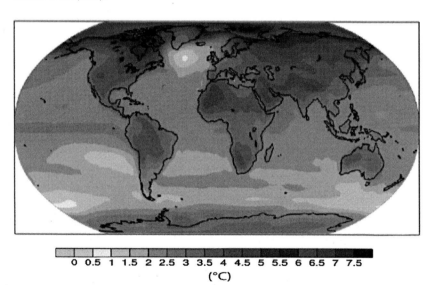

0 0.5 1 1.5 2 2.5 3 3.5 4 4.5 5 5.5 6 6.5 7 7.5
(°C)

Figure 3.8. Temperature changes in A1B 'Business as Usual' scenario for 2090–2099.
Source: IPCC (2007).

GCM climate models strongly suggest how serious the pace and degree of climate change may well be. Namely, there is less than a five percent chance that global warming this century will be less than 2 °C, but a twenty-five percent change that it will be greater than 5 °C. The realistic climatic impacts of temperature increases in the range of 5 °C compared to pre-industrial temperature levels significantly increase the risk of dangerous self-reinforcing feedbacks and abrupt large-scale shifts in the climate system (see figure 3.9).

The greatest risk of reaching such a tipping point is indeed in the high-latitude circumpolar Arctic region, where, as noted previously, the temperature increases have been greatest and the GCM models have a high degree of uncertainty with regard to cryosphere processes. First, the rapid retreat of Arctic Sea ice (see figure 3.10) has been exceeding even the simulation-model predictions that the Arctic Sea would reach near ice-free September conditions by 2040 (Holland, Bitz and Tremblay 2006). Greater warming in the Arctic has led to greater summer sea-ice melting, which creates self-reinforcing positive feedbacks. Less surface ice cover means lower surface albedo and more radiant energy available to be absorbed to melt even more ice. The resulting increase in the

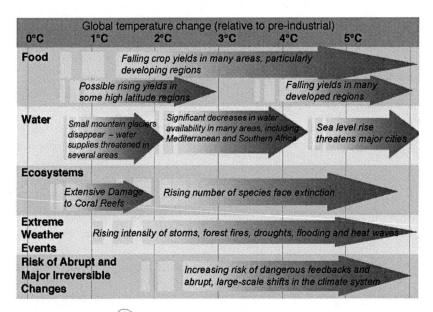

Figure 3.9. Projected impacts of climate change.
Source: Stern Review.

ice-free water surface absorbs still more short-wave infrared radiation, which reinforces warming temperatures.

It appears this feedback system is continuing to be ever more strongly felt (Schmid 2008). Second, the GCM models so far have not been able to adequately incorporate ice sheet and glacier dynamics and have consistently erred on the conservative side; namely, glaciers are retreating and surging faster than the models predict. A multitude of published scientific papers have reported on the hypothesis that warmer Arctic region temperatures could account for the observed increase in the volume of lubricating surface meltwater via fracture crevasses and moulins reaching the ice-bedrock interface, accelerating ice flow and increasing the loss of ice mass. For example, in the last decade alone, accelerated ice discharge not only in the west but also particularly in the east doubled the Greenland ice sheet mass deficit from ninety to 220 cubic kilometres per year (Rignot and Kanagaratnam 2006: 986–990). Recent analysis of satellites and other observations reveals that the speed-ups in ice sheet flow (fifty to one hundred percent) are even higher than earlier observations, but the relative speed-up of outlet glacier flow is far smaller (less than fifteen percent) (Joughin et al. 2008). The critical unknown is whether or not an Arctic-warming tipping point has already been reached.

One might ask what do these changes in the Greenland ice sheet and possible Arctic-warming tipping point portend for, or have to do with, the Russian North's climate change impacts? Well, for example, longer periods of ice-free coastal waters will increase coastal erosion from wave action, which will threaten coastal settlements and infrastructures. Changes are already evident in coastal/biological productivity, as are adverse effects on ice-dependent marine wildlife. While some regional fisheries may experience beneficial effects in the short run, and others will experience adverse effects, acidification is a long-term threat to all marine biological productivity and harvesting. On the other hand, beneficial effects of a less severe climate in the North and Siberia, while dependent on local conditions, include such things as reduced energy expenditures for heating, increased agricultural and forestry opportunities, more navigable river and sea routes and marine access to resources and offshore oil, gas, and ocean-floor mineral deposits (Anisimov et al. 2007: 655–661, 668–669). For Russia, all circumpolar nations and global trade, it appears likely that the dream of many for an ice-free (Canadian) Northwest Passage, which happened for the first time in the late summer of 2007, or an ice-free Russian Arctic Sea route will likely become a reality for increasingly longer periods annually.

While on the positive side a more ice-free Arctic Sea means that it will play a greater role as a carbon sink, on the negative side the resulting acidification of polar waters is predicted to have deleterious effects on calcified organisms and hence deleterious consequences for the entire aquatic food chain. Then, too, as noted previously, carbon dioxide has the relatively unusual property of being inversely soluble in water with regard to temperature. Thus, as ocean water temperatures increase, the ocean's ability to absorb carbon dioxide decreases and its

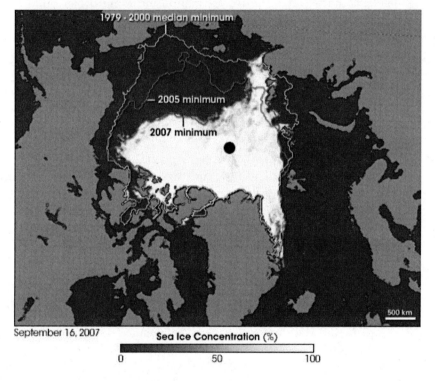

Figure 3.10. Arctic Sea Ice Minimums.*
Source: NASA (2007).

* This image shows the Arctic as observed by the Advanced Microwave Scanning Radiometer for EOS (AMSR-E) aboard NASA's Aqua satellite on 16 September 2007. In this image, the white indicates high sea ice concentration, the darker color and labels indicate the minimum Arctic sea ice boundaries for selected years. The black circle at the North Pole results from an absence of data as the satellite does not make observations that far north.

ability to serve as a carbon dioxide buffer for the atmosphere weakens, and if sea water temperatures rise too high, the oceans could become a new net source of atmospheric carbon dioxide. On the other hand, far more dire ecological disruption consequences would ensue before Arctic Ocean water temperatures would become warm enough to become net carbon dioxide sources.

Other global warming impacts include shorter periods of snow cover, longer frost-free periods, longer growing seasons and higher than average precipitation levels, especially as rain, thawing and changes in the northern Asian ice-rich permafrost occur with high potential for subsidence and damage to infrastructure, including urban buildings and utilities, oil and gas extraction and transportation facilities. By 2050 the highest discontinuous risk regions for these problems will be around the Arctic coast. The medium-risk zone includes such large population centres as Yakutsk, Noril'sk and Vorkuta and most of the Baikal-Amur and Trans-Siberian railways (Anisimov et al. 2007: 675; Instanes et al. 2005: 907–944; Anisimov and Belolutskaia 2004: 73–81; Anisimov and Lavrov 2004: 78–81; Tutubalina and Rees 2001: 191–203; Khrustalev 2000: 238–247).

The entire issue of permafrost thawing and the climatic role of the huge west Siberian lowland bogs are two of the most relevant issues related to climate change in Russia. Between the mid-1950s and 1990, there was an increase in the thickness of the active permafrost layer (i.e., the layer that melts in the summer and freezes in the winter) of more than twenty centimeters, according to historical data collected at the Russian meteorological stations for the continuous permafrost regions of the Russian Arctic (Frauenfeld et al. 2004; Zhang et al. 2005). On the other hand, for the same period, several specialized permafrost research sites in the central part of Sakha (Yakutia) revealed no significant changes in the thickness of the active layer (Varlamov et al. 2001; Varlamov 2003).

Everything else being equal, low snowfall alone can reduce the insulating effect of snow and lead to deeper winter freezing. However, everything is not equal and shorter periods of snow cover, longer frost-free periods and increased precipitation as rainfall all function as self-reinforcing positive feedbacks, leading to rising temperatures and faster permafrost thawing. When water freezes it expands about ten percent in volume, and conversely, when permafrost melts, land subsidence occurs. The greater the depth of melting, the greater the subsidence;

with differential local melting, differential subsidence and disruption will damage infrastructure and buildings and rupture oil and gas pipelines. During the last decades of the Soviet Union, there were numerous articles about thousands of such pipeline breaks in the North because of local permafrost melting combined with shoddy pipe welds performed under pressure to fulfill overly ambitious pipe-laying plans. During the course of a series of personal interviews conducted in Moscow in 1989, 1994 and 2000, many physical geography researchers were concerned that the entire low-lying Yamal Peninsula could disappear due to subsidence from permafrost melting. Thus, the melting of permafrost indirectly poses a huge potential strategic risk to the energy security of Western Europe and hence the United States.

Another major reason for very serious concern about permafrost melting is the fact that Siberia's bogs are a storehouse of enormous quantities of GHGs, mainly in the form of methane hydrates. Their release could very well result in the catastrophic warming of the earth because methane molecules are twenty-six times more potent than carbon dioxide molecules in their greenhouse warming effect (Mrasek 2008; "Northern Bogs" 2006). The west Siberian bogs contain some 70 GtC (gigatons of carbon) of methane representing twenty-five percent of all the methane stored on the globe's land surfaces (Pearce 2005: 12). If released, it could more than double the 762 GtC currently resident in the atmosphere (IPCC 2007: 6–13; Field and Raupach 2004; NGS 2008: 32–33). While on the one hand, warm temperatures increase floral biological activity that functions as a carbon sink, on the other hand, warmer temperatures also stimulate the detritus chain releasing both methane and carbon dioxide from the decay of undecomposed plant matter (Sever 2005; Bohn et al. 2007; Sample 2005a; Sample 2005b; Feifer 2006). The relative strength of these two feedback pathways is incredibly significant for the future of the planet's climate given the fact that approximately 900 GtC are frozen in permafrost zones globally and of which 500 GtC have been flash frozen in the Siberian tundra regions alone (Walter et al. 2006; McDonald et al. 2006; Smith et al. 2004).

Irrefutable evidence of the thawing of the Siberian permafrost lies in two phenomena, which may at first seem contradictory. First, over the past thirty years, the total lake surface area and number of lakes in the Siberian permafrost zone have increased by +14 percent and +4 percent, respectively, while in the southern zones of discontinuous permafrost the declines in lake area and number of lakes have ranged from –11 percent to minus –13 percent and from –6 percent to minus –9 percent, respectively, resulting in net losses of both lake area and number. The increases in lake area and number in the zones of continuous permafrost are clear evidence of melting and water ponding on top of the permafrost, whereas the latter lake drainage occurs as the permafrost degrades even further. Both processes have been leading to the accelerated release of carbon dioxide and methane (Smith et al. 2004; Smith et al. 2005).

Climatic Change Contrarians

Despite the overwhelming hard scientific evidence from empirical observation, measurement and systems modelling, there are still so-called climate skeptics or 'climate contrarians' publishing both in Russia and the West on the above enumerated climate changes and potential impacts in Russia and elsewhere. Two of these contrarians are Yuri Izrael, the director of the Russian Academy of Sciences' Institute of Climatology and Ecology, and Vladimir Melnikov, the director of Russia's Institute of the Earth's Cryosphere (Taylor 2005). Much of the climate science in Russia is centred on Izrael and he is renowned for both his skepticism about causes of global warming and his argument that global warming would be beneficial to Russia. His influence led to the prominent positioning of climate skeptics at the 2003 World Climate Change Conference in Moscow. Despite 250 members of the Russian Academy of Sciences having signed a nongovernmental organization petition in favour of Russia's ratification of the Kyoto Protocol, Izrael very likely played a critical role in the May 2004 decision of the academy not to support ratification (Korppoo, Karas and Grubb 2006).

Without having ever interviewed these people or met them in person, one is hard-pressed to understand their position, other than the fact that many people in Russia think the benefits of global warming for Russia exceed its potential costs, especially the direct and indirect costs (e.g., lower economic growth) of climate change adaptation and mitigation. In general, however, internal disputes over Russian climate-related policies and ratification of the Kyoto Protocol seem very much to have been based on differing interdepartmental and intramural assessments regarding the financial and bureaucratic benefits and costs of addressing, honestly and scientifically, global warming and climate change policies, rather than on the validity of scientific evidence of global warming. An overview of the various positions taken by various Russian stakeholders in these internal debates and concerns over Kyoto is presented in a later part of this chapter.

Outside of Russia, well-funded and orchestrated efforts to discredit climate science have been uncovered in the United States. For example, the facts are quite clear that between 1998 and 2005 ExxonMobil funnelled nearly US$ 16 million to a network of forty-three advocacy organizations in a deliberate effort to confuse the public about global warming science and sow seeds of doubt about global warming and the human role in climate change via fossil fuel consumption and land cover/land use changes (Union of Concerned Scientists 2007). In fact, the source of the previous citation, the Heartland Institute, has, since 1998, received nearly forty percent of its total funds (US$ 561,500) from ExxonMobil, specifically designated for climate change projects (Union of Concerned Scientists 2007: 31). While the case of ExxonMobil's deliberate climate change/global warming disinformation campaign has received the most detailed exposure and analysis, it has been just one of many fossil fuel energy companies and industry associations that have expended considerable funds to neo-liberal and conservative think-tanks and given campaign contributions, lobbied politicians and funnelled campaign money to politicians in a thus far successful effort to not only prevent US ratification of Kyoto but preclude any federal effort to curtail carbon dioxide emissions. Even more disturbing, the US media and blogs, such as ClimateScienceWatch, have written about numerous well-documented examples of the Bush administration's political efforts to interfere with climate science and censor US government scientists (e.g., "Censorship of Government Scientists" 2008; Harper 2008; Hansen 2008). As the American example attests, climate change policy-making is high politics and the global warming debate in the United States, Russia and elsewhere is one in which a number of interest groups, often drawing upon the vocabulary of science, aims to make their voices heard.

Basic UNFCCC and Kyoto Protocol Information

Many readers of this book may not be familiar with the key features and history of the Kyoto Protocol despite the voluminous media accounts about Kyoto over the past decade. Accordingly, the objective of this section is to provide a concise overview of some of the important Kyoto-related terms, concepts, features and instruments (for more complete information, see Korppoo, Karas and Grubb 2006; UNEP; United Nations 1998). UNFCCC stands for the United Nations Framework Convention on Climate Change and the Kyoto Protocol, signed on 11 December 1997, at Kyoto, Japan, as an amendment to the UNFCCC. The Kyoto Protocol was opened for formal country signatures on 16 March 1998. In order for the Kyoto agreement to enter into force, two core requirements had to be satisfied. First, at least fifty-five countries had to formally ratify the agreement, and second, the combined carbon dioxide emissions of these fifty-five ratifying countries had to represent at least fifty-five percent of the world's 1990 carbon dioxide emissions. The agreement set GHG reduction targets for the 2008–2012 period for six GHGs, including carbon dioxide, methane, nitrous oxide, hydrofluorocarbons, perfluorocarbons and sulphur hexafluoride.

In December 2000 the IPCC Kyoto-related talks in The Hague stalled, largely due to US stonewalling shortly after the contested and uncertain results of the US Presidential election. Soon after taking office in 2001, President George Bush stated that the United States would not ratify Kyoto. Bush's Kyoto stance, and for that matter his administration's resistance to both acknowledge the complex reality of global warming and the role of human actions in fossil fuel consumption and land use changes as major causes, and hence the failure of the US government to play any significant leadership role in dealing with climate change, presented a crucial and fairly unique opportunity for Russia to show herself as a multilateral power player and positive global environmental leader. This was true because in the Kyoto base year of 1990 for calculating GHG reduction targets, the United States, Australia and Russia contributed 55.8 percent of the Annex I nations' global GHG emissions. The United States was responsible for about one-third, Russia 17.4 percent and Australia the remainder. Through the summer of 2004, none of these three nations had ratified Kyoto. Thus, with the United States refusing to ratify Kyoto, the only way the agreement could come into force was if Russia ratified it.

Russia and the Kyoto Protocol

First, it is pertinent to summarize the various negotiating positions that Russia held during the lengthy and contentious Kyoto negotiation process. For example, Russia opposed quantitative restrictions on Kyoto mechanisms, taxes on the implementation of Kyoto mechanisms, special status for the CDM (Clean Development Mechanism) and the treating of Russia's emission surplus due to its economic meltdown in the 1990s as "hot air". It also opposed "supplementarity", owing to its potential negative effects on the development of carbon markets. On the other hand, Russia supported an early start to JI (Joint Implementation) projects and carbon emissions trading, a flexible approach to compliance, counting forests as carbon sinks, international support for capacity-building in IET (international emissions trading), a regulatory role for state and government involvement, the reinvestment of emission trading revenues into climate change mitigation projects and the banking of carbon credits and forward contracts (e.g., Avdeeva 2005; Korppoo, Karas and Grubb 2006; Korppoo and Moe 2007).

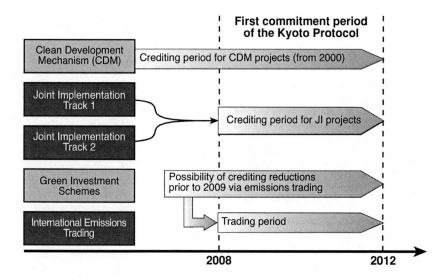

Figure 3.11. Mechanisms for international emissions transactions under the Kyoto Protocol.
Source: Korppoo, Karas, and Grubb, eds. (2006).

During Russia's protracted internal deliberations prior to ratification, the arguments for and against Russian ratification of the Kyoto Protocol can simply be summarized as a series of bulleted items (see Avdeeva 2005; Henry and Sundstrom 2007: 47–69; Korppoo 2002: 387–393; Korppoo and Moe 2007; Korppoo, Karas and Grubb 2006; Tangen et al. 2002).

Arguments for ratification of the Kyoto Protocol:

- the climate change impacts: permafrost, sea level rise;
- enhanced foreign direct investment (FDI) from JI;
- the revenue from likely sales of Russia's emission surplus;
- the investments via Kyoto mechanisms could support modernization and innovation in the energy sector;
- the improvements in energy efficiency are crucial for future economic growth;
- GHG reductions could improve the domestic physical-ecological environment;
- Russian ratification could improve Russia's image as a supporter of global multilateralism; and
- ratification and implementation could smooth the way for Russia's entry into the WTO (World Trade Organization).

Arguments against ratification of the Kyoto Protocol:

- climate change impacts may be positive for high-latitude Russia;
- the extent of anthropogenic climate change is (very) uncertain;
- revenues from ratification and compliance are likely to be low;
- the costs would be too high for domestic compliance;
- the Kyoto Protocol is unfair because not all countries have taken on emission (reduction) commitments;
- the second phase or post-2012 GHG limits could conflict with Russia's ambitious economic growth goals;
- US withdrawal makes the Kyoto Protocol nearly pointless; and
- the Kyoto Protocol is at best ineffective and more radical approaches are necessary.

In the final analysis it appears that the following factors were most crucial in Vladimir Putin's final decision in favour of ratification. At the Marrakech meetings in 2002, Russia was successful in bargaining for a thirty percent reduction below the 1990 baseline levels for calculating "carbon credits" due to its steep economic decline. This created a potential US$ 10 billion windfall for the sale of Russian "hot air" carbon credits. The adoption of such things as the CDM, JI and Green Investment Schemes and IET mechanisms were Kyoto Protocol features considered favourable for Russia. Finally, the decision was probably based much more on political considerations than on scientific or even financial ones, most important of which was likely the European Union's (EU's) support for Russia's membership in the WTO. On the one hand, lack of US ratification has weakened the prospects for Russian revenue in the carbon-offset markets. On the other hand, Russia's ratification and the United States' failure to ratify elevated Russia's image as a multilateral power player and its position for influence in post-2012 climate negotiations has concomitantly reinforced the United States' image as an obstructionist unilateralist.

Finally, let us turn briefly to highlight some of the events that unfolded during Russia's domestic decision to ratify the Kyoto Protocol. In December 2003 the World Wildlife Federation conducted a survey of the Duma, which revealed that less than twenty-five percent favoured ratification, greater than twenty-five percent opposed ratification and greater than fifty percent thought ratification was possible. Andrey Illarionov, economic adviser to President Putin, can well be considered to have been the most vocal critical spokesperson of the Russian opposition to ratification. In January 2004 the chair of the State Duma's International Affairs Committee announced that parliamentary hearings would be held in the spring of 2004. This led to a great deal of controversy from the late winter to the autumn of 2004. For example, at the Duma hearings, three committees (ecology, economy and international affairs) issued a joint statement that the Russian ratification of Kyoto would be "inexpedient" and without purpose given the clear US position and the nonparticipation of major developing countries such as China and India.

The former situation can be translated as a concern that the value of potential carbon credits would be vastly diminished without US participation, and hence the United States needed to purchase carbon credits. The latter argument was in close alignment with a major US stated reason for refusing to ratify the Kyoto Protocol. On the other hand, the Russian Industry and Economy Ministry and the Ministry of Economic Development and Trade urged Putin to ratify. Presumably, the potential for FDI, industrial modernization and profits from the sale of carbon credits were the prime reasons for their position (Avdeeva 2005: 293–294; Korppoo, Karas and Grubb 2006: 6–23).

In May 2004 Putin began WTO accession talks with the EU while proclaiming there was no link between Kyoto and the WTO on Russia's part. On 23 September 2004, the Russian Ministry of Natural Resources (read: coal, oil, gas and metal and mineral mining interests) formally recommended Kyoto approval. Three days later, Illarionov compared the Kyoto Protocol to fascism. On 30 September 2004, the Russian Cabinet of Ministers approved the federal law to ratify Kyoto. On 22 October 2004, by the overwhelming margin of 334 to 74, the State Duma voted to ratify. President Putin signed off on the treaty on 5 November 2004 and Russia's formal submission of its ratification documents to the United Nations occurred on 18 November 2004. This final Russian action allowed Kyoto to come into force ninety days later on 16 February 2005 (Korppoo, Karas and Grubb 2006: 10–21).

Opportunities and Challenges for Russia's Kyoto Implementation

The Kyoto implementation mechanisms diagramed in figure 3.11 potentially provide some positive opportunities for Russia as a result of her Kyoto ratification. For example, table 3.2 includes some of the potential FDI by economic sector that could come to Russia as JI projects. To benefit from Kyoto ratification directly, Russia and other nations need to put in place some elements in order to achieve institutional compliance. Briefly, there are four major types of compliance elements. First, there is a fairly detailed and complex series of what have become known as PAMS, or domestic policies and measures, ranging from legal to economic to technologic. Second, annual GHG inventories according to IPCC guidelines must be implemented. Third, a registry to track domestic emissions and implementation of the Kyoto mechanisms and commitments needs to be established. Finally, all of the above must be reported to the UNFCC Secretariat annually.

Russia still had major data problems and compliance gaps late in 2008, many of which were hampering progress on JI projects or leading to outright termination of even the planning stages for such domestic and FDI projects (e.g., Elder 2008). For example, forestry inventories were not consistent with IPCC requirements and their quality varied considerably between regions. Data for gas flaring and coal mine methane were not available. GHG emissions for the waste sector and agriculture were simply not available. There were a number of problems with industrial activity data and a lack of data for transport, municipal and residential fuel consumption (Korppoo and Moe 2007; Korppoo, Karas and Grubb 2006: 85–137). Table 3.3 represents the status and an overview of the relative difficulty of Russia being able to comply with Kyoto at approximately the time of Russian ratification.

On the other hand, as a summary compliance table, table 3.3 does not by any means indicate that Russian progress towards implementation was absent. A number of foreign consultants, as well as Russian sci-

Energy sector	
Power	combined cycle gas turbines; distributive networks; clean coal technologies; fuel switching
Oil and gas	reduction of gas flaring and venting; reduction of gas leakage in transmission; improvement of compressors; oil refining; retrofitting CHP
Renewable energy	wind; solar; biomass; hydro; geothermal; fuel cell efficiency; equipment modernization; design, processes and end use
Industrial sector	
Energy efficiency	CHP; lighting; motors; boilers
Iron and steel	production processes
Chemicals, paper	retrofitting; replacing obsolete equipment metallurgy
Forestry	land use change; reforestation
Waste fuel recovery	methane landfill capture; cement sector
Residential/construction	insulation; double-glazing; energy metering; fuel switching; efficient combustion; insulating pipes; better roofs; passive solar; optimizing pumps

Table 3.2. Potential JI projects by economic sector.
Source: Korppoo, Karas, and Grubb, eds. (2006).

Element of compliance	Current status in Russia	
Emission	Russia below target	+ +
Policies and measures	Enough to show activities	+
Registry	A simple registry is easy, quick and cheap to establish	−
Reporting	Easy to improve if better inventies and more cooperation between administrative units	−
Inventories	Data missing, quality not consistent with IPCC requirements	− −

+ + will not cause problems
+ will not cause serious problems
− will cause problems but easy to solve
− − will problems, difficult to solve

Table 3.3. Russian Kyoto compliance summary.
Source: Korppoo (2004).

entists, were involved in the estimates of the potential GHG emission reductions that could be achieved in the Russian natural gas sector. The data in table 3.4 represent both a tangible example of Russian efforts to comply with Articles 4 and 12 of the FCUNCC and Article 7 of the Kyoto Accord. The data represent GHG emission data projected out to 2020 under two different scenarios: a so-called moderate scenario and an 'innovatively active scenario.' What these operational terms mean is not entirely clear, but presumably the latter scenario is a combination of structural change, innovation in the energy sector leading to greater efficiency and a high level of economic growth. In both scenarios Russia would not reach its 1990-based carbon dioxide emissions cap by 2020. If accurate, this means that Russia would be able to play a significant role in global carbon trading markets. But will there really be a global demand for such a role?

Greenhouse gas	Unit of measurement	1990	2004	2010	2015	2020
Moderate scenario						
CO_2	Mt CO_2	2,283	1,616	1,736	1,843	1,956
	% of 1990	100	70.8	76.0	80.7	85.7
Innovatively active scenario						
CO_2	Mt CO_2	2,283	1,616	1,820	2,009	2,218
	% of 1990	100	70.8	79.7	88.0	97.2
CH_4	Mt CO_2e	406	292	320	344	371
	% of 1990	100	72.0	78.8	84.9	91.5
N_2O	Mt CO_2e	233	118	133	147	163
	% of 1990	100	50.7	57.2	63.2	69.8
F-gases	Mt CO_2e	39	48	56	63	71
	% of 1990	100	123.0	144.0	161.5	182.0
Sum of Kyoto gases	Mt CO_2e	2,961	2,074	2,329	2,563	2,823
	% of 1990	100	70.0	78.7	86.6	95.3

Table 3.4. Characteristics of Kyoto gas emission scenarios in the Russian Federation to 2020.
Source: *4th National Communication in Compliance with Articles 4 & 12 of the Framework Convention of United Nations about Climate Change and Article 7 of the Kyoto Protocol* (2006).

What Challenges Lie Ahead for Russia and Will a Clear Russian Climate Policy Manifest Itself?

In summary, ratification of the Kyoto Protocol was relatively easy, but implementation and compliance have not been, and will not be, as easy and problem-free for Russia. First, Russia has been slow to implement compliance processes and did not open its doors to domestic and foreign investors to start trading carbon credits until late March 2008. Bureaucratic and ministerial infighting over control of the program has already led to the cancellation of dozens of environmentally friendly projects and has jeopardized others. The IET mechanism was only set to run for forty-eight months and Russia has already missed the first three months or more (Elder 2008). Given the unstable geopolitical situation in the Middle East and elsewhere, the volatility of crude oil prices, the uneasy state of the global energy economy and differential economic growth rates, it is still not at all clear what financial and other benefits Russia will reap from her ratification of the Kyoto Protocol (for example, see Elder 2008; Redman 2008). European carbon markets appear very unstable and the global economic downturn augurs well for neither the sale of Russian carbon markets nor possibly even continued growth in Russian oil and gas exports to Europe (Elder 2008).

The situation is made murkier still by difficult problems facing Russia's oil industry ("Russia's Oil Industry: Trouble in the Pipeline" 2008). There are significant technological, institutional, legal and organizational limitations and difficulties still to be resolved in Russia prior to its fully complying with Kyoto. There is a serious need to marry and bring into alignment all climate change policy components with other Russian strategic development goals and tasks. The most serious potential conflict may occur if Russia's economic transition is slow in reducing its energy intensity and if at the same time rapid economic expansion results in its GHG emissions rising much faster than many had projected, creating a "Kyoto Cross", a sort of 21st-century perverse "Scissors Crisis". In the near term, given Russia's flush oil and gas revenues, it seems likely that Russian political considerations will dominate over economic ones. Finally, unless some of the worse potential climate change impacts are felt across Russia's landscape and by her people more rapidly and disruptively than anyone would estimate, it seems Russian strategic energy issues will dominate over climate change issues. Accordingly, then, it will be a very warm wind indeed that ushers in a sound and discernable Russian climate change policy, which nonetheless may be too little too late.

REFERENCES

4th National Communication in Compliance with Articles 4 & 12 of the Framework Convention of United Nations about Climate Change and Article 7 of the Kyoto Protocol. 2006. Moscow.

Anisimov, O. A. 2007. "Polar Regions (Arctic and Antarctic)." In Climate Change 2007: Impacts, Adaptation and Vulnerability. Contribution of Working Group II to the Fourth Assessment Report of the Intergovernmental Panel on Climate Change, ed. M. L. Parry, O. F. Canziani, J. P. Palutikof, P. J. van der Linden and C. E. Hanson. Cambridge: Cambridge University Press, 653–685.

Anisimov, O. A., and M. A. Belolutskaia. 2004. "Predictive Modelling of Climate Change Impacts on Permafrost: Effects of Vegetation." Meteorol. Hydrol. 11: 73–81.

Anisimov, O. A., and C. A. Lavrov. 2004. "Global Warming and Permafrost Degradation: Risk Assessment for the Infrastructure of the Oil and Gas Industry." *Technologies of Oil and Gas Industry* 3: 78–83.

Avdeeva, T. G. November 2005. "Russia and the Kyoto Protocol: Challenges Ahead." *Review of European Community and International Environmental Law (RECIEL)* 14: 293–302.

Bohn, T. J. et al. October–December 2007. "Methane Emissions from Western Siberian Wetlands: Heterogeneity and Sensitivity to Climate Change." *Environmental Research Letters* 2, 045015, doi: 10.1088/1748-9326/2/4/045015.

"Censorship of Government Scientists." 2008. [http://www.climatescience watch.org/index.php/csw/C20/] [consulted 20 June 2008].

Elder, M. 25 March 2008. "Carbon Credits Get Cool Reception." *The Moscow Times*.

Farzin, Y. H. Fall 2000. "Kyoto Greenhouse Gas Emissions Reduction Targets: Economic Issues and Prospects." *Agricultural and Resource Economics Update*. [http://www.agecon.ucdavis.edu/extension/update/articles/fall2000_2.pdf] [consulted 16 May 2008].

Feifer, G. 18 September 2006. "Climate Change Cited in Siberian Landscape Shift." *NPR: All Things Considered*.

Field, C. B., and M. R. Raupach, eds. 2004. *The Global Carbon Cycle: Integrating Humans, Climate, and the Natural World*. Washington, DC: Island Press.

Frauenfeld, O. W. et al. 2004. "Interdecadal Changes in Seasonal Freeze and Thaw Depths in Russia." *Journal of Geophysical Research* 109, D05101, doi: 10.1029/2003JD004245.

Hansen, J. 23 June 2008. "Twenty Years Later: Tipping Points Near on Global Warming." The Huffington Post. [http://www.huffingtonpost.com/dr-james-hansen/twenty-years-later-tippin_b_108766.html] [consulted 24 June 2008).

——. 13 July 2006. "The Threat to the Planet." *New York Review of Books* 53: 12: 12–16.

Hansen, J. et al. 26 September 2006. "Global Temperature Change." *Proceedings of the National Academy of Sciences* 103: 39: 14,288–14,293.

Harper, T. 24 June 2008. "Earth Near Tipping Point, Climatologist Warns." *The Toronto Star*. [http://www.thestar.com/News/World/article/447808] [consulted 24 June 2008].

Henry, L. A., and L. M. Sundstrom. November 2007. "Russia and the Kyoto Protocol: Seeking an Alignment of Interests and Image." *Global Environmental Politics* 7: 4: 47–69.

Holland, M. M., C. M. Bitz and B. Tremblay. 12 December 2006. "Future Abrupt Reductions in the Summer Arctic Sea Ice." *Geophysical Research Letters* 33, L23503, doi: 10.1029/2006GL028024. [http://www.ucar.edu/news/releases/2006/arctic.shtml].

Instanes, A. et al. 2005. "Infrastructure: Buildings, Support Systems, and Industrial Facilities." In *Arctic Climate Impact Assessment, ACIA*, ed. C. Symon, L. Arris and B. Heal. Cambridge: Cambridge University Press, 907–944.

IPCC (Intergovernmental Panel on Climate Change). 2007. "Understanding and Attributing Climate Change." Chapter 9 in *Climate Change 2007: The Physical Science Basis: Summary for Policy Makers*. Cambridge: Cambridge University Press.

Joughin, I. et al. 17 April 2008. "Seasonal Speedup along the Western Flank of the Greenland Ice Sheet." *Science DOI*: 10.1126/science.1153288.

Khrustalev, L. N. 2000. "On the Necessity of Accounting for the Effect of Changing Climate in Permafrost Engineering." In *Geocryological Hazards*, ed. L. S. Garagulia and E. D. Yershow. Moscow: Kruk Publishers, 238–247.

Korppoo, A. December 2004. "Russia and Compliance under Kyoto: An Institutional Approach." The Royal Institute of International Affairs: Chatham House.

——. 2002. "Russian Ratification Process: Why is the Rest of the World Waiting? Research Letter." *Climate Policy* 2: 387–393.

Korppoo, A., J. Karas, and M. Grubb, eds. 2006. *Russia and the Kyoto Protocol: Opportunities and Challenges*. Washington, DC: Brookings Institute: Chatham House.

Korppoo, A., and A. Moe. 2007. "Russian Climate Politics: Light at the End of the Tunnel?" Climate Strategies briefing paper. [http://www.climate-strategies.org/uploads/Russia_politics_bp.pdf] [consulted 15 November 2007].

Manning, M. 2008. "Climate Change 2007: Observations and Drivers of Climate Change." Paper presented at the IPCC briefing at WMO Congress, Geneva, Switzerland, 15 May. [http://www.ipcc.ch/pdf/presentations/briefing-geneva-2007-05/observation-and-drivers.pdf] [consulted 16 June 2008].

Marland, G., T. A. Boden and R. J. Andres. 2006. "Global, Regional, and National Annual CO_2 Emissions from Fossil-Fuel Burning, Cement Manufacture, and Gas Flaring: 1751–2003." In *Trends: A Compendium of Data on Global Change*. Carbon Dioxide Information Analysis Center, Environmental Sciences Division, Oak Ridge National Laboratory, US Department of

Energy. Oak Ridge, TN: CDIAC. [http://cdiac.esd.ornl.gov/ftp/ndp030/] [consulted 10 May 2008].

McDonald, G. M. et al. 13 October 2006. "Rapid Early Development of Circumarctic Peatlands and Atmospheric CH_4 and CO_2 Variations." *Science* 314: 285–288.

Mrasek, V. 17 April 2008. "Melting Methane: A Storehouse of Greenhouse Gases Is Opening in Siberia." Spiegel On Line. [http://www.spiegel.de/international/world/0,1518,547976,00.html] [consulted 21 March 2008].

NGS (National Geographic Society). April 2008. *Special Report: Changing Climate.* Washington, DC: National Geographic Society.

National Report of the Russian Federation on the Emission Commitments. 2007. Moscow.

"Northern Bogs May Have Helped Kick-Start Past Global Warming." 13 October 2006. *Science Daily.* [http://www.sciencedaily.com/releases/2006/10/061012183530.htm] [consulted 30 April 2008].

Parker, R. 10 March 2008. "China CO_2 Emissions Rising Faster Than Expected." *Future Pundit.* [http://www.futurepundit.com/archives/005062.html] [consulted 6 April 2008].

Pearce, F. 2005. "Climate Warning as Siberia Melts." *New Scientist Magazine* 11: 2512: 12.

Redman, J. 11 April 2008. "The World Bank's Carbon Deals." *Foreign Policy in Focus.*

Richter-Menge, J. et al. 2006. "State of the Arctic Report." NOAA OAR Special Report. Seattle, WA: NOAA/OAR/PMEL.

Rignot, E., and P. Kanagaratnam. 17 February 2006. "Changes in the Velocity Structure of the Greenland Ice Sheet." *Science* 311: 5763: 986–990.

Russian Federation. Ministry of Economic Development and Trade. 2006. *Russian Federation: Report on the Evidence of Progress in Fulfillment of the Obligations of the Russian Federation According to the Kyoto Protocol.* Moscow: Ministry of Economic Development and Trade.

"Russia's Oil Industry: Trouble in the Pipeline." 10 May 2008. *The Economist,* 71–72.

Sample, I. 12 August 2005a. "Melting Permafrost Poses Greenhouse Crisis." *The Guardian.*

———. 11 August 2005b. "Warming Hits 'Tipping Point' Siberia Feels the Heat It's a Frozen Peat Bog the Size of France and Germany Combined, Contains Billions of Tonnes of Greenhouse Gas and, for the First Time Since the Ice Age, It Is Melting." *The Guardian.*

Schmid, R. E. 2 May 2008. "Major Arctic Sea Ice Melt Is Expected This Summer." Associated Press.

Sever, M. July 2005. "Carbon Leaching out of Siberian Peat." Geotimes. [http://www.geotimes.org/july05/NN_arcticpeatCO2.html] [consulted 3 March 2008].

Smith, L. C. et al. 3 June 2005. "Disappearing Arctic Lakes." *Science* 308: 1429.

——. 16 January 2004. "Siberian Peatlands a Net Carbon Sink and Global Methane Source Since the Early Holocene." *Science* 303: 353–356.

Tangen, K. et al. 2002. *A Russian Green Investment Scheme: Securing Environmental Benefits from International Emissions Trading.* Climate Strategies.

Taylor, J. M. 1 November 2005. "Russians Debunk Permafrost Scam: Siberia Not Melting, Methane Gases Remain Stable." Heartland Institute. [http://www.hearland.org/Article.cfm?artid=17978] [consulted 30 March 2008].

Thompson, D. W. J. et al. 29 May 2008. "A Large Discontinuity in the Mid-Twentieth Century in Observed Global-Mean Surface Temperature." *Nature* 453: 646–649.

Tutubalina, O. V., and W. G. Rees. 2001. "Vegetation Degradation in a Permafrost Region as Seen from Space: Noril'sk (1961–1999)." *Cold Reg. Sci. Technol.* 32: 191–203.

Union of Concerned Scientists. January 2007. "Smoke, Mirrors and Hot Air: How ExxonMobil Uses Big Tobacco's Tactics to Manufacture Uncertainty on Climate Science." [http://www.ucsusa.org/assets/documents/global_warming/exxon_report.pdf] [consulted 3 February 2009].

United Nations. 1998. *Kyoto Protocol to the United Nations Framework Convention on Climate Change.* [http://unfccc.int/resource/docs/convkp/kpeng.pdf] [consulted 8 May 2008].

UNEP (United Nations Environment Programme). "Manual on Compliance with and Enforcement of Multilateral Environmental Agreements." United Nations Environment Programme, Division of Environmental Law and Conventions. [http://www.unep.org/dec/onlinemanual/Resources/Glossary/tabid/69/Default.aspx [consulted 20 November 2007].

Varlamov, S. P. 2003. "Variations in the Thermal State of the Lithogenic Base of Landscapes in Central Yakutia." *Proceedings of the Second International Conference, The Role of Permafrost Ecosystems in Global Climate Change*, 12–17 August 2002, Yakutsk, Russia, 52–56.

Varlamov, S. P. et al. 2001. "Thermal Response of the Lithogenic Base of Permafrost Landscapes to Recent Climate Change in Central Yakutia. *Proceedings of the International Conference, The Role of Permafrost Ecosystems in Global Climate Change*, Yakutsk, Russia, 3–5 May 2000.

Walter, K. M. et al. 7 September 2006. "Methane Bubbling from Siberian Thaw Lakes as a Positive Feedback to Climate Warming." *Nature* 443: 71–75.

Worrell, E. et al. 2001. "Carbon Dioxide Emissions from the Global Cement Industry." *Annual Review of Energy and Environment* 26: 303–329.

Zhang, T. et al. 2005. "Spatial and Temporal Variability of Active Layer Thickness over the Russian Arctic Drainage Basin." *Journal of Geophysical Research* 110, D16101, doi: 10.1029/2004JD005642.

Chapter Four

Recent Developments
in the Russian Fisheries Sector

Anne-Kristin Jørgensen

Introduction

In the city of Murmansk on the Kola Peninsula, the fisheries theme is omnipresent. The city's coat of arms is graced by a fish and a trawler under a stylized northern light. There is a large fisheries port, a fisheries research institute and a plethora of fishing and fish processing companies. "Fisherman's Day" on the second Sunday of July is not just any professional holiday—it is a cause for major celebrations where everybody takes part.

However, many of those dependent on the fisheries—a key factor in the economy of northwestern Russia—probably view the celebrations with mixed feelings. In the course of the last decade and a half, the Russian fisheries sector has earned a reputation as being inefficient, criminalized and unreformable. Official yearly catches are down to a third of the amounts produced towards the end of the Soviet period, the fishing fleet is in poor condition and the land industry is withering away. Fundamental disagreements among decision makers on how the sector should be managed have frustrated all attempts to create a stable legal and institutional framework for the fisheries, despite a general consensus on the fact that stability and predictability are crucial factors if the current stagnation is to be overcome.

The first part of this chapter examines the performance of the Russian fisheries in the post-Soviet period, as well as the main conflicts that have marred Russian fisheries policy and management since the breakup of the Soviet Union. In the second part of the chapter, more detailed attention is given to the recent (2007–2008) reform attempts, and to an assessment of the chances that these attempts will succeed.[1]

The Soviet Legacy

The development of Soviet marine fisheries began in the 1920s with the establishment of fishery kolkhozes and, subsequently, trawler fleets in the Barents Sea and the Far East (Pautzke 1997). The Soviet fisheries sector soon came to be dominated by a relatively small number of large state-owned fishing fleets, whose main task was to provide the country's inhabitants with sufficient amounts of protein in the form of affordable fish products (Vylegazhnin and Zilanov 2000). Consequently, the majority of fishing activities were oriented towards plentiful pelagic species like pollock, herring, capelin and mackerel. From the late 1950s, a significant amount of the total catch was taken in distant waters outside the African and South American continents. The distant-water fishery was heavily subsidized by the state.

The Soviet economy was organized according to the sector principle,[2] so all functions related to the fisheries were subsumed under the umbrella of the Ministry of Fisheries. The country was divided into five main fisheries regions, or 'fisheries basins'—the Northern, Far East, Western (Baltic), Black Sea and Caspian. All fisheries-related activities in each basin were supervised by a regional management body that served as the ministry's extended arm in the region. In the Northern fisheries basin, which encompassed Murmansk and Arkhangel'sk Oblasti, as well as the Autonomous Republic of Karelia, this management organization was called Sevryba (Northfish) (Hønneland and Jørgensen 2002).

According to Hønneland (2004), the Northern fisheries basin employed some eighty thousand people at the end of the Soviet period. Of these, more than seventeen thousand were employed by the largest fishing fleet, Murmansk Trawl Fleet, and more than six thousand by the Murmansk Fish Combinate, the largest shore processing facility. The regional "fisheries complex" was a highly integrated system, with Sevryba at the centre of a structure encompassing the industry proper (fishing fleets and processing plants), as well as a large number of other organizations responsible for supportive functions like supplies, sales and research. Ivanova (2005) argues that, despite Sevryba's status as a federal body, the regional influence on the Northern fisheries basin was quite substantial in the Soviet period. She points out that Sevryba managers were part of the regional fisheries community, and that operative decisions were mostly taken on the regional (Sevryba) level.

Russian Fisheries in the Post-Soviet Period: Stuck in Transition?

The breakup of the Soviet Union meant the end of the sector principle in the economy, and the once monolithic fisheries complex rapidly disintegrated. Productive and management functions were split from each other, and a further process of fragmentation took place within each of the two spheres. In the course of a few years, many of the fishing fleets were split up into a multitude of smaller companies and partly or wholly privatized. Both the state companies and the new private ones adapted to the introduction of market economy principles by orienting themselves almost exclusively towards high-profit activities. The fleets, consisting predominantly of aging and fuel-consuming vessels, were almost completely withdrawn from the distant fishing grounds and the pressure on fish stocks in the Russian Exclusive Economic Zone (EEZ) steadily grew. Moreover, the traditional focus on cheap and plentiful species of fish for the home market was abandoned, as the fishing companies switched to species fetching good prices in Russia's neighbouring countries to the east (Japan and Korea) and west (mainly Norway), where an increasing share of their catches were landed.[3]

Frequent changes in the legal and institutional framework—first and foremost the system for quota allocation—made fishing companies wary of making long-term commitments, e.g., by investing in the modernization of their fishing fleets. Instead, most actors strived to maximize short-term gains—often by overfishing their quotas, which further increased the pressure on stocks in the EEZ.[4] Due to incomplete legislation and weaknesses in the control system, quota restrictions could usually be violated with impunity. It is assumed that a large part of the revenues from the fishing activities—legal and illegal—ended up in foreign bank accounts as a safeguard against an uncertain future. Due to this capital flight and the lack of investments, the fisheries soon stood forth as a crisis-ridden sector where most companies had a hard enough time coping with day-to-day survival.

The fish processing industry in Russia's coastal areas was not able to adapt to the new circumstances as swiftly and easily (relatively speaking) as the fishing fleets. Hopelessly old-fashioned, overdimensioned and leaning on outdated modes of production, they completely lost out to foreign companies in the competition for raw materials. Even those who managed to secure regular deliveries of fish one way or another usually found that their products were uncompetitive at home and unmarketable abroad. The enormous fish combinates in Murmansk and other coastal cities soon came to resemble dying dinosaurs, although most were able to keep up some sort of production on a small scale.

It may be argued that all these problems were unavoidable side effects of the transition from one system to another. Unfortunately, in the fishing industry, 'transition' seemed somehow to turn into a permanent state. As the turn of the millennium came and went without any substantial changes in its state of affairs, an image of the fisheries as thoroughly criminalized and unreformable took hold among the Russian public.

Although more than fifteen years have now passed since the onset of transition, the situation in the Russian fishing industry remains bleak. The resources are depleted from more than a decade of extreme fishing, some almost to the point of extinction.[5] The fishing fleet is in a serious state of decay, consisting mostly of old, fuel-inefficient and technically outdated vessels.[6] The fisheries sector numbers nearly five thousand companies, with an average of 0.7 vessels per company (Russian Federation 2008). As logically follows, a significant number of these 'fishing companies' have no vessels at all, and there is also a large number of microcompanies with one or two boats at their disposal. Many of the former belong to the group of "fisheries rent-seekers" who have secured quota rights on the basis of former fishing activities but make their profits by illegally selling their quotas to other companies (Mentyukova 2007).

The lion's share of the most valuable resources is still exported, not only because foreign buyers are able to pay higher prices but also because vessels landing their catches in Russia are subject to time-consuming and often very costly control procedures from as many as fifteen to twenty-five different control bodies.[7] As a result, the decay of the Russian land industry continues and imported fish products have come to occupy a large share of the Russian seafood market. Ironically, many

---

of these imported products are made from Russian raw materials landed abroad.

Post-Soviet Fisheries Management: The Vicious Cycle of Reform

In the area of fisheries management, the post-Soviet period has been
characterized by two central lines of conflict. On the one hand, there is
the overarching political struggle between Moscow and the regions over
delimitation issues, which in the area of fisheries translates into the
question of ownership of fish resources. On the other hand, there is the
more sector-specific struggle between proponents of "traditional" management values and proponents of "modern" ones.[8]

The borders between the "traditionalists" and the "modernizers"
are by no means clear-cut. Somewhat simplified, the traditionalist camp
is made up of those belonging to, or identifying with, the Soviet "fisheries complex": regional authorities in the fisheries-dependent regions,
the land industry, most of the traditional fishing companies and most of
those making up the fisheries bureaucracy. The most profiled exponent
of modern management values has been the Ministry of Trade and
Economic Development, supported by some fishing companies and in
some cases by other federal authorities.

Again, somewhat simplified, the traditionalists see the fisheries as a
"strategic" branch of the economy, whose main objective is to provide
jobs in the fishery-dependent regions and contribute to the food security of Russia. The traditionalists are mostly market skeptics, and many
have expressed the view that the fishing industry is by its very nature
dotatsionnyy (i.e., that it should be subsidized by the state). The modernizers, on the other hand, believe that the fisheries should be treated like
any other business, and that the main objective of the industry should
be profitability. The Ministry of Trade and Economic Development has
been particularly preoccupied with raising the revenues from the fishing industry to the state budget.

The outline above is an idealized description of the complex web of
criss-crossing interests and shifting alliances that have formed developments in the Russian fisheries sector since the demise of the Soviet
Union. The main point is that the lack of consensus between main players on core management principles and values has made it very difficult
to work out a stable legal and institutional framework for the sector. As

indicated in the preceding section, this lack of stability has undercut both the willingness and the ability of industry actors to play by the rules.

The conflict over the institutional set-up of Russian fisheries management can also be read along the line of traditionalists versus modernizers. The former believe that a single independent body—preferably a ministry—should be in charge of all fisheries-related issues. One of the traditionalists' main arguments is that splitting up functions will lead to a loss of oversight, bureaucratic infighting and general inefficiency. The modernizers are skeptical, partly because they think the Soviet model, with separate ministries for every industrial branch, is obsolete, and partly because they believe that leaving people from the "fisheries complex" in sole charge of fisheries management is equal to inviting corruption.

Indeed, the State Committee for Fisheries does have a reputation for being notoriously corrupt even by Russian standards. Since the early 1990s, the head of the committee has been replaced on average once a year, and the position is jokingly referred to as *rasstrel'naya*—derived from the verb, *rasstrelyat*—'to execute by shooting' (Ovchinnikov 2007). Still, there has been no shortage of high-profile politicians and bureaucrats willing to shoulder that particular responsibility—a fact usually ascribed to the potential for personal enrichment that seems to be part and parcel of the job as the country's 'head fisherman.'

The state committee itself has been through eight major reorganizations since 1991, with changes both in its status and its name,[9] in addition to various internal upheavals. The development of the institutional set-up during this period can be described as a vicious circle of reform: Poor managerial results and frequent accusations of misuse of office regularly led to demands for reform. However, the continuous reorganizations swallowed time and resources that may have been put to better use, and the high rate of personnel turnover resulted in a loss of valuable expertise and experience. As might be expected, the performance of the committee went from bad to worse, which paved the ground for new reform demands.

When the three-level system of ministries, services and agencies was introduced in connection with an administrative reform in 2004, the Fisheries Committee was disbanded and the political and legislative functions in the area of fisheries were handed over to the Ministry of Agriculture. The committee itself was transformed into the Fisheries Agency under the ministry and put in charge of practical implementation of the fisheries policy, while the Veterinary Service (also subordinate to the ministry) was given responsibility for fisheries control.[10] Since this reorganization was part of a general reform affecting all parts of the state bureaucracy, most observers expected that this time the new system had come to stay—or at the very least for a longer period. However, as we shall see, in 2007 the State Committee for Fisheries re-emerged on the scene like the proverbial phoenix from the ashes.

The hardest battles in the area of management principles have been fought over the issue of quota allocation. Here, the traditionalists have expressed their preference for distributing the quotas for free and also according to fishing history (i.e., with preference given to those who are already active in the fisheries—companies based in the coastal regions rather than Muscovites and foreigners). They have been fiercely opposed to the idea of selling quota shares at auction—a brainchild of the Ministry of Trade and Economic Development—and to the introduction of levies for quotas (Hønneland 2001).

The modernizers have argued that selling quotas at auction would result in a number of positive effects. First and foremost, it would ensure that some of the revenues from the fisheries would revert back to the state. Moreover, they maintain, quota auctions would counteract corruption, since the fisheries bureaucrats would not be able to manipulate the results of the auctions. As for quota levies, they too would ensure that some revenues would be added to the budget, and they would be a fair compensation for granting a limited number of actors the right to exploit resources that in principle belonged to the state, and thus to all Russians (Hønneland 2001).

For most of the period from 1991 until today, quotas have been allocated for free on the basis of fishing history. From 2001 to 2003, part of the quotas for the most valuable species was sold at auction. This meant that a number of new companies—mostly from Moscow and partly backed by foreign capital—were able to enter the fisheries. When the auctions were abolished again and the principle of fishing history reinstated as the main basis for quota allocation, the new actors remained eligible for quotas since they had taken part in the fisheries one, two or three years in a row. The abolishment of the auctions was followed by the introduction of quota levies, which has remained in place until today. Consequently, one could say that in the area of quota allocations, a sort of compromise has been reached between the traditionalists and the modernizers.

The lack of consensus over core issues related to fisheries management has greatly hampered the process of working out a stable legal framework for the fisheries. For most of the post-Soviet period, the fisheries sector has been mainly regulated by a stream of presidential decrees and government resolutions, as well as orders and provisions on the ministerial and committee levels (Hønneland 2004). These regulations have typically been short lived, often contradictory, difficult to implement and poorly enforced. In 2004 Russia finally adopted a framework law on fisheries. This concluded a thirteen-year-long process where a number of drafts had been laboriously worked out and then rejected either by the Federal Council or the president, each time leading to the establishment of a so-called conciliatory commission to get the work on the law back on track. The conflict between traditionalists and modernizers was also evident in this legislative process, since the inclusion of legal provisions for quota auctions and quota levies was among the most contentious issues after 2001. However, the overarching bone of contention was the question of whether fish should be defined solely as a federal or partly as a regional resource, with the consequences this would have for regional participation (or nonparticipation) in resource management, particularly where quota allocations were concerned (Hønneland 2001).

Considering the "strengthening of the power vertical" under President Vladimir Putin, it is not surprising that the federal centre came out victorious on most points when the law on fisheries was finally adopted. However, as follows in the next section, this breakthrough by no means meant that the law had found its form once and for all.

Recent Developments in Russian Fisheries Management, 2007–2008

The 2004 reorganization of the fisheries bureaucracy and the subsequent adoption of the law on fisheries were followed by some three years of relative stability, in the sense that both the management institutions and the legal framework remained almost unchanged. However, this did not result in any substantial improvement of the state of affairs in the fisheries sector. The problem of overfishing continued; the fishing fleets remained export oriented, contributing to the further deterioration of the land industry and investment levels remained low, which meant that the pressing issues of fleet renewal and modernization were left unsolved (Russian Federation 2008).

The first indications that a new wave of reform was underway came when President Putin made his annual speech to the Federal Assembly in April 2007 (Russian Federation 2007a). For the first time, fisheries-related issues were given more than a passing mention in the president's address on the state of the nation. After posing the rhetorical question about whether Russia was really harvesting the maximum benefit from its natural resources, Putin pointed out that although fisheries issues had recently received a lot of public attention, no visible progress had been made in the industry. He went on to argue for the necessity of putting a stop to the practice of allocating fishing quotas to foreign companies, indicating that reserving the quotas for Russian companies would help develop the land industry. Furthermore, he called on the government to work out a system of measures to improve customs control and prevent overfishing. Finally, he expressed great worry over the state of the Russian civilian fleet (presumably including the fishing fleet) and spoke of the need to restore the country's shipbuilding industry.

In May 2007 Putin fired Stanislav Ilyasov as head of the Federal Fisheries Agency and appointed in his place Andrey Krayniy, the director of Kaliningrad Fisheries Port and a graduate from the Presidential Academy.[11] In late August, at a State Council meeting in Astrakhan devoted to the situation in the fisheries sector, the president reiterated his dissatisfaction with the state of affairs. He directed his critical remarks mainly to the Minister of Agriculture, Aleksey Gordeev, and then he addressed Krayniy, more or less saying that he entrusted it to him to solve the problems ("Rybnyiy den' pravitel'stva" 2007). A couple of days previously, then prime minister Mikhail Fradkov had made a statement on the advisability of having a single authority in charge of the various functions related to the fisheries ("Yedinoe vedomstvo po voprosam rybnogo khozyaystva" 2007). Thus, it was clear to all that a new major reorganization was imminent.

Institutional Developments:
The Brief Return of the Fisheries Committee

The Russian State Committee for Fisheries was officially restored by presidential decree on 26 September 2007. According to the decree, the committee would take over the functions of the Ministry of Agriculture

---

in the sphere of fisheries, as well as those of the Veterinary Service related to fisheries control. Moreover, the committee would be directly subordinate to the Russian government (Russian Federation 2007b). Thus, the committee had, for all practical purposes, been endowed with the powers of a ministry.

However, the Ministry of Agriculture was by no means ready to surrender all of its influence in fisheries matters. Minister Gordeev made it clear that, being responsible for the country's general policy in the area of food and food security, his ministry was bound to have a say on many issues related to the fisheries (Russian Federation 2007b). He also pointed out that the resurrected committee did not fit very well into the new state bureaucratic structure created in 2004 (Mironova 2008). Some observers took these statements to indicate that Gordeev would not be content with a certain influence in fisheries matters but intended to fight for the return of the committee to the ministerial fold. In May 2008, when President Dmitry Medvedev established his government, they were seemingly proven right: The Fisheries Committee was disbanded and once again transformed into an agency under the Ministry of Agriculture.

However, new complications soon ensued. Representatives of the fisheries sector were outraged with the decision to disband the committee, not least since this happened in the middle of a difficult process involving the elaboration and implementation of several important new regulations (Mironova 2008). Following intense lobbying from the fisheries interests, President Medvedev made a creative halfway move: The ex-committee remained an agency, but it was removed from the Ministry of Agriculture and made directly subordinate to the prime minister. Actually, this set-up officially came into being via an initiative from Minister Gordeev, which seems strange at first glance. However, the Russian media interpreted this move—probably correctly—as tactical on Gordeev's part. Some speculate that the agency will be left alone over the summer to deal with the new regulations and make sure the 2008 fishing season is going smoothly, but that it will then be returned to the ministry in the fall (Mironova 2008).

Judging from previous experience, this new round of organizational upheaval is bound to hamper current attempts to reform the fisheries sector. A core question is how these developments will influence matters in the area of fisheries control. In 1998 the responsibility for controlling fishing vessels at sea was removed from the Fisheries Committee to the Federal Border Service. In 2004 the responsibility for controlling vessels in port was handed over from the new Fisheries Agency to the Veterinary Service (Hønneland 2005). In both cases, the reorganization led to a lot of tension between the fisheries authorities and the organizations taking over their responsibilities. The process of handing over functions and resources was drawn out, bitter and muddled, and the quality of fisheries control dropped significantly during both transition periods. As long as the overarching institutional questions remain unsettled, it is likely that the interagency tug-of-war over fisheries control will continue behind the scenes and that the much-called-for improvements in this area will not materialize.

Policy Developments: Main Objectives and Principles of the Krayniy Administration

In his capacity as head of the Fisheries Agency, Andrey Krainiy is the main exponent for Russian fisheries policy, and he has been quite a visible public figure in 2007–2008. At the same time, his statements and positions embody some of the contradictions, as well as the general driving forces, shaping this policy. At first glance, the policy statements made, and conceptual documents worked out, since he first took office in May 2007 seem to indicate that traditionalist views have won the upper hand in the area of policy-making. Thus, even if the resurrection of the committee turned out to be a pyrrhic victory for the traditionalists, they could find some comfort in the fact that Krayniy remained the head of the Fisheries Agency.

In interviews and media performances, Krayniy has put great stress on social welfare, food security and national independence. Among his favourite subjects have been the necessity of raising fish consumption to the recommended twenty-six kilograms per year per inhabitant by making fish products more affordable, and the importance of redirecting Russian catches to Russian ports in order to revive the land industry, reduce the country's dependence on imported seafood and make over-fishing more difficult. Actually, a concrete date was set—1 January 2009—when all catches taken in the Russian EEZ must initially be landed and declared on Russian territory (Ledeneva 2008). Moreover, Krayniy has hardly given a single interview without going into his plans for reviving Russia's blue-water fisheries by creating a state-owned fishing company that would specialize in fisheries in distant waters and function as a locomotive behind which the commercial fleet might follow.[12] Not least, his harsh utterances on several occasions on the necessity of purging the fishing fleet of foreign actors and foreign capital seem to place him firmly in the traditionalist camp.[13]

On the other hand, Krayniy does not share the view held by some traditionalists that the fisheries must necessarily be a subsidized branch of the economy. Although he claims that systems for credit subsidies and fuel subsidies have to be put in place in order to revive the fisheries sector, he has made it clear that the sector must become economically viable and that the main burden of necessary investments must be born by the industry itself. Thus, another favourite subject of Krayniy's has been the consolidation of the fisheries sector and how this is to be achieved mainly through structural measures rather than direct state support.

The most important of these structural measures, which is supposed to be implemented by 2009, is the introduction of ten-year fishing quotas.[14] The rationale behind this move is the fishing companies' aversion towards long-term investments, which has been ascribed (probably correctly) to the ever-changing rules of the game in Russian fisheries. In particular, the principles of quota allocation have been subject to very frequent changes. In 2003 it was decided that quota shares would be awarded to companies for five years at a time, ensuring at least some predictability. However, the hoped-for increase in investment levels did not occur. Industry representatives have pointed out that with current vessel prices, a modern ocean-going trawler needs at least five to ten years of fishing to work off the initial investment. The industry has unanimously welcomed the plans for introducing ten-year quotas, although some have argued that even ten years is too short a time horizon to make investments attractive.

Another structural measure is directed against the unlawful but widespread practice of trade in quotas between companies. As pointed out previously, many companies acquiring quota rights on the strength of previous fishing history, or by buying quotas in 2001–2003, have no boats of their own. Some have been leasing vessels from other companies in order to take the quotas, but there has also emerged a numerous class of rent-seekers who make their profits by selling their quotas to other companies. In order to rid the sector of these "sofa-fishermen" and redistribute their quotas to active fishing companies, it has been decided that from 2009 onward, quotas shall not be awarded to companies without vessels (Mentyukova 2007).[15]

Apart from Russia providing 'real' fishing companies with larger quotas and thus strengthening its economy, it is expected that this measure will induce companies to merge into larger entities. Those who have quotas but no vessels may join forces with those who have vessels but no quotas.[16] Such an outcome would be seen as very positive by the authorities, since it is their explicit goal to reverse the fragmentation of the fisheries sector. Larger companies are considered more economically effective than smaller ones, their activities more transparent and their general attitude more responsible. Krayniy thus refers to large companies (i.e., companies with an annual turnover of at least three hundred million dollars a year) as "our natural partners in the struggle against illegal fishing" ("Podoshla ryba" 2008).

Krayniy has been very outspoken about his dislike for the quota auctions, but he has presented concrete plans for a system whereby fish catches are sold at auction. According to these plans, when mandatory landing on Russian territory of fish caught in the Russian EEZ is implemented in 2009, any company wanting to sell its fish to foreign buyers has to do so via auctions.[17] The Russian fisheries authorities claim that the auction system will eliminate long chains of middlemen between fishing companies and consumers, thus making fish products more affordable. Also, they believe the auction system will prevent the making of shady deals in connection with the buying and selling of fish (Russian Federation 2008).

Although mandatory landing of catches in Russia does not mean that fishing companies are forced to sell their catches to Russian buyers, a new economic incentive has been introduced to make this option more attractive: a reduction of quota levies to only ten percent of the full rate for those who sell their fish at home (Shschedrunova 2007). In addition, if it is correct that many companies currently land and sell their catches abroad simply in order to avoid catch control, one might indeed expect the new system to put more fish on the Russian market.

Legal Developments: Turning Intentions into Law

Those familiar with Russian fisheries policy in the post-Soviet period will probably have concluded from the contents of the previous section that there is not much new under the sun. They would be right inasmuch as all the main objectives and principles for the revival of the fisheries sector put forward by the committee under Krayniy have, at

---

some point, been included in the strategies of previous administrations—administrations that have consistently failed in putting their plans into practice. The doubling of fish consumption, the redirection of Russian fish to Russia and the reconquering of the lost fishing grounds of the "World Ocean"—these slogans have been reiterated ad nauseam to the point where one tends to automatically dismiss them as wishful thinking. However, developments in the legislative arena in 2007 seem to indicate that the current fisheries administration is making some headway on at least some of the issues singled out as priorities.

Possibly the boldest move that was made in the field of fisheries legislation in 2007 was the addition of a new article to the law on fisheries in April 2007—actually, before Krayniy's appointment—introducing new measures to combat overfishing. Among these was the mandatory destruction of confiscated fish products made from particularly valuable or threatened species. A main objective of this regulation was to put a stop to the corrupt schemes whereby caviar stemming from illegal fishing was issued with false papers stating that it had been confiscated by the authorities and was sold on their behalf (Mentyukova 2007). Allegedly, Russian authorities have been trying unsuccessfully for years to adopt this regulation, and it took the direct involvement of President Putin to finally push it through (Davydov 2008). Other measures contained in the new article included the introduction of administrative confiscation of illegal catches and of vessels and fishing gear used for the purpose of illegal fishing, as well as the mandatory destruction of confiscated fishing vessels unsuccessfully put up for auction.

The most comprehensive round of legislative reform came in late 2007 in the form of Law No. 333, introducing changes to the law on fisheries (Russian Federation 2007a). This legislative initiative hardly left a single article of the original law intact. Some of the changes were purely technical ones, but there were a large number of substantial alterations as well. Among the measures that were codified by law were the allocation of commercial quotas to companies for a ten-year period (Article 33) and the mandatory landing in Russia of catches taken in the EEZ (Article 19).

Many of the changes introduced in Law No. 333 are aimed at improving the fisheries control system. One new provision (Article 12) simplifies the procedures by which fisheries licences are revoked, as well as specifies in more detail the conditions (number and gravity of violations) for revoking licences. Presumably, this will make it easier to use this punitive measure in practice. Moreover, it is now explicitly stated in the law (Article 44) that the results of state monitoring of the fish resources can be used as a basis for the conviction of offenders. If this measure proves "implementable," it would be a great victory for the fisheries authorities, who have fought other bureaucratic structures and mighty lobbyists for years for the right to use data from the satellite monitoring of vessels as proof in court.

In addition to those mentioned above, there are a number of lesser—but possibly important—alterations, the aims of which seem to be: (i) to reduce bureaucratic barriers that complicate lawful fisheries activities; (ii) to reduce bureaucratic and other barriers that complicate the prosecution and/or punishment of offenders and (iii) to shift priorities away from the control and prosecution of minor violations to the control and prosecution of major ones.

Conclusion

For the Russian fisheries sector in general, and for the traditionalists in particular, 2007 definitely brought some progress. A "professional" was appointed head of the Fisheries Agency, then the Fisheries Committee was resurrected, and by the end of the year, the decision to introduce ten-year quotas had been codified in law. However, as the disbandment of the committee in May 2008 clearly shows, it would indeed be premature to declare any sort of victory on behalf of the traditionalists. As for Krayniy, although his rhetoric seems to place him firmly in their camp, one cannot fail to notice that his populist statements in the traditionalist vein are often followed by more sober and subdued observations and arguments that indicate a more pragmatic leaning. Most of the measures he has suggested as solutions to the fisheries sector's problems are not dependent on the finance ministry's willingness to loosen the purse strings but rest on a blend of structural and market economy measures. Thus, while the current management policy may be served to the public under a rich traditionalist sauce, the hard framework of that same policy seems to be based on the pet principle of the modernizers—the concept of an economically viable and profitable fishing industry.

In fact, Krayniy's penchant for traditionalist rhetoric paired with a pragmatic sense of what market economy measures can achieve reminds one strongly of the political ways of the recent Russian president. Moreover, Putin and his government demonstrated an unprecedented interest in fisheries issues throughout 2007, and this renewed focus on the fisheries was evident even before Krainiy took office. Thus, although Krayniy stands forth as a high-profile politician, it may be argued that the political will of the president has been the main driving force behind the revitalization of Russian fisheries politics in 2007. But even if we assume that the recent attempts at reform have the full-hearted backing of the political leadership, this is hardly any guarantee of their success. In Russia, however high the priority of a political initiative, it always runs the risk of death by bureaucratic obstruction.

Indeed, the unhealthy relationship between bureaucrats and businessmen that has characterized the Russian fisheries sector for a decade and a half has probably played a significant part in the spectacular failure of previous attempts at reform. To quote *Ekspert* magazine in the introduction to an interview with Krayniy:

> The Russian fisheries have traditionally been considered one of the most corrupt sectors of the economy. Attempts to make it more civilized have never been crowned with success: all good intentions have stranded on the resistance on the part of Russian and foreign businessmen and bureaucrats who have had an interest in keeping the market out of control. ("Podoshla ryba" 2008)

In other words, both the businessmen and the bureaucrats have been interested in maintaining the status quo. The former because the lack of control and clear rules has made it possible to derive large profits from illegal fishing, and the latter because, in such a chaotic situation, there has been ample opportunity for them to get a share of the spoils.

It seems a reasonable assumption that this deadlock of mutual interests can hardly be overcome until the status quo is made less attractive to both parties. Apart from the various political measures geared towards making legal fishing activities more viable (such as the ten-year quotas), there are some other factors that would point towards a 'legalization' of the business. First, there is the banal fact that many of those who have been in the fisheries for a while have probably secured their future many times over. Thus, they may have reached the point where they are ready to 'go legal.' Second, although the business has thus far shrugged off all of the sawing-off-the-branch-you-are-sitting-on type of arguments with yawning indifference, the effects of fifteen years of overfishing are now becoming very concrete. Some of the most "currency-intensive"[18] species have been harvested almost to extinction, and for others, the large amounts taken above the quotas have saturated the market and caused prices to drop sharply.

If the largest business actors are interested in a change of affairs, this might turn out to have some real effects, since the smaller companies—though undoubtedly well-schooled in the art of bribery—hardly have the same capability of influencing policy outcomes. But, then, what about the bureaucrats? Resting comfortably upon the branch of corruption, they can hardly be expected to welcome the chainsaw of law and order. It is therefore unfortunate that it is the bureaucrats who have the greatest say when it comes to setting the rules of the game. There are numerous examples of how Russian bureaucrats, faced with the appalling option of having to live on their wages, have put in place new and complicated regulations (or new applications of old ones) in order to ensure the dependence of business actors upon their 'help.' The best that can be hoped for in the short-to-medium term is probably a strategic alliance between the fisheries bureaucracy and the key actors in the fisheries business—Krayniy's "natural partners in the struggle against illegal fishing"—which discreetly incorporates the issue of compensation for those representing the bureaucracy in the partnership. One need not look farther than the Russian oil and gas sector to find examples of such a solution.[19]

It may be that the Russian fisheries sector has finally hit bottom, and that the only way—for the moment—is up. On the other hand, the modern history of the sector indicates that the way up will almost certainly be long and thorny, and in the end, there are no guarantees that the current attempts at reform will not follow the time-honoured practice of taking a nose-dive before even leaving the ground.

NOTES

1. This chapter is based primarily on the primary and secondary literature cited directly in the text, but it also relates to the author's own experience as an observer of the Russian fisheries as a researcher and in other capacities over the last two decades.

2. The country's economic interests were divided into a number of sectors, each headed by a separate ministry.

3. For a more detailed description of this development, with a particular focus on the northern fisheries, see for Hønneland (2001) or Ivanova (2005).

4. In the Soviet period there were few incentives to overfish the quotas, given the lack of private buyers who might have bought the illegal catches.

5. The most well-known case is that of the caviar-producing sturgeon.

6. According to the Russian fisheries authorities, sixty-eight percent of all fishing vessels currently belong in this category (Russian Federation 2008).

7. This is a problem frequently pointed out by the industry and the fisheries authorities alike. The number of control bodies is around twenty in all (Koltunova 2008).

8. Aspects of this conflict have been described by Hønneland (2004) and Ivanova (2005).

9. For most of this time the committee has had an independent or semi-independent status, but four times it has been dissolved and incorporated into, or made subordinate to, the Ministry of Agriculture. For details, see Hønneland (2004).

10. In full, the Veterinary Service is called the Federal Service for Veterinary and Phytosanitary Control.

11. Andrey Krayniy's c.v. is available in Russian at [http://www.fishcom.ru/page.php?r=9].

12. In one interview, Krayniy identified the return to the "World Ocean" and the redirection of Russian fish to Russian ports as "the two main strategic tasks" of the committee ("Podoshla ryba" 2008).

13. However, Krayniy has made it clear that foreigners must be bought out (rather than just thrown out) of the Russian fisheries, pointing out at the same time that the fisheries (as opposed to the processing industry) are closed to foreigners in many countries in the world ("U Rossii i Yaponii v oblasti rybolovstva bolshoe budushee!" 2007).

14. Krayniy has referred to this measure as the most important form of support that can be given to the fishers (Mentyukova 2007).

15. The expression "sofa-fishermen" is Krayniy's own.

16. Krayniy forecasts "a feverish sell-out of small companies" ("Podoshla ryba" 2008).

17. Those who sell their catches on the home market will have the option of using the auction system but they will not be obliged to do so.

18. This expression (*valyutaemkie* in Russian) is widely used for species that fetch a high price on foreign markets.

19. Indeed, some statements of President Putin's on the fisheries sector in 2004 were interpreted by several analysts as forecasting a development in the fisheries sector parallel to that in the oil and gas sector. That is, the fisheries sector would be dominated by a limited number of "fish oligarchs" who would be granted special treatment as a reward for law-abiding behaviour and general support for the authorities and their policy in the area of fisheries (see, for instance, "Kreml' sdaet rybu" 2004).

REFERENCES

Davydov, D. 31 January 2008. "Mafiya ne bessmertna. Roskomrybolovstvo beretsya eto dokazat" (The mafia is not immortal, and the Fisheries

Committee intends to prove it). *Izvestiya*. [http://www.izvestia.ru/obsh-estvo/article3112557/].

Hønneland, G. 2005. "Fisheries Management in Post-Soviet Russia: Legislation, Principles and Structure." *Ocean Development & International Law* 36: 179–194.

———. 2004. *Russian Fisheries Management. The Precautionary Approach in Theory and Practice*. Boston: Martinus Nijhoff Publishers.

———. 2001. "Centre-Periphery Tensions in the Management of Northwest Russian Fisheries." In *Centre-Periphery Relations in Russia. The Case of the Northwestern Regions*, ed. H. Blakkisrud and G. Hønneland. Aldershot, UK: Ashgate.

Hønneland, G., and A. K. Jørgensen. 2002. "Implementing International Fisheries Regimes in Russia—Lessons from the Northern Basin." *Marine Policy* 26: 5: 359–367.

Ivanova, M. 2005. "The Northern Fisheries of the Russian Federation: Institutions in Transition." M.A. dissertation, Norwegian College of Fisheries Science, University of Tromsø. [http://www.nfh.uit.no/dok/maria_ivanova.pdf].

Koltunova, O. 18 February 2008. "Pod znakom ryby" (Under the sign of pisces). *Kompaniya*. [http://www.ko.ru/document.php?id=18198].

"Kreml' sdaet rybu" (The Kremlin surrenders the fish). 23 June 2004. Gazeta.ru. [http://www.gazeta.ru/comments/2004/06/a_127450.shtml].

Ledeneva, L. 14 February 2008. "Glava Goskomrybolovstva Andrey Krayniy otvetil na voprosy zhurnalistov" (Head of the State Committee for Fisheries, Andrey Krainiy, answered questions from journalists). *Komsomol'skaya Pravda*. [http://www.kp.ru/daily/24049.4/102533/].

Mentyukova, S. 19 October 2007. "Ryba-eto ne sel'skoe khozyaystvo, tam tekhnologii sovsem drugie" (Fish is not agriculture, the technology is completely different). *Kommersant*. [http://www.kommersant.ru/doc.aspx?DocsID=816415].

Mironova, Ju. 3 June 2008. "Krainiy po rybe" (The latest on fish). *Vremya Novostey*. [http://www.vremya.ru/2008/96/4/205164.html].

Ovchinnikov, A. 29 August 2007. "Glava Rosrybolovstva Andrey Krainiy: Deshevoy brakonerskoy ikry bol'she ne budet!" (Head of the State Fisheries Committee Andrey Krainiy: There will be no more cheap caviar from poachers!). *Komsomol'skaya Pravda*. [http://www.kp.ru/daily/23958/72246/].

Pautzke, C. G. 1997. "Russian Far East Fisheries Management." *North Pacific Fishery Management Council Report to Congress*. [http://www.fakr.noaa.gov/npfmc/summary_reports/rfe-all.htm].

"Podoshla ryba" (The fish has come). 18 February 2008. *Ekspert*. [http://www.fishcom.ru/page.php?r=15&id=21].

Russian Federation. 2008. *O merakh napravlennykh na razvitie rybokhzyaystvenno-go kompleksa* (On measures directed towards the development of the fisheries complex). Background material for a meeting of the Russian Government on 24 January 2008. [http://www.fishcom.ru/page.php?r=14&id=89].

——. 6 December 2007a. *O vnesenii izmeneniy v Federal'nyy zakon O rybolovstve i sokhranenii vodnykh biologicheskikh resursov i otdel'nye zakonodatel'nye akty Rossiyskoy Federatsii* (On changes to the federal law on fisheries and conservation of aquatic biological resources and some other legislative acts of the Russian Federation). Federal Law No. 333. [http://212.15.102.244/bpa/bpa_doc.asp?KL=5283&TDoc=47&nb=0].

——. 26 September 2007b. "Minsel'khoz ostanetsya bez ryby" (The agriculture ministry is left without fish). State Committee for Fisheries. [http://www.fishcom.ru/page.php?r=14&id=12].

——. 2007c. *Annual Address to the Federal Assembly, April 26, 2007*. [http://www.kremlin.ru/eng/speeches/2007/04/26/1209_type70029type82912_125670.shtml].

"Rybnyiy den' pravitel'stva" (The government's fish day). 31 August 2007. GZT.ru. [http://www.gzt.ru/business/2007/08/31/180930.html].

Shschedrunova, E. 3 November 2007. "Narod i vlast" (People and power). Radio Mayak. [http://www.fishcom.ru/page.php?r=15&id=2].

"U Rossii i Yaponii v oblasti rybolovstva bolshoe budushee!" (There is a great future for Russia and Japan in the field of fisheries!). 16 November 2007. Kiodo Tsusin. [http://www.fishcom.ru/page.php?r=16&id=128].

Vylegazhnin, A. N., and V. K. Zilanov. 2000. *Mezhdunarodno-pravovye Osnovy Upravlenia Morskimi Zhivymi Resursami* (International legal foundations for the management of living marine resources). Moscow: Ekonomika.

"Yedinoe vedomstvo po voprosam rybnogo khozyaystva" (One body in charge of fisheries issues). 28 August 2007. RIA Novosti. [http://fishres.ru/news/news.php?id=6270].

Chapter Five

Northern Offshore Oil and Gas Resources: Policy Challenges and Approaches[1]

Arild Moe and Elana Wilson Rowe

Introduction

From being on the brink of bankruptcy in 1998, Russia made a remarkable economic comeback, largely driven by high oil and gas prices. Oil, and especially gas, are to an overwhelming extent produced in the northern parts of Russia and the potential for further development of the industry is also to be found in the North, both onshore and offshore. While the tension manifested in Russian northern politics and development, namely the balancing of market and geopolitical/strategic concerns, is evident throughout the petroleum industry, it is especially prominent in offshore development. This is because the development of petroleum resources on the continental shelf will be difficult, if not impossible, to realize without the involvement of foreign competence and capital. At the same time, offshore oil and gas are clearly defined as strategic natural resource assets and, consequently, fall under the evolving legislation and policies on strategic resources that explicitly limit such non-Russian involvement. In many ways, the study of offshore policy development illustrates broader challenges facing the oil and gas industry within Russia, such as balancing state control and the need for foreign and private investment and creating policy for cost-effective development in a largely uncompetitive monopoly environment. This study, with a close tracing of policy development, also gives an indication of some of the challenges involved in the creation of strategic long-term policy within Russia more generally.

The aim of this chapter is to assess the place of offshore petroleum development in the context of overall Russian energy priorities and to examine the evolution of offshore policy and strategy at both the federal and company levels. The chapter first reviews some of the key developments in Russian energy policy since 2005, before examining Russian governmental offshore policy development. The offshore strategies of the two companies that are likely to play a prominent role in Russian offshore development, Rosneft and Gazprom, as well as the interactions thus far between them are then outlined. In tracing the often troubled and halting evolution of federal policy and practice, the question of the extent to which the strategic importance assigned to offshore petroleum reserves is translating into coordinated strategic action and long-term policy-thinking is raised and discussed in the concluding section to the chapter.

Becoming 'Strategic': The Geopolitical Significance of Russia's Natural Resources

Energy, in particular oil and natural gas, played a very important role in the Soviet economy. The Soviet Union was the world's largest producer of oil, as well as gas, and the petroleum industry was an integrated part of the state structure. After 1991 the oil industry was first reorganized into separate companies and then to a large extent privatized. The gas industry in Russia was not broken up but instead became one company—Gazprom—with dominant state ownership. The reorganization of the oil industry took place at a time when economic and technical problems that had been building up over several years were being felt in terms of rapidly falling output, exacerbated by the general political and economic transformation the country was going through.

When Vladimir Putin came to power, strengthening the Russian state, after a long period of disorganization, was his central aim. The oil industry was again performing well after private owners had introduced new technology and methods, and the sector was earning large profits due to an increasing world market price. The economic significance of the sector for Russia was again highlighted, and many came to see oil and gas exports as Russia's main assets on the global stage. While President Putin's vision of a strong centralized federal government playing a leading role in the management of key economic sectors like energy can be traced to several years earlier (Balzer 2004), increased state control over Russian natural resources and profits became a characteristic of his second presidential term (2004–2008). It was manifested in the dismantling of the private company, Yukos, the largest oil producer in Russia, with its main assets subsequently taken over by the state-dominated company, Rosneft. Gazprom, which has close to a monopoly in the gas business, has had its position reinforced legally and has been allowed to swallow other companies. The vocabulary of 'strategic resources' has been a key feature of this increased attention, reflected both in new legislation to govern new projects and in efforts to restructure the existing portfolio of large oil and gas projects within Russia.

The legislation on strategic resources, which had long been debated and examined in various branches of government before its final approval in April 2008, identifies economic sectors in which substantial involvement and investment of foreign-owned companies would require explicit permission from governmental authorities. The law covers forty-two industries that are defined as strategic to Russia's defense and security (e.g., arms and aircraft), fishing and seafood production and precious metals and hydrocarbons, among others. Foreign private investors must now gain approval from the Russian government before acquiring more than a fifty percent stake in a strategic company, with a stricter level of twenty-five percent set for companies owned by foreign governments and international organizations. This package of legislation included the new law on foreign investment in strategic sectors, as well as accompanying changes in existing laws, notably the law on mineral resources. The mineral sector is singled out for stricter regulations than the general norm and comprises "geological studying of underground resources and (or) exploration and exploitation of minerals". Deposits of oil reserves of more than seventy million tons and gas deposits of more than fifty billion cubic metres (BCM) are now termed "resources of federal significance". This still leaves numerous fields below the threshold, although offshore fields are defined as being of federal significance notwithstanding their size.

Private foreign investors who want to acquire, alone or as a group, more than ten percent of a Russian company engaged in using mineral resources of federal significance need advance approval from the authorities. Possibly, if the shares are distributed between unrelated investors, foreigners may own up to twenty percent of a company combined, without special permission. Yet, this is not clearly spelled out in the law. For foreign-government-controlled investors, the rules are stricter. They encounter a corresponding five percent limit.

An explicit goal of the new legislation is to increase the predictability for foreign investors and, to some extent, codify regulations that have already been applied informally. The new law is said to be based on a 'permission principle' with few absolute prohibitions. Indeed, the new law gives considerable discretion to the executive branch, and a liberal-minded government could, based on the law, give foreign investors significant roles in exploration and extraction of hydrocarbons. The implementation of the law remains to be seen, but the tone of the law and the present dominant discourse and recent political action make a broadly liberal interpretation of the law less plausible.

Overall, the new legislation has important implications for the general development of the petroleum sector in Russia. The legislation removes competition on the continental shelf; further increases the privileged positions of Gazprom and Rosneft; complicates the operations of private Russian oil companies, notably Lukoil and TNK-BP, and introduces a new layer of bureaucracy. Given that a good deal of disagreement persists in Moscow in terms of both the letter and the spirit of the law, it is likely that the process of developing implementation mechanisms will be slow and contested and may hamper development of both onshore and offshore energy projects.

While the legislation moved rather slowly and was discussed for nearly three years, Russia's state apparatus worked comparatively quickly to reorganize existing oil and gas projects so as to place state and state-owned petroleum companies in leading roles. The attempt to realize a leading role for state and state-owned companies and to minimize the position of foreign and nonstate-owned endeavours in the oil and gas sector in advance of the legislation on strategic resources is exemplified by the pressure placed on the Sakhalin-2 consortium. Sakhalin-2 operated in Russia under a production-sharing agreement (PSA) that allowed the companies involved (Shell, Mitsui and Mitsubishi) to recoup their initial investments in this offshore oil project in the Russian Far East before they were required to start substantially sharing project profits with the Russian state. Dissatisfaction with the PSA project came to a head when the Sakhalin-2 consortium announced a US$ 10 billion price overrun during phase two of the project—a budget increase that would have further delayed the point at which the Russian state would have a right to a substantial percentage of the project's profits.

The public announcement of the budget overrun was followed by an environmental review of the project by the government, which led to the suspension of a key expert review/approval by the Ministry of Natural Resources. This was widely seen as a method for exerting pressure on the Sakhalin-2 consortium partners and resulted in Gazprom gaining a fifty-percent-plus-one share of the consortium on favourable terms (see Bradshaw 2006). The focus on the project was also part of a general dissatisfaction with PSAs, which were signed in the 1990s under Boris Yeltsin's administration during a period of relatively low hydrocarbon prices and Russian economic transition. With the high oil prices of today, the structure of these agreements came to be seen as unacceptably disadvantageous.

The inclusion of Gazprom in the Sakhalin project was in keeping with the Kremlin's overall efforts to reassert control over Russian energy development by putting state-controlled companies in charge of existing projects. Outside of the Sakhalin project, the Russian offshore remains undeveloped and, consequently, Russian authorities are operating with a more or less 'clean slate.' In an energy market increasingly looking northwards, and with Russia facing problems in keeping up oil production and balancing gas supplies with projected domestic demand and export commitments, offshore resources are becoming increasingly significant.

The Russian Offshore Strategy

Russia has a continental shelf of 6.2 million km², of which four million are considered to be of potential interest for oil and gas production (Strategiya 2006). According to Russia's Ministry of Natural Resources, one-third of Russia's initial gas resources and twelve percent of its oil resources are located on the continental shelf (Varlamov 2007). This corresponds to 13.5 billion tons of oil and seventy-three trillion m³ of natural gas. Of this, two-thirds are said to be located in the Barents and Kara seas (Strategiya 2006). The ministry has, on different occasions, published very optimistic statements about future output, such as that the shelf could produce ninety-five million tons of oil and 320 BCM of natural gas by 2020 (see Trutnev 2005). Offshore production today is only around five million tons of oil, exclusively from Sakhalin.

While offshore resources are often presented as an important element in Russia's future energy balance, efforts to develop a comprehensive offshore strategy began relatively late. Throughout the 1990s, Russia did not really have a plan for development of offshore resources and very little attention was devoted to offshore exploration. In the words of Natural Resources Minister Yury Trutnev: "Since 1993, no serious exploration of the RF [Russian Federation] continental shelf has in fact been undertaken. The amount of exploration operations was reduced to a tenth compared with the mid-1980s when most of the known fields were discovered" (Trutnev 2006).

The closest we come to an offshore strategy from this period are the plans developed by Gazprom, which were endorsed on the political level but remained unimplemented (see, for example, Moe and Jørgensen 2000). Offshore resources were considered a long-term option, and Gazprom gave little priority to such development after the company had secured control over promising fields in the Barents Sea. Gazprom's interests changed, however, a few years ago with liquefied natural gas (LNG) becoming an increasingly interesting business prospect (among other motivating factors discussed below). Meanwhile, the government has also taken steps to work out a strategy for offshore development (Naumov 2007).

The government started a process in October 2003 and the Ministry of Natural Resources worked out a "strategy for exploration and development of the oil and gas potential of the continental shelf of the Russian Federation until 2020" that was presented at a meeting of the Russian government in March 2006 but has yet to be adopted officially (Strategiya 2006). Nevertheless, the Ministry of Natural Resources and affiliated structures, as well as other actors, continue to refer to this document as the offshore strategy and its main points are therefore worth reviewing. Overall, the strategy points out the vast potential of the offshore fields and argues for the realization of ambitious production goals—ninety-five million tons of oil and 150 BCM of natural gas offshore by 2020. However, the strategy also points out the obstacles to the realization of those goals. These obstacles include

- low levels of exploration;
- high investment risks;

- high exploration and development costs due to remote locations;
- a poorly developed infrastructure supporting production and transportation of offshore resources;
- an unattractive and unstable fiscal regime and high government take;
- a bureaucratic system of state management and issuance of user rights for offshore resources; and
- an insufficiently developed legal framework not adapted to the specifics of offshore activity.

The strategy sets out to address these problems. One important issue is the financing of geological exploration/surveys. According to the strategy, the state should finance regional surveys, with resource users (the companies) paying for exploration and appraisal drilling. However, the state should finance all exploration in "disputed, [foreign] border areas, of zones with a high potential" and also "areas where for defense and security reasons" only state companies can be admitted. What these clauses mean is not exactly defined, but they indicate that foreign policy and security concerns loom large in official thinking about offshore activities.

To support and facilitate exploration by companies, which will clearly account for the lion's share of exploration costs, the strategy points out several mechanisms:

- adopting a legal system for the purchase of geological information;
- instituting a long-term plan for licencing rounds;
- extending licence periods to seven to ten years;
- recognizing finder's rights, meaning that the company discovering a field shall receive the right to develop it without a new auctioning process;
- improving the fiscal regime and reducing and differentiating taxes on production;
- developing infrastructure to stimulate offshore activities; and
- supporting the Russian machine-building industry in developing offshore technology.

In addition, the strategy prescribes a series of measures to enhance the environmental safety of offshore operations.

The strategy was accompanied by an ambitious "complex plan of action" outlining specific tasks and timelines, in which some of the issues raised above were concretely addressed.

- The extension of licence periods was accepted via an amendment to the law on mineral resources in the late fall of 2007.

- Finder's rights had already been introduced by a government resolution before the final draft of the strategy was published, but the procedure seems to leave considerable discretion to the authorities, and the principle contradicts the law on mineral resources, in which auctioning is required (a revised or new law on mineral resources is still in progress).

- The improvement of the fiscal regime is a broad issue. However, a system for a differentiated mineral resources tax was implemented in 2007. However, it has only been applied to eastern Siberia. It is expected that it will be extended to most of the offshore areas.

- Another measure that has been given attention is the establishment of a state shipbuilding holding, which was decided on in early 2007. This relates to the plan of action, since an explicit goal is to build platforms and ships for offshore activities (Chugunov 2007).

Still, two years after the presentation of the strategy, only some of the mechanisms listed above have been established—and then only partly. Clearly, there has been a serious delay in implementing the action plan.

The lack of thrust is apparent and may be partially explained by the fact that the strategy has not been fully endorsed by the government. There are several reasons for this. The Ministry of Natural Resources presented a "state strategy for exploration and development of the oil and gas potential of the continental shelf of the Russian Federation", which can be viewed as a predecessor to the present strategy, to the government in December 2004. According to the natural resources minister, the document had at that time been endorsed by all of the ministries and agencies (Trutnev 2005). In this earlier document, PSAs were presented as a major instrument to attract investments. It also proposed that the

Ministry of Finance and the Ministry of Economy consider a series of tax measures to improve the investment climate, including reduced taxes and duties, tax holidays and credits to operators, uplift, tax exemption for exploration work and customs exemption for importation of unique equipment.

A high-level interagency commission was established in July 2005 to finalize the strategy (Mezhvedomstvennaya Komissiya 2005). Apparently, in this process, the Ministry of Natural Resources' proposals met with resistance and the final draft, as summarized above, appeared watered down. PSAs had more or less gone out of fashion again, and it seems that the proposed tax revisions had also met with resistance. Thus, major mechanisms had disappeared from the strategy, and this left the ministry's almost frantic appeals about offshore development without much clout.

Yet, there is another reason why the Ministry of Natural Resources did not succeed. There is no doubt that there has been an increased focus on offshore resources over the last few years. This has attracted increased attention from several agencies, each with their own agenda. The Ministry of Energy and Industry, which has been marginalized in resources management, worked out their own strategy—the "program for complex development of hydrocarbon resources in Russia's northwestern region until 2020". The major theme of this document (which the authors have not seen) is to maximize the use of domestic scientific and industrial potential (Naumov 2007). It has been accompanied by a concept for a "national action program for technical and technological support for development of the oil and gas potential of the continental shelf of the Russian Federation", worked out by the ministry's two subordinate agencies, Rosenergo and Rosprom (Makhlin 2006). This work has also run into difficulties. It was supposed to be presented to the government in the fall of 2006, but two years later a final draft had not yet emerged (Grigor'ev 2007). Realizing that its own strategy had been far from sufficient, in 2007 the Ministry of Natural Resources started cooperating with the Ministry of Economic Development in order to prepare a "federal target program for development of the continental shelf" (Veletminskiy 2007). The status of this process is unknown.

In total, it is clear that a coherent strategy has not been adopted on the federal level. As is often the case in Russia, when the introduction of indirect measures and framework conditions becomes log-jammed, the idea of creating a new state structure arises. Unsurprisingly, then, the question of who should develop offshore resources remains a topic of debate. The Ministry of Natural Resources has for some time proposed the creation of a state company to take care of offshore exploration, arguing that this body could "distribute blocs more efficiently. After having received geological data we could put blocs on the shelf into use".[2] In early December 2006, the creation of a new gigantic state company, which would own a controlling stake in all of the projects on the Russian shelf and be formed from parts of Gazprom, Rosneft and Zarubezhneft, was discussed explicitly at a meeting of the Security Council ("National Project Kremlin Shelf" 2006).

This plan, however, seemed to have been abandoned by late February 2007, when the president of Rosneft stated that the federal government planned to divide all new offshore oil and gas fields between Rosneft and Gazprom. The Ministry of Natural Resources was reported to be considering four unnamed options for how to divide the fields between the companies, with the intention of releasing a plan in the summer of 2007 (Medetsky 2007). Then, in April 2008, the Minister of Natural Resources announced that blocs on the continental shelf would be divided between Gazprom and Rosneft according to their expected "profile"—oil or gas (Kommersant 2008). This happened at the same time as the new legislation for strategic resources made it clear that henceforth only experienced Russian state-owned companies would be given licences for the continental shelf—in practice, Gazprom and Rosneft.[3]

The implication of the minister's announcement seems to be that the projects will be divided on an uncontested basis. There still could be points of contention, however, even if direct competition is removed from the licencing phase. Some of these potentially problematic issues are taken up in the remaining sections of this chapter. In any case, the government, by its declaration combined with the restrictions in the new legislation on foreign investment, has to a large extent ceded control of the developments in the offshore sector to Gazprom and Rosneft. Consequently, the offshore strategies of these companies, and the extent to which and how they are already competing and cooperating, is of relevance to understanding how an offshore regime might develop.

Gazprom and Rosneft's Offshore Strategies and Interaction

Both Gazprom and Rosneft have stated specific interests in offshore stakes and have generated plans meant to facilitate offshore development. In mid-April 2007 Gazprom submitted a memo to the Ministry of Natural Resources, listing deposits in the Kara and Okhotsk seas for which it would like to receive licences. In May 2007 Rosneft sent the ministry a similar list of offshore fields for which it would like to obtain licences, including locations in the Okhotsk, Barents and Laptev seas. This corresponded with Rosneft's announcement of its intention to produce twenty-five million tons of oil and forty BCM of gas from new areas in the Sea of Okhotsk by 2020 and twenty million tons of oil and seventy BCM of gas from the Barents Sea (*The Sakhalin Times* 2007).

Capital, however, may become a constraint for both companies in commencing a new phase of expensive offshore development. Both Rosneft and Gazprom share the characteristic of operating under a relatively large debt of twenty-five billion and forty billion, respectively. Rosneft spent more than twenty-five billion in acquiring Yukos assets, taking loans from a consortium of Western banks to cover the cost. The acquisition transformed Rosneft into the country's largest oil company (Elder 2007). Gazprom is now the world's second-largest energy company and has a monopoly on gas export. However, for Gazprom to maintain its output, an estimated investment of US$ 18 billion per year between now and 2030 is needed (Simmons and Murray 2007).

Rosneft's Offshore Strategy

Interestingly, in Rosneft's growth strategy[4] and production and development plan,[5] no mention of the northern offshore is made except in its relationship to Sakhalin. In a more informal March 2006 statement, however, Rosneft named the Sakhalin-3 projects (Kirinsky Block) and shelf deposits in the Kara, Barents and Chukotka seas as of interest for acquisition (Rosneft 2006a).[6] In many ways, Rosneft's offshore strategy can perhaps be most usefully understood as part of their regional strategy for the Russian Far East, rather than as an offshore strategy per se.

However, Rosneft's concrete actions and projects reveal an orientation towards the offshore and the North outside the Far East. Rosneft has worked extensively to further develop the export capacity of their Arkhangelsk terminal, with a floating storage facility and an offshore tank farm, with the aim of overcoming problematic capacity constraints in Transneft's northwestern pipeline system. Although this increased capacity is primarily meant to support oil production in northern Russia and the Timano-Pechora oil province, it may represent capacity for future growth in the North, including offshore. Rosneft has also ordered three ice-breaking shuttle tankers from a Spanish shipyard, primarily intended for transport between Arkhangelsk and Murmansk (Vzglyad.ru 2006), but such tankers could also be relevant for transport from offshore fields. In addition, Rosneft has agreed to launch a shipping service for offshore oil projects in cooperation with the state-run shipping company Sovkomflot ("National Project Kremlin Shelf" 2006).

In Rosneft's gas strategy, Rosneft states that natural gas is becoming an increasingly important part of the company's business, particularly in relationship to integrated oil and gas projects off Sakhalin. This expansion into gas marks a point of closer interface with Gazprom and its monopoly export network. The gas from these far eastern areas is "intended for parts of Russia currently not covered by existing pipelines and rapidly growing Asian export markets".[7] Regardless, gas is still not a top priority in Rosneft's planned and existing offshore projects. For example, in relationship to the Sakhalin-4 and -5 fields, Rosneft is planning on re-injecting all of its associated gas during the initial production of crude oil to maintain reservoir pressure. After all of the crude oil is recovered, Rosneft may produce gas if its production and transportation are commercially viable.[8] With Sakhalin-3 and the West Kamchatka projects, all the gas will be re-injected except for small amounts used to power the project's pumping stations onshore.

As will be discussed in greater detail below, the question of Rosneft gas has already been problematic in terms of the Sakhalin-1 consortium's initial plans to export gas to China via a proposed pipeline. Rosneft, as part of this consortium, seems to have blocked that move, possibly foreseeing the potential conflict with Gazprom, and has suggested as an alternative LNG and tankers (White and Ball 2007). Rosneft's leaders were reportedly very dissatisfied with the ultimate outcome of selling Sakhalin-1 gas to Gazprom for regional domestic use.

For Rosneft, expanding into gas clearly means developing new forms of cooperation with Gazprom. This need is clearly stated in the company's "Vision and Strategy" section on their website: "While management believes Rosneft will be technically able to produce approximately 40 bcm of gas by 2012, attaining this level of production will depend on Rosneft's ability to sell the gas . . . which is dependent upon the negotiation of an agreement with Gazprom that is currently under discussion". The question of how such a cooperation might function is returned to below, following a brief review of Gazprom's offshore and oil strategies.

Gazprom

Gazprom accounts for approximately eighty-seven percent of Russian gas production and controls the lion's share of Russian gas reserves. Gazprom runs the integrated trunk pipeline system and holds an export monopoly. However, Gazprom faces a significant challenge in maintaining supply after 2010, due to falling output in three out of four of its major fields. Increased offshore activity is presented as a key element in the company's response to this challenge. A "concept for development of hydrocarbon resources on Russia's continental shelf until 2030" was adopted in 2003.

Based on this concept document, Gazprom prepared a more detailed program in 2005 that divides the continental shelf into four regions (Kirillov 2007: 9):

1. Pechora Sea: mainly oil—includes Prirazlomnoye and Dolginskoye and structures close to them;
2. Northeastern Barents Sea: mainly gas—Shtokman and satellites;
3. Ob and Tazov Bay: mainly gas—Severo-Kamennomsykoe, Kamennomyskoe-More, and others; and
4. Kara Sea: mainly gas—offshore section of Kharasavey and Kruzenshtern, offshore fields Leningradskoe and Ruzanovskoe.

The order of development of these regions has been determined by the size of their resources, the distance to existing infrastructure and the optimization of industrial development. Gazprom's announced plans can be summarized as follows:

- Offshore oil production in the Pechora Sea will start first. It has a higher priority now due to Gazprom's stronger engagement in oil. However, a firm year for the start-up of Prirazlomnoye has not been set.

- Shtokman is to be put into production in 2013-2014 to fill up the Nordstream pipeline and meet the demand for LNG in the Atlantic region, as well as domestic supplies. Adjacent fields will be connected at a later stage.
- The largest field in Ob-Tazov Bay will be brought into production in 2015–2017. Later, offshore fields, like Chugoryakhinskoye, will be connected.
- The fields in Kara Sea will be brought on stream around 2028–2029 when onshore fields on the Yamal peninsula have peaked.

Altogether, according to Gazprom, implementation of this plan will amount to a production level of 180 BCM of natural gas and eleven million tons of oil in 2030. However, these plans must not be mistaken for a projection of what is actually going to happen. The timelines proposed, for example, for the Shtokman field, already seem unrealistic. They presuppose, for instance, that Gazprom will be given a more or less free rein offshore. This special role offshore has, of course, been confirmed by the new legislation discussed earlier. However, even if the company enjoys a very strong political position today, it is not certain that it will do so in five years. Rather, it is more important to read the plans as aspirations as of today. It is then useful to suppose that the company will engage in decision-making in the near future aimed towards realizing this plan to the extent possible. A more comprehensive evaluation of the resolve of both Gazprom and Rosneft with regard to offshore development would have to take into account a fuller picture of the strategies and investment opportunities of these two companies. This falls outside the scope of this chapter. Yet, one would logically expect that the monopoly position now given to the two companies for offshore gas and offshore oil will not be an incentive to increase their offshore efforts, other factors remaining unchanged.

Interaction between Gazprom and Rosneft

Pundits often describe Gazprom and Rosneft as being locked in a political and economic competition that has only become more intense since their failure to merge in 2005 and in their efforts to acquire the remaining assets of the bankrupt Yukos. This competition is seen not only as one of business competition but political competition as well. Gazprom has been associated with now President Dmitri Medvedev (formerly deputy prime minister), while Rosneft's link to Putin's inner circle is Igor Sechin, who was deputy chief of staff in the presidential administration and was named deputy prime minister in the Putin government. Medvedev and Sechin have served as chairmen of the board of Gazprom and Rosneft, respectively.

Recent statements from the Ministry of Natural Resources indicate that Gazprom's profile as a gas producer and Rosneft's as an oil producer are meant to suffice for dividing up the continental shelf between the two, thereby forgoing competition between the two companies. However, if we look at onshore oil and gas development as a corollary, it becomes clear that the picture is not so simple. Although Gazprom is without a doubt the dominant Russian gas producer, oil companies also play a role in the Russian gas market and independent gas producers, along with major Russian oil companies, control about one-third of Russia's natural gas reserves. Many of the oil companies are responsible for the vast quantities of gas flared each year as they do not have the incentives and access needed to bring this gas to the market. However, flaring may be ruled unlawful by 2011 and legislation is currently being discussed that would greatly limit flaring, such as enforcing the use of ninety-five percent of the associated gas in primarily oil projects (Simmons and Murray 2007). This may be another driving force behind Rosneft and Gazprom's increased cooperation, should Rosneft wish to sell its gas on the Gazprom-controlled export market.

The relationship between Gazprom and Rosneft is likely to become even more interactive due to: (i) the important place now given to state-run energy endeavours; (ii) the thus far equally privileged relationship given to these companies in terms of offshore resources and (iii) the increasingly artificial divide between oil and gas projects and companies. But will it lead to cooperation or more competition? Despite the rhetoric of competition surrounding the political affiliations of each company, there certainly exists a level of cooperation between the two of them. Gazprom and Rosneft had previously (in 2001) entered into an agreement to join forces for the development of the Prirazlomnoye oil field and Shtokman gas condensate fields, and had set up the fifty-fifty Sevmorneftegaz joint venture to implement the agreement ("Gazprom, Rosneft and Statoil Sign Memorandum of Understanding" 2004). The partnership was dissolved when Gazprom bought out Rosneft, which needed cash for its purchase of Yuganskneftegaz. The partitioning of

Yukos also changed the power constellations in the fuel and energy sector and the announced merger between Gazprom and Rosneft was shelved.

However, merely a year after the failed merger efforts, Rosneft's president, Sergei Bogdanchikov, could describe cooperation with Gazprom as "regular" and note that eighty percent of Rosneft's gas was delivered to consumers via Gazprom's transport systems (Rosneft 2006b). In November 2006 Gazprom and Rosneft signed a partnership deal on strategic cooperation for joint work in oil, gas and electricity production, as well as joint bids on energy contracts. The main aim of the partnership agreement was to avoid confrontation and extensive competition on the domestic and foreign markets between the two companies, although the agreement may further reduce the influence and space for international energy companies as well. The agreement document states specifically that the companies plan on jointly developing tenders and participating in auctions for subsoil-use rights and plan to implement projects together on a fifty-fifty basis. They will also cooperate in developing and creating geological and geophysical information databases and exchanging information during exploration. More specifically, under the agreement, Gazprom will acquire natural gas from Rosneft at the west Siberian fields that link up to Gazprom's gas transportation system at a 2006 production level. Further agreements related to new fields and an expanding transport system will be made in subsequent agreements. It should be noted that the agreement did not lay out any specific projects. The agreement will remain in place until 2015, with the option of five-year renewal periods ("Gazprom and Rosneft Shelve Rivalry, Form Partnership" 2006).

Both Rosneft and Gazprom are now actively involved in oil and gas consortiums that have reached production phases off Sakhalin, rendering the Sea of Okhotsk an interesting current test case for how the companies will interact offshore. Eastern Siberia and the Far East have recently been made a prioritized area for regional gas development. The state's program on integrated gas production, transportation and supply system in eastern Siberia and the Far East places emphasis on both supplying gas domestically and increasing exports to China and other Asian Pacific countries. The program was approved on 15 June 2007 by the government commission responsible for fuel and energy sector issues, and Gazprom was appointed the coordinator of program implementation, with special emphasis placed on meeting the growing domestic gas market in the region. Then deputy prime minister Medvedev argued that the strategy of the Russian Federation was to have one company as the sole exporter of gas produced in Russia and he stressed that this is the best strategy for economic effectiveness in the Russian Far East ("Gazprom Is Seeking Agreement to Buy 100% of Sakhalin-1 Gas" 2007).

While Gazprom's focus on, and role in, the Far East and eastern Siberia is a relatively recent one (with Gazprom's 2007 entrances into the Sakhalin-2 consortium and the Kovytka project[9]), Rosneft has been in many ways more established in the region via its involvement in the Sakhalin projects. Rosneft owns over thirty percent of the oil and gas reserves and resources in the Far East and has argued that the "more the company's reserves are concentrated locally, the greater the synergies it can achieve from its activities" (Rosneft 2007). There are signs that Gazprom's aggressive entry into the Far East fields and markets caused tension between the two companies. For example, on one regionally important issue, Gazprom appeared to have won the day. By mid-August it was clear that Sakhalin-1 gas would be used in Russia's domestic market rather than exported directly to China. Gazprom has been working to consolidate the Chinese market and had blocked Exxon Mobil from selling its Sakhalin-1 gas to China ("Sakhalin-1 Gas: Final Destination Unknown" 2007). Officially, Rosneft puts a positive spin on this development, noting that "while the PSA governing Sakhalin-1 allows for gas export independent of Gazprom, collaboration with Gazprom could be desirable in the event that pipelines to northeastern China become the favored export route".[10]

At a 30 June 2007 meeting of Rosneft's shareholders, a commitment to cooperating with Gazprom was reiterated. Bogdanchikov stated, "Gazprom needs gas pipelines and fields, and we are positioning ourselves as an oil company, although we are also involved in the gas business. Our plans for the period up to 2020 will increase the proportion of our earnings from gas sales to 30%. Using Gazprom's potential in a number of vital areas (linked with transport and export), will of course also benefit Sakhalin".[11] Despite this announced cooperation, rivalry between the companies is reportedly intense, and the relationship between the top leaders is said to be contentious.

Conclusion

The interaction between Rosneft and Gazprom on Sakhalin illustrates some key aspects of their interrelationship and has much to say about what Russian offshore development may look like in the medium term. While these two state-controlled energy companies do cooperate on some issues, competition between them can be seen as the primary characteristic of their interactions. In this way, although a fundamental principle of Russian energy policy is that of national control, one can discern room for change, and this tracing of the circuitous development of offshore policy indicates some challenges relating to the energy sector more broadly and to Russian policy-making processes more specifically.

Firstly, the relationship between the state-controlled companies and the increasing overlap between their traditional areas of commercial dominance encompasses a level of volatility. Also, having traced the often circuitous changes in Russian offshore policy and the variety of sometimes contradictory ideas that have been presented over the past two years, another important feature of Russian offshore policy becomes clear: It remains unconsolidated and plays out against a backdrop of either ad hoc decision-making or competition between key elements of the state (or perhaps both). Ideas that seemed to have been completely abandoned later resurface and new strategies and proposals continue to be developed, which perhaps speaks to different governmental bodies attempting to put their stamp upon, and secure a role in, offshore development policy. The ongoing development of the legal framework for strategic resources and its actual implementation, with the important questions it raises about foreign involvement, adds additional complexity to the policy environment in Moscow, presenting obstacles to strategic and unified policy work.

At the same time, many Russian actors involved in this political-commercial milieu seem to recognize the importance of creating stable rules for investors. 'Stability' and 'facilitating investment' are keywords of President Medvedev's political vocabulary. However, it may also be misleading to anticipate an 'offshore regime' or an 'offshore policy' in the singular. Perhaps we may not see a unified regime at all. Instead, the government may choose to adopt particular approaches to particular projects, responding to the circumstances of the moment.

NOTES

1. This article was produced with project funding from the PETROSAM program of the Research Council of Norway. The project, "RUSSCASP - Russian and Caspian energy developments", is carried out by the Fridtjof Nansen Institute, the Norwegian Institute for International Affairs and Econ Pöyry as consortium partners and also includes other institutions and researchers (see http://www.fni.no/russcasp/index.html).
2. See Deputy Minister Varlamov in Veletminskiy (2007).
3. The third state oil company, Zarubezhneft, which was set up to work in projects abroad, has declared that it feels competent to participate on the Russian continental shelf and could be interested, particularly in the Barents Sea ("'Zarubezhneft' gotova na rossiyskiy shel'f" 2008).
4. See [http://www.rosneft.com/printable/Upstream/growthstrategy].
5. See [http://www.rosneft.com/printable/upstream/productionanddevelopment].
6. Rosneft is also carrying out an exploration project on the West Kamchatka shelf in cooperation with the Korean National Oil Company.
7. See [http://www.rosneft.com/printable/upstream/gasstrategy].
8. See [http://www.rosneft.com/printable/Upstream/Exploration/ExplorationAssets/Sakhalin-5].
9. In addition, Gazprom Neft received Russian governmental permission to explore the Lopukhovskoye field until 2010, possibly in partnership with Statoil (this was not confirmed by a Statoil representative) ("Gazprom Left, Norway's Statoil to Explore Lopukhovskoye Field" 2007).
10. See [http://www.rosneft.com/printable/Upstream/Productionanddevelopment].
11. See Rosneft, General Shareholders' Meeting, [http://www.rosneft.com/printable/Investors/shareholdersmeeting/meeting767/meeting/i].

REFERENCES

Balzer, Harley. 2005. "The Putin Thesis and Russian Energy Policy." *Post-Soviet Affairs* 21: 3: 210–225.

Bradshaw, Michael. 2006. "Sakhalin-II in the Firing Line: State Control, Environmental Impacts and the Future of Foreign Investment in Russia's Oil and Gas Industry." *Russian Analytical Digest* 8: 6-11. [http://www.geog.le.ac.uk/staff/mjb41/articles/Sakhalin2_in_the_Firing_Line_State.pdf] [consulted 5 February 2009].

Chugunov, Dmitriy. 15 March 2007. "Rossiya budet stroit' korabli" (Russia will build ships). *Rossiyskaya Gazeta*.

Elder, Miriam. 4 September 2007. "After Devouring Yukos, Rosneft Is Hungry for Cash." *International Herald Tribune.*

"Gazprom and Rosneft Shelve Rivalry, Form Partnership." 29 November 2006. Gazpromstock.com. [http://www.gazpromstock.com/2006/11/29/gaz prom-and-rosneft-shelve-rivalry-form-partnership] [consulted 1 February 2008].

"Gazprom Is Seeking Agreement to Buy 100% of Sakhalin-1 Gas." 11 May 2007. *The Sakhalin Times.*

"Gazprom Left, Norway's Statoil to Explore Lopukhovskoye Field." 20 July 2007. *The Sakhalin Times.*

"Gazprom, Rosneft and Statoil Sign Memorandum of Understanding." 9 September 2004. Gazprom. [http://www.gazprom.ru/eng/news/2004/09/13809.shtml] [consulted 1 November 2007].

Grigor'ev, Mikhail. 2007. "Kak nam obustroit' shelf" (How shall we develop the shelf?). *Mirovaya energetika* 4: 30.

Kirillov, Denis. 2007. "Vykhod v more" (Exit to the sea). *Gazprom.*

Kommersant. 17 April 2008. "'Gazprom' i 'Rosneft' idut na dno" (Gazprom and Rosneft go to the bottom).

Makhlin, Mikhail. 20 June 2006. "Neftegazovyiy dayving." *Rossiyskaya Gazeta.*

Medetsky, Anatoly. 28 February 2007. "State to Divvy Up Offshore Projects." *Moscow Times.*

Mejvedomstvennaya Komissiya. 5 July 2005. *Utverjdeny sostav i poljenie o Mejvedomstvennoi Komisii po podgotovke proekta strategii izucheniya I osvoeniya neftegazovogo potentsiala kontinental'nogo shel'fa RF I kompleksnogo plana deistvii po ee realizatsii.* [http://www.mnr.gov.ru].

Moe, Arild, and Anne Kristin Jørgensen. 2000. "Offshore Mineral Development in the Russian Barents Sea." *Post Soviet Geography and Economics* 41: 2: 98–133.

"National Project Kremlin Shelf." 15 December 2006. Gazeta.ru.

Naumov, Stanislav. 19 April 2007. "Prioritety promyshlennoi politiki dlya osvoeniya kontinental'nogo shel'fa" (Priorities of commercial policy for the development of the continental shelf, speech by the director of the Department of Economic Analysis and Planning under the Ministry of Energy and Industry Stanislav Naumov at the roundtable 'The Arctic—a 'hot spot' of the 21st Century"). [http://www.minprom.gov.ru/appear-ance/ report/41/print] [consulted 1 February 2008].

Rosneft. 23 February 2007. "Interview with Sergey Bogdanchikov, President of Rosneft on the Television Program Vesti/FES." [http://www.rosneft.com/

printable/news/news_in_press/10705.html] [consulted 15 November 2007].

———. 2006a. "Rosneft President Presents Development Strategy and Potential Projects to Russian and Foreign Media." [http://www.rosneft.com/printable/news/news_in_press/9967.html] [consulted 15 November 2007].

———. 2006b. "Bogdanchikov Informs President Putin of Rosneft Consolidation Decisions." [http://www.rosneft.com/printable/news/news_in_press/9966.html] [consulted 15 November 2006].

"Rosneft Seeking Additional Licenses to Work Offshore." 28 May 2007. *The Sakhalin Times.*

"Sakhalin-1 Gas: Final Destination Unknown." 20 July 2007. *The Sakhalin Times.*

Simmons, Daniel, and Isabel Murray. 2007. "Russian Gas: Will There Be Enough Investment?" *Russian Analytical Digest* 27: 7: 2–5.

Strategiya. 2006. *Strategiya izucheniya osvoeniya neftegazovogo potentsiala kontinentalnogo shelfa Rossiyskoy Federatsii do 2020 Proekt* (Strategy for exploration and development of the oil and gas potential of the continental shelf of the Russian Federation until 2020). Draft. [http://www.mnr.gov.ru].

Trutnev, Yury. 2006. *O povyshenii effektivnosti osvoyeniya uglevorodnikh resursov kontinental'nogo shel'fa Rossiiskoi Federatsii* (Concerning the enhancement of efficiency of hydrocarbon resources development on the continental shelf of the Russian Federation). *Mineral'nye resursy rossiiskogo shel'fa—2006 (Mineral Resources of the Russian Shelf—2006).* Moscow: Geoinformark.

———. 15 May 2005. *Doklad Ministra prirodnikh resursov RF Yuriya Trutneva na zesedanii pravitel'stva RF na temu "O merakh po izucheniyu I povysheniyu effektivnosti osvoyeniya mineral'no-syr'evykh resursov kontinental'nogo shel'fa Rossiiskoi Federatsii"* (Report of the Minister of Natural Resources Yuriy Trutnev at the government session on "measures for exploration and increased efficiency in the development of mineral resources on the continental shelf of the Russian Federation"). [http://www.MNR.gov.ru] [consulted 1 February 2008].

Varlamov, Dmitry. 2007. Speech by Deputy Natural Resources Minister Varlamov at RAO/CIS Offshore St. Petersburg. [http://www.mnr.gov.ru].

Veletminskiy, Igor. 29 March 2007. "Razvedka nedrami." *Rossiyskaya Gazeta.*

Vzglyad.ru. 2006. [http://www.vzglyad.ru/news/2006/2/9/21966.html].

White, Gregory, and Jeffrey Ball. 7 May 2007. "Rough Patch." *Wall Street Journal.*

"'Zarubezhneft' gotova na rossiyskiy shel'f" (Zarubezhneft is ready for the Russian continental shelf). 9 June 2008. *RBK Daily.*

Chapter Six

Growth Poles and Ghost Towns in the Russian Far North[1]

Timothy Heleniak

Introduction

T he importance of the resources of the Far North for Russia's current and future economic growth is undeniable (Smith and Giles
2007). However, the population size and settlement patterns that
the Soviet Union employed to exploit the resources of the region would
not have been possible in a market economy. According to most estimates, Siberia and the Russian Far North were extremely overpopulated and there were huge costs of spatial inefficiency under the Soviet system (Mikhailova 2005). The breakup of the Soviet Union, the economic
transition and the liberalization of its society has caused significant
changes to the economic structure and migration patterns of the regions
of Russia, including those in the northern and eastern peripheries.

Between 1989 and 2006 there has been an out-migration of seventeen percent of the population from the Russian Far North, or one out
of every six people. At the extreme are Magadan, where fifty-seven
percent of the pretransition population has left, and Chukotka, where
three-quarters of the population have migrated from the region under
deteriorating social and economic conditions. On the other hand, some
settlements, particularly those in the Khanty-Mansiy and Yamal-
Nenets okrugs in west Siberia based on oil or natural gas exploitation,
are regions of in-migration during the post-Soviet period. Thus, the
economy and settlement patterns of the Russian Far North have not
universally shrunk (as is often thought to be the case) but shrivelled,
with the economies of some regions shrinking considerably while

others have been able to take advantage of new economic conditions and grow.

These new conditions have necessitated changes in policy towards the population of the Far North and development practices in the region. The new economic and social conditions have necessitated new forms of labour supply, with an increased role played by the private sector. Yet, at the same time there is a need to deal with the social and economic consequences of the inherited northern population, as well as the consequent social and physical infrastructure. The purpose of this chapter is to trace the evolution of policy towards northern development and population from the Soviet and immediate post-Soviet periods to the present.

The term 'Far North' (*kraynyy sever*) is a social construct. Russia is undeniably a northern country, for no other country has so much of its territory lying in high latitudes and north of the Arctic Circle. This is important for the country's national psyche, as well as its economic importance. The boundaries of Russia's 'northernness' seem to be expanding, along with its growing economic might, to include territories north of its northern land borders, including all of the Arctic Sea and the North Pole. With climate change and the thawing of sea ice, this might become important, depending on the extent of undiscovered resources in the Artic seabed (Dore 1995).

The idea of a 'Far North' was first introduced in 1932 with the specific aim of establishing zones with higher wages for the purpose of attracting the necessary labour force to exploit the resources of the region (Stammler-Gossmann 2007). The boundaries of this region have been altered over the years depending on changing development priorities. The 'Far North' referred to in the rest of this chapter is based upon the current Russian government definition. This definition cuts across oblast-level units, and because most demographic and economic statistics are presented only for oblasts, a slightly different set of sixteen regions is used for the analysis of population and migration patterns in the chapter (a list of regions, along with their populations and patterns of population change, is shown in table 6.1).

The analysis in this chapter is based on a combination of statistics showing changes in the size and composition of the population of the Far North, as well as policy documents of the Russian government that reflect changes in its policy towards northern development generally and the population and labour force of the region specifically. The last

---

Soviet census conducted in 1989 and the first Russian census carried out in 2002 provide convenient statistical benchmarks for analyzing changes in the size and composition of the northern regions. Annual population estimates and migration flow statistics are also used. There are an increasing number of surveys of migrants in Russia, some specifically of northern migrants, which can provide additional insight.

Following this introduction, the chapter is divided into two major sections. The first describes patterns of migration and population change in the Russian Far North. This section begins with an overview of migration across the former Soviet Union, followed by a specific analysis of migration in the Russian Far North. This is followed by an analysis of mobility of the Russian population and characteristics of migrants leaving the Russian Far North, and the impact that these migration streams have had. The second section in the chapter summarizes Russia's changing policy towards the population of its northern periphery, with a separate treatment of regions of growth and decline.

Patterns of Migration and Population Change in the Russian Far North

Brief Overview of Migration in Post-Soviet Russia

Neoclassical economic theory posits that one of the major drivers of migration among countries and regions is differences in income. While there was certainly migration within Russia and between Russia and the other former Soviet Union (FSU) states during the Soviet period, the patterns were quite different from what they might have been if the country had operated under market conditions—mobility was likely lower, in part because of the flat income distribution among the FSU states and regions within them. When it existed, the Soviet Union was a closed migration and economic space. Many decisions regarding the spatial distribution of the population and economic activity were guided by the central planning apparatus rather than the market. There were restrictions on the population's movements in the form of the *propiska* or resident permit system. There was also an elaborate system of taxes, subsidies and financial transfers that caused concepts of 'profitability' to be different under central planning than under market conditions.

Region	Total population		Percent change 1989–2006			Absolute change 1989–2006		
	1989	2006	Total	Natural increase	Migration	Total	Natural increase	Migration
Russian Federation	147,022	142,754	-2.9	-6.9	4.0	-4,268	-10,165	5,897
The North	9,774	8,260	-15.5	1.8	-17.3	-1,514	174	-1,688
Karelian Republic	790	698	-11.7	-8.3	-3.4	-92	-66	-27
Komi Republic	1,251	985	-21.3	-1.3	-19.9	-266	-16	-249
Arkhangel'sk Oblast	1,570	1,291	-17.7	-6.2	-11.6	-279	-97	-182
Nenets Autonomous Okrug*	54	42	-22.2	5.4	-27.6	-12	3	-15
Murmansk Oblast	1,165	865	-25.8	-1.3	-24.5	-300	-15	-286
Khanty-Mansiy Autonomous Okrug	1,282	1,478	15.3	11.6	3.7	196	149	48
Yamal-Nenets Autonomous Okrug	495	531	7.2	13.9	-6.7	36	69	-33
Tuva Republic	308	308	0.2	12.6	-12.5	0	39	-38
Taymyr Autonomous Okrug	56	39	-30.4	5.7	-36.1	-17	3	-20
Evenki Autonomous Okrug	25	17	-30.9	5.8	-36.6	-8	1	-9
Sakha Republic (Yakutia)	1,094	950	-13.2	10.4	-23.5	-144	114	-258
Chukotka Autonomous Okrug	164	51	-69.2	4.6	-73.8	-113	8	-121
Kamchatka Oblast	472	349	-26.0	0.9	-26.9	-123	4	-127
Koryak Autonomous Okrug*	40	23	-42.0	0.5	-42.5	-17	0	-17
Magadan Oblast	392	172	-56.2	1.2	-57.4	-220	5	-225
Sakhalin Oblast	710	526	-25.9	-3.3	-22.6	-184	-23	-161

* Data for these areas are also included in the larger geographic unit of which they are a part.

Note: 'The North' as defined here is made up of the sixteen regions designated as such in the study.

Table 6.1. Population trends in the Russian North, 1989–2006 (Beginning of year; in thousands)

Sources: See note 2.

With the breakup of the Soviet Union into fifteen independent states, the transition to a market economy and the lifting of most restrictions on migration movements, the economic fortunes of countries and regions have changed considerably, resulting in large-scale shifts in the patterns and directions of migration movements. The ratio of the FSU state with the highest GDP (gross domestic product) per capita to the lowest has gone from 6.2 in 1990 to 11.8 in 2004.[3] Likewise, the ratio of the Russian region with the highest gross regional product to the lowest went from five in 1990 to thirty-six in 2002.[4] Thus, regional income disparities, which had played a minor role in influencing migration patterns during the Soviet era, have become a major factor during the post-Soviet period.

At the international level, Russia has become the major migration magnet in the region, with a net immigration of 5.8 million between 1989 and 2004, while collectively the other FSU states have had a net emigration of 9.6 million (obviously, including emigration to outside the FSU space, as well as some statistical discrepancy). Among FSU states, Armenia, Georgia, Kazakhstan, Tajikistan and Moldova have had emigration of fifteen percent or more of their populations. Another factor important to migration in the post-Soviet space was that at the time of the breakup, sixty million people, over twenty percent of the Soviet population, were members of one of many ethnic diasporic groups living outside of their defined homelands.[5] Much of the early migration movements across the post-Soviet space can be attributed to the diasporic migration of people moving to what they perceived to be their ethnic homelands. However, the period of intense diasporic migration seems to have past and most recent migration appears to be economically motivated (Mansoor and Quillin 2007).

The Soviet system attempted to equalize living standards among all regions, between urban and rural areas and across urban settlements of different sizes. The restructuring of the economic geography of the post-Soviet space has produced increased disparities in living standards and large internal migration streams. Many capital and other larger cities in the FSU states have gained large numbers of migrants from smaller cities and rural areas (Heleniak 2004). With enterprises now operating under market conditions, some have become more profitable while many others have become much less so as the costs of both inputs and outputs have shifted considerably. With large numbers of either newly profitable or now insolvent enterprises, regions across the post-Soviet space have seen their economic fortunes diverge considerably, with some becoming boom regions and many others becoming ghost towns or regional pockets of poverty. One of the regions where both of these trends can be seen most apparently is across the large expanse of the Russian Far North.

Northern regions containing large amounts of resources, which had been undervalued under central planning, have become growth poles of the new Russian economy and also regions of in-migration. Simultaneously, the costs associated with industrialization and maintaining settlements in the distant regions of Siberia and the Russian Far North have caused steep increases in the cost of living, and many enterprises become unprofitable resulting in large population losses. Much of the data and analysis in this chapter pertains to the eighty-nine regions in Russia, but this masks important analysis of disparities and migration streams at lower levels.[6] This occurs because of the paucity of readily available data at lower levels of geography. According to a World Bank study of poverty in Russia, while inequality among regions is important, it is actually inequality within regions that dominates (World Bank 2005c). Thus, to the extent possible, consideration of increased disparities and migration patterns within northern regions will be considered.

Migration in the Russian Far North

While there was a general eastward trend of migration outward from central Russia towards Siberia for centuries, it was during the Soviet period under central planning that this buildup of Siberian and northern cities was undertaken on a massive scale. Though the development practices that the Soviet Union employed towards its northern regions could have only existed under a centrally planned system, there was evidence of neoclassical economics at work with the use wage and other financial incentives to draw people to the North and east (Gerber 2006). The migration continued right up until the end of the Soviet period, although there were signs that it was slowing during the 1980s. According to one estimate, using a broader definition of the Russian North, the region was overpopulated by 14.6 million people as compared to Canadian development practices (Mikhailova 2005).

Figure 6.1 shows the regional patterns of net migration during the post-Soviet period as people have been attempting to overcome this spatial misallocation by migrating away from these overpopulated regions. Between 1989 and 2006, there has been a net migration of 1.7 million people out of the regions defined as the 'Far North.' Most other regions of Siberia and the European North, which are included in the categorization of "regions equivalent to the Far North," have also experienced out-migration. With some natural increase, the population of the region has fallen by 15.5 percent over this period (table 6.1). Unlike Russia, there were more births than deaths in the Far North over the entire period as a result of having a younger age structure. However, for the Far North as whole and for many northern regions, the number of deaths began to exceed the number of births around the year 2000 and thus in many regions, the populations are declining because of both out-migration and negative natural increase. Over the entire period, all northern regions, except for the Khanty-Mansiy Autonomous Okrug, have had out-migration. Ten of the sixteen northern regions have had one-quarter or more of their populations migrate out since 1989.

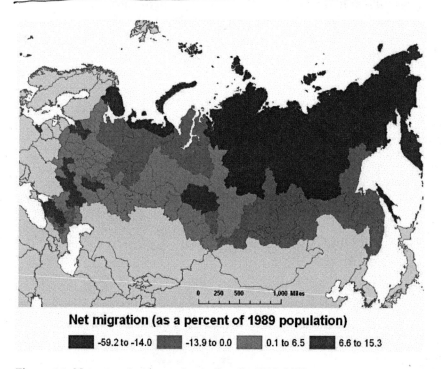

Net migration (as a percent of 1989 population)

-59.2 to -14.0   -13.9 to 0.0   0.1 to 6.5   6.6 to 15.3

Figure 6.1. Net migration by region in Russia, 1989–2002.
Source: Goskomstat Rossii, Demograficheskiy yezhegodnik (Demographic Yearbook), selected editions.

Figure 6.2 shows the temporal trends of net migration in the Russian Far North for the period of 1989 to 2006. Many northern regions started losing people in the late 1980s, and by 1990, all of the northern regions had more people leaving than coming. The peak period of out-migration was the first half of the 1990s, with the peak year being 1992, when prices were liberalized and economic reforms began. While there are still more people leaving the Far North than coming to the region, the rate of net out-migration has slowed considerably since this peak in the early 1990s.

This trend of slowing migration turnover in the Far North is consistent with the pattern experienced elsewhere in Russia and across the former Soviet Union. There is a two-part explanation for this increase and then decrease in migration turnover across the Russian Far North and the rest of the post-Soviet space. With the breakup of the Soviet Union and beginning of economic reforms, there was a rapid rise in income and unemployment disparities among the regions, but these inter-regional variances in wages and unemployment then levelled off after 2000 (Gerber 2005b; Mansoor and Quillin 2007). As will be examined in more detail below, there was a portion of the population prone to migrating under changing circumstances who moved under these new conditions, but as the situation stabilized, the migration turnover rate

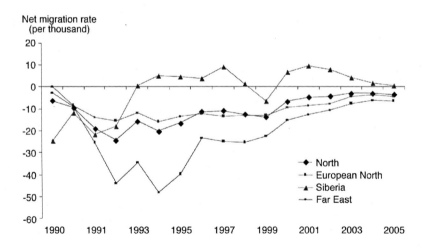

Figure 6.2. Net migration by region in the Russian Far North, 1989–2005.
Source: Goskomstat Rossii, selected publications.

did as well. One study in Russia of individual migration characteristics found that the same types of people tended to migrate during the Soviet and post-Soviet periods and that differing regional economic perform-ance rates contributed to new migration patterns (Gerber 2005a).

Figure 6.2 also shows net migration patterns for three groups of northern regions: the European North (Karelian Republic, Komi Republic, Arkhangel'sk Oblast, Nenets Autonomous Okrug and Murmansk Oblast); Siberia (Khanty-Mansiy Autonomous Okrug, Yamal-Nenets Autonomous Okrug, Tuva Republic, Taymyr Autonomous Okrug and Evenki Autonomous Okrug) and the Far East (Sakha Republic, Chukotka Autonomous Okrug, Kamchatka Oblast, Koryak Autonomous Okrug, Magadan Oblast and Sakhalin Oblast). The regions of the European North have consistently had out-migration over the period of 1989 to 2005 and at roughly the same rates as the Far North as a whole. The regions classified as Siberia initially had out-migration in the early 1990s, when the oil and gas industries were restructured, but then switched to in-migration as the industries in these regions began to take advantage of the resources they possessed under the new market conditions, as well as benefiting from infusions of both foreign and domestic investment. Later, the only year Siberia had out-migration was in 1999, the year following the 1998 fiscal crisis. It was the more distant regions of the Far East that had the highest rates of out-migration, which have been consistently higher than in the Far North as a whole. While the levels of out-migration have changed, the rank order of migration patterns among northern regions has stayed more or less the same. In other words, those northern regions losing relatively large numbers of people in 1990 were also losing relatively large numbers in 2005.

Northern Migration by Destination

This section turns to a discussion of migration in the Russian Far North by origin and destination, which provides more nuance and insight. Much of this is based on migration statistics that are compilations of the declarations that people are required to make when moving within Russia. Since 1992, when legal restrictions on mobility were lifted, peo-ple moving within Russia are not required to obtain permission to do so. However, they are still required to register their movements and there are various incentives to do so, such as the requirement to register in order to gain access to public services. Like any migration measurement system, there are certainly movements that are not captured, but in general, they do provide a fairly complete picture of migration within the country.[7]

While the general impression of the Russian Far North during the 1990s is that it was a region that was depopulating rapidly as a result of massive out-migration, the reality is a bit more complex. Even during the first half of the 1990s, the peak period of net out-migration from the Far North, there were six people migrating to the northern regions for every ten people leaving them. Over the past decade, this ratio has risen to eight in-migrants to every ten out-migrants, thus depicting a situation of considerable migration and labour market turnover rather than just one-way exodus. As shown in figure 6.3A, both in-migration and out-migration have fallen over time, with the narrowing of the gap between the two accounting for the slowdown of overall net out-migration from the Far North.

During the early 1990s, just after the breakup of the Soviet Union, international migration movements across the borders of the new states were fluid and poorly controlled (and in some cases, poorly measured). The Bishkek Agreement allowed visa-free travel among the newly independent states and initially there was considerable migration among the states, much of this ethnically motivated as many people sought to move to what they perceived to be their homelands, believing that their lives would be better (ICFMP Development 2005; Mansoor and Quillin 2007). In 1993, among northern regions, thirty-four percent of out-migrants went to foreign countries, while forty-eight percent of in-migrants were from outside of Russia (see figure 6.3B). Over the 1990s, the international borders of the newly independent states ossified and movements across them became more regulated, especially those of Russia, which had become the migration magnet among FSU states. As can be seen in figure 6.3B, the migration exchanges of northern regions became increasingly with other regions of Russia and less with countries outside of Russia. In-migration from foreign countries fell to thirteen percent in 2005 and out-migration to foreign countries to seven percent. Thus, the general pattern for the Far North has been one of net in-migration from foreign countries and net out-migration to the rest of Russia. Much of this is fueled by the Khanty-Mansiy and Yamal-Nenets regions gaining large numbers of foreign migrants to work in the oil and gas fields.

One study based on a large sample of migration histories found that rates of internal migration across Russia have not changed between the Soviet and post-Soviet periods (Gerber 2005a). However, trends on migration turnover from official statistics show quite a different picture, which has also been noted in a study of internal migration (Ionstev and Aleshkovski 2006). Based on these data, for all of Russia the number of

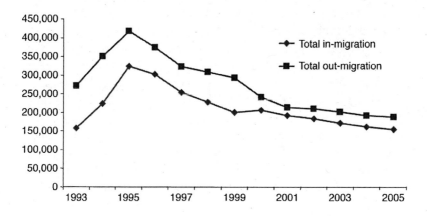

Figure 6.3A. Migration to and from the Russian North, 1993–2005.

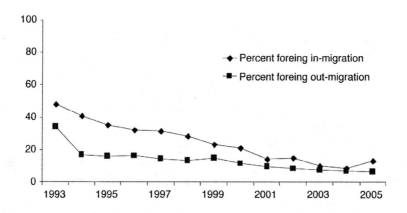

Figure 6.3B. Migration exchange between the Russian North and foreign countries, 1993–2005.

Source: Goskomstat Rossii, selected publications.

people migrating each year declined from 3.0 percent in 1991 to just 1.5 percent in 2005.[8] While there has likely been some deterioration in the share of all moves captured by the migration statistics system, those not captured certainly do not amount to half of all moves, and thus the broad trend of decreased mobility seems likely. Mobility in the Russian Far North is similar to that in the country as a whole, going from 2.8 percent of all people moving in a year in 1995 to 1.5 percent in 2005.

In addition to the overall decreased mobility among Russians, both in the Far North and elsewhere, there seems to be an increased tendency towards local migration movements and away from long-distance migration. As shown in figures 6.4A and B, based upon either figures for arrivals or departures, the same trends emerge: people in the Far North who choose migration as a strategy of adaptation, selecting a local destination rather than one that is far away. Some of this is part of a trend across the Far North of consolidation into larger urban settlements as jobs, services and quality of life deteriorates in smaller northern towns (Gray 2005; Heleniak 2008a; Thompson 2008). Thus, increasingly, labour markets in many northern regions are becoming segmented. Tuva, ever the outlier among 'northern' regions, seems to becoming a self-contained migration space, with eighty-six percent of in-migrants coming from elsewhere in the region and seventy-seven percent of out-migrants staying within the region. Again, the Khanty-Mansiy and Yamal-Nenets okrugs seem be exceptions to the general northern migration rule. Far smaller percentages of movements are within both of these regions and larger percentages are within other regions of Russia as people in these regions seem to be competing on a national labour market. In some regions of the Far East, such as Chukotka, Kamchatka and Magadan, there appears to be smaller amounts of intraregional exchange and more with other Russian regions than the Far North as a whole.

A factor contributing to this reduced number of inter-regional movements is the increased cost of transport after government subsidies were removed (Round 2005; Thompson 2004). Thus, the distance decay across the Far North is becoming increasingly a factor impeding migration (Spies 2007). This seems to be leading to the creation of poverty traps, where people are not able to migrate away from regions with deteriorating economies (Ionstev and Aleshkovski 2006). As Thompson says about Chuktoka in the 1990s, "people became more fixed in place as movement became more expensive, less reliable, or just as often, simply impossible" (2008). Many northern regions are so distant from the populated centres of the country that the populations and economies cannot take advantage of agglomeration economies of scale. One of the central themes of the study by Hill and Gaddy is that Russia needs to shrink its economic geography by increasing the linkages between population centres and markets (2003).

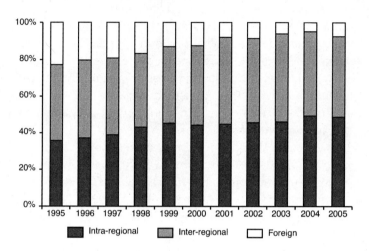

Figure 6.4A. In-migration by destination in the Russian North, 1995–2005.

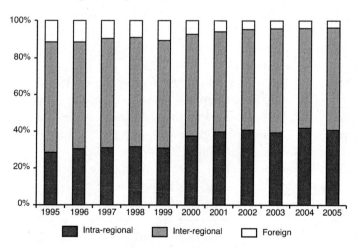

Figure 6.4B. Out-migration by destination in the Russian North, 1995–2005.
Source: Goskomstat Rossii, Chislennost' i migratsiya naseleniya Rossiyskoy Federatsii v 20— g. (Numbers and Migration of the Population of the Russian Federation in 20—), selected editions

Intuitively, most would expect that there is a negative relationship between regions with high rates of in-migration and low rates of out-migration (Plane and Rogerson 1994). Regions with good economic conditions should attract a lot of in-migrants and few people should want to leave. Conversely, regions with poor economic conditions (such as many of the Far North regions) should have high rates of out-migration and attract few in-migrants. However, in many migration systems, a positive relationship has actually been found to exist between regions of in-migration and out-migration, and in some cases the relationship is quite strong. This is the case among Russian regions in the post-Soviet period where there has been a consistently positive and quite strong correlation between regions of high in-migration, at the same time being regions of high out-migration.

A scatter plot of the relationship between the out-migration and in-migration rates for the regions of Russia in 2004 is shown in figure 6.5. In that year the correlation coefficient (r) between the in-migration and out-migration rates was 0.68. Over the period 1993 to 2004, when data have been available, the correlation coefficient has averaged 0.62, indicating a relatively strong relationship between regions of in-migration and out-migration. In figure 6.5 selected northern regions are highlighted, as are selected other regions. As can be seen, many northern regions, both prosperous and poor, are among the regions in Russia with both high rates of in-migration and high rates of out-migration. Thus, migration has hardly been unidirectional away from most northern regions, as might have been expected.

Three explanations have been put forward to explain the situation where this positive relationship has been found within a migration system (Plane and Rogerson 1994). However, these explanations are often more applicable to more prosperous regions and do not fully account for less well-off regions combining the expected high rates of out-migration with the unexpected high rates of in-migration. The first explanation is labour market turnover. In prosperous regions, people are earning good incomes and looking to advance, and that desire to advance might include looking for opportunities outside of the region. This could certainly apply to some of the more prosperous northern regions, such as Khanty-Mansiy Okrug, which has a high rate of in-migration but where only one in five migrants stay.[9] In less prosperous northern regions, it might be because the exodus from these regions has created a number of vacancies that can only be filled by people from outside the

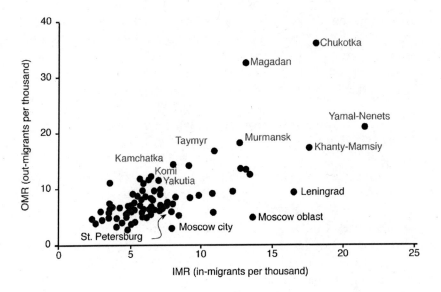

Figure 6.5. Relationship between in-migration rates and out-migration rates by region in Russia, 2004

Source: Rosstat, Chislennost' i migratsiya naseleniya Rossiyskoy Federatsii v 2004 godu (Numbers and Migration of the Population of the Russian Federation in 2004), Moscow: 2005, pp. 30–38.

region. As Gray observed in Chukotka in the mid-1990s, there seemed to be constant movement in the region's capital (Gray 2005). This observation applied to movements away from the region, internal movements into the city and the high turnover of jobs and apartments, but it could also apply to high rates of in-migration. During most of the 1990s, Chukotka consistently had a high rate of out-migration, but it also had among the highest rates of in-migration in Russia.

The second explanation has to do with age structure. Many regions of recent high in-migration have large numbers of people in the highly mobile, early-labour-force age bracket. This was certainly the case in most northern regions in 1990 at the beginning of the economic transition, but with that exodus, many of these young mobile people seem to have been replaced by another cohort of young mobile people. The third explanation is related to the second and has to do with migrant stock. Regions with large numbers of young footloose people have a hard time retaining them as economic conditions deteriorate. This was certainly the case in the Far North, leaving a population of hard-core stayers.

Taken together, these three explanations do not fully account for the trend of many northern regions also being places of attraction, but there is an important policy implication. It does demonstrate that people, including many young educated people, are still willing to migrate and work in the Far North, albeit perhaps not permanently.

Mobility of the Population of the Far North and Place-Specific Social Capital

It has often been said that Russians had a low rate of mobility compared to people in other countries, in part because of the Soviet legacy of not using migration as an adaptation strategy (Gerber 2005a). The inflexible housing market and lack of well-developed rental and mortgage markets also acted as barriers to migration. In a survey of recent migrants from the Far North, the availability of housing was a key element in their decision to migrate, more so than a job (Institute 1998). The average Russian moves just twice in his or her lifetime, compared to seven times for the average Brit, and thirteen times for the average highly mobile American (Ionstev and Aleshkovski 2006). Yet, these averages hide the fact that in any society, some people do not move while others are quite mobile. When designing migration assistance or regional development programs, it is important to keep in mind such migration tendencies. Also, the nature of regions will change as a result of in- and out-migration. As documented above, there have been some dramatic population shifts as a result of migration across the Russian Far North since 1990.

Duration of residence exerts a negative influence on migration (Plane and Rogerson 1994). The longer people live in one place, the less likely they are to move as they build up social capital specific to a region and the physical costs of moving become high. These ties to a community inhibit migration (Gerber 2005a). Duration of residence is related to characteristics such as age, sex and marital status. In addition to economic and other incentives, other strong motives for migration include family reunification and a desire to return to place of origin (Gerber 2005b). Surveys of migrants from the Far North have shown that the most cited reasons for choosing a destination are the fact that there are family or friends living there or that people lived in the region during childhood (Institute 1998).

With these tendencies in mind, the possible migration decisions of the population of the Far North just prior to the onset of the economic transition can be analyzed. As seen in figure 6.6, in 1989 forty-nine percent of the population of Russia still lived in the region in which they were born, while only thirty-seven percent of the population of the Far North were living in their region of birth. In Khanty-Mansiy, Yamal-Nenets, Chukotka and Magadan only about a quarter of the population had been born there, indicating that these were regions of newcomers with fewer place-specific social ties. Also, fifteen percent of the population of the Far North had been born outside of Russia, mostly in Ukraine and Belarus, against just seven percent for all of Russia. In addition to Russia, Ukraine and Belarus were among the most developed in the FSU and both had large numbers of people with the skills and background needed by northern enterprises. However, with uncertainty regarding citizenship and benefits following the breakup of the Soviet Union, many would leave the Far North for their newly independent titular states, believing that their economic prospects would be better there. Again, especially large numbers of people in the same four Far North regions—Khanty-Mansiy, Yamal-Nenets, Chukotka and Magadan—had large portions of their populations, between twenty-three and thirty percent, who had been born outside of Russia.

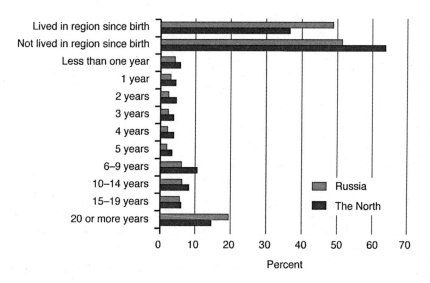

Figure 6.6. Length of residency of the population of Russia and the Far North, 1989.
Source: The Interstate Statistical Committee of the CIS and East View Publications Inc., 1989 USSR Population Census (CD-ROM), Minneapolis, MN,: 1996.

As seen in the table, of those who had been born outside of the Far North but lived there in 1989, many were recent arrivals. Especially larger portions of the populations of the Khanty-Mansiy and Yamal-Nents okrugs were recent arrivals, with forty-two and fifty-one percent, respectively, having migrated to the region over the previous five years. According to theory, if somebody moves once, they will be more likely to move again in the face of changing conditions, such as those the regions of the Far North encountered. Those who had lived for a shorter period in the region would leave, as they had less 'northern' social capital and some remaining in the materik, plus most viewed their stay in the North as temporary anyway (Institute 1998).

Characteristics of Migrants and the Impact on the Population of the Far North

In any population, characteristics of movers are quite different from nonmovers, such as in the Far North where there have been such large population movements over the past fifteen years. Prior to the economic transition, compared to the rest of Russia, the population of the Far North tended to be less Russian and to have disproportionately higher shares of Ukrainians, Belarusians and, of course, Siberian natives. The population also tended to be younger, more male and more educated. In order to understand some of the policy measures towards the northern population, this section discusses population change among northern regions according to several key demographic characteristics: ethnicity, education, gender and age.

Eleven of the sixteen regions defined here as being part of the Far North are homelands of various Siberian and northern ethnic groups, seven of which are homelands to *malochislenny narod severa* (small-numbered peoples of the North). Broadly speaking, there are two northern economies. One is a rural economy of northern and Siberian natives engaged in traditional activities, and the other is a non-native, predominantly Slavic population working in various extractive and support enterprises. The waves of migration of non-native groups to the Far North during the Soviet period dropped natives to rather miniscule shares in some regions, including their homelands.

The out-migration during the post-Soviet period has consisted mostly of non-natives and has reversed some of the demographic superiority of Russians and Russian speakers, but they remain a significant presence.

In spite of this out-migration, the Russian share of the population of the Far North fell only slightly, from 70.9 to 69.8 percent of the population, and ethnic Russians remain the majority of the population in all but two northern regions (Heleniak 2008b). The titular share of the eleven northern and Siberian homelands increased in all but Karelia. In Chukotka, which has had the largest population decline of any region, the Russian share fell from sixty-six to fifty-two percent, while the indigenous share increased from ten to thirty-one percent, though this does not seem to have translated into increased indigenous political power (Gray 2005). The closest any of the Siberian groups are to being a majority in their own homeland are the Koryaks, who increased their share of the population of Koryak Autonomous Okrug from twenty-five to forty-one percent.

In 1989 the regions of the Far North tended to have more educated populations than the rest of Russia. There are three reasons for this. First, the Far North was a region of migrants and more educated people in Russia have higher rates of mobility, as is the case in most countries (Gerber 2005a). Second, the economic structure of the Far North required a more educated labour force. Finally, there were restrictions on migration to many northern regions, allowing enterprises to be selective of whom they would hire. During the post-Soviet period, the regional pattern of change in educational levels has mirrored that of net migration (Heleniak 2008b). Stated differently, those regions in Russia that gained larger numbers of people through migration gained disproportionately large numbers of highly educated people, while those regions that lost larger numbers of people through out-migration, as was the case in many regions of the Far North, lost larger portions of their most educated populations.

Surveys of migrants from the Far North have confirmed this pattern of migrants being more educated than those left behind (Institute 1998). Many northern regions also tend to lack higher education facilities, causing the out-migration of young people, a situation also found in northern regions outside of Russia. The decline in the more educated segments of many northern regions has implications for regional economic growth, since more educated people tend to be more productive and innovative. In spite of the out-migration of many educated people from the Far North, their populations remain on average more educated than the rest of the country.

Globally, there are about 101 males per 100 females. However, Russia has among the lowest gender ratios in the world, with just

87.2 males per 100 females in 2002, down slightly from 87.7 in 1989. Because the Far North encompassed regions of in-migration and because it had an occupational structure that had a higher share of traditionally male jobs, the gender ratio in 1989 of 100.7 males per 100 females was well above the Russian average. The out-migration from the North was predominantly male, lowering the overall gender ratio to 94.3 males per 100 females, bringing it closer to the Russian average. The largest decline in the gender ratio in the Far North was among those in the most mobile age range of fifteen to thirty-four. Though the gender ratio declined in every northern region, in all but one it remained above the Russia average.

There is a well-documented selectivity of migration by age with peak mobility taking place in the young working ages. For regions, there are implications for economic growth and the mix of fiscal spending, depending on whether they have a relatively young or old population. Russia tends to have an older population in the core of the country in central Russia and a young periphery, including much of Siberia and the Far North. This is because many of the Far North peripheral regions have been the destination of so many people in the most mobile ages. Places with growing local economies are particularly attractive to younger migrants, and those with declining economic opportunities tend to lose larger numbers of younger people (Moore and McGuinness 1999).

This situation of economic growth and then decline can describe many northern regions in the Soviet and post-Soviet periods. During the economic transition period, there was a thirty-eight-percent decline in people twenty-five to thirty-nine years of age in the Far North. There were increases in all age groups above age forty (except for those at the retirement age of fifty-five to fifty-nine), the result of an aging population with lower mobility rates. In 1989 all the northern regions had median ages less than the Russian average. While all of them still do, the median age in the Far North has moved closer to the Russian average. Many of the migration assistance programs are aimed at pensioners, because it is so costly to support such a large nonworking population with the higher living costs in the Far North. However, many of these programs are undersubscribed as it is not so easy to leave when people are older and have built up considerable place-specific social capital.

Russia's Changing Policy towards the Population of Its Northern Periphery

The preceding summary and analysis of migration patterns in the Far North has demonstrated that the majority of the flows and their composition happened according to migration theory. It was also shown that there is a certain segment of the northern population that will resist migrating in the face of deteriorating conditions because of place-specific social ties. The population of the Far North has retained most of its demographic peculiarities, but the out-migration over the past fifteen years has brought many of these indicators closer to the Russian average. The period of rapid turnover and outflow seems to have passed and the population and migration flows to and from the region seem to have settled into a steady state. One surprise is that the migration patterns between the Far North and the rest of Russia are not as unidirectional as might have been expected. The region seems to have retained some of its previous attraction as a migration destination for young people in order to earn high wages from a temporary spell of employment. This section will discuss the two different types of northern regions and trace the evolution of Russian labour policy in the Far North from the Soviet period to the present.

Northern Regions in Recession and Resurgence

Because the economy of the Far North was simultaneously overdeveloped and underdeveloped (Blakkisrud and Hønneland 2006), there are two concurrent components to the new northern labour policy. One is to train and recruit skilled young workers for employment in expanding resource-extraction regions, and the second is resettlement assistance for pensioned, disabled, unemployed and other nonworking people (Oleinik 2004). Each situation has different policy implications that need to be both regionally and demographically differentiated. There are enormous regional disparities in terms of socio-economic conditions across Russia and among regions of the Far North. An important factor to keep in mind with either regional development or migration assistance programming in the Far North is that intraregion inequality accounts for most of the inequality in Russia (World Bank 2005c). Most of the poor in Russia, as well as the Far North, live in regions whose gross regional product per capita is close to the national average.

There is an obvious need to ensure a supply of skilled workers to crucial northern enterprises. This seems to be occurring, led by the private sector, albeit there seems to be considerable migration turnover in many northern regions. One method that is often touted as a solution to overcome the distances and harsh climate of the Far North is the increased use of the *vakhtovyi*, or shift-work, method. Shift-work methods can exist on a variety of spatial and temporal scales. While the Far North has long employed various forms of shift work, it seems as if the potential for such methods was underutilized during the Soviet period and that the emphasis was on the building of large permanent settlements. Surveys of people involved in shift work in the Far North found that travelling long distances to work in northern resource enterprises does not decrease job satisfaction, and that long-distance commuting is a good method for combining employment in high-wage northern oil and gas industries with living in a more pleasant environment outside the North (Spies 2007; Spies 2006). There does not appear to be much systematic data to determine how many people employed in the Far North are working within shift-work arrangements, or how this compares to the corresponding share during the Soviet period.

At the opposite extreme has been the closure or abandonment of numerous smaller northern settlements (Thompson 2008). This has been due to the depletion of the resource upon which the settlement was based; increased production costs, especially transport costs, making economic activity unprofitable under new conditions; and the increased costs and deterioration of living conditions in smaller northern settlements due to the withdrawal of state support (Ribova 2000). The massive transport effort required to support the network of distant northern settlements was greatly cut back when the costs of supplying this sparse settlement network became apparent. Because of the distances between northern settlements, there are no local economies of scale (Huskey 2005; Huskey and Morehouse 1992). The result has been both a deliberate and spontaneous policy of consolidating the population into fewer settlements in order to reduce costs (Thompson 2004; Dyachenko 2004). This policy of closing "unpromising settlements" and either reducing or consolidating the population has not been accomplished by entirely voluntary methods (Round 2005; Thompson 2003). In some cases, infrastructure has been undermined or utilities cut in order to hasten the 'natural death' of a settlement. This process of settlement closure continues as more than one hundred *neperspektivny naseleniyye punkty* (nonvi-

---

able settlements) in Komi, Buryatia Sakha, Magadan, Chukotka and Nenets Okrug have been identified for closure (Committee for Problems of the North and Far East 2007).

Overall, the number of settlements across the Far North declined by ten percent between the 1989 and 2002 censuses (Heleniak 2008a). This process of consolidation seems most extreme in the far northeast corner of Russia. In Magadan, when census-takers arrived in 2002, they found that forty-two percent of what had been previously inhabited settlements were abandoned or had become ghost towns. In Chukotka, the new economic conditions led to poverty traps where people were not able to migrate, especially given the barter-type economy that Russia had in the 1990s (Thompson 2008). Increased mobility, often with state support, has been suggested as a solution to these deep pockets of poverty, as it has been found that increases in income in Russia often raise migration rates (World Bank 2005c). One of Roman Abramovich's aims when he took over as governor of Chukotka was to concentrate the population in order to achieve scale economies in service delivery, such as hospitals, schools, energy supply and airports (Thompson 2004). This seems to have had an impact, as the number of cities in Chukotka was reduced from twenty to sixteen between the 1989 and 2002 censuses, the number of small towns from eighteen to thirteen and the number of villages from sixty-six to forty-one (CIS Statistical Committee 1996; Rossii 2005).

The Evolution of Russia's Northern Labour Policy

The Soviet Union's approach to supplying a labour force to the Far North went through several phases, which, taken together, resulted in many more people and larger settlements in the Far North than in northern regions elsewhere in the world. The first phase, of course, was forced labour in the form of the infamous Gulag system (Armstrong 1965; Bond 1985). It was through the use of conscripted labour that much of the urban and transport infrastructure of the Far North was built. The second overlapping phase was the use of various northern wage increments that were introduced in 1932 (Stammler-Gossmann 2007).

Following the death of Joseph Stalin, by the end of the 1950s, most of the forced labour camps had been closed and the system of northern benefits and privileges became more important (Luzin, Pretes and Vasiliev 1994). A second phase identified by Armstrong (1965) was to appeal to young workers to help in the development of remote areas as a part of building Communism. Related to this was the policy of *ogna-bor* (government-organized recruitment) and the mandatory placement of graduates in hard-to-fill positions, including in the Far North. The third phase was to add other benefits to northern wage increments and to improve housing and social conditions. By the end of the Soviet period, many northern regions were better supplied with hard-to-find consumer goods than the rest of Russia (Thompson 2008). In addition to these measures aimed at securing a labour force for the *osvoenoe severa* (opening of the North), there was also the construction of a huge and heavily subsidized transportation infrastructure, in order to overcome the enormous distances from central Russia to the Far North, and large fiscal transfers to make the system sustainable.

The economic transition away from central planning and the decentralization of finance led to a number of unintended consequences across Russia and the rest of the Soviet Union, including the realization that the population size of the Far North was a tremendous financial burden on the Russian government. The sectoral shifts that accompanied the economic transition of de-emphasizing industry in favour of services has had significant spatial implications, perhaps to the largest extent in the Far North (World Bank 2005a). It has been said that the Soviet economic system contained a number of spatial inefficiencies. This was not quite the case, as the system worked fine in a centrally planned economic system with administratively set prices and within the closed economic space of the Soviet Union. The huge distances across Russia to the Far North were collapsed by the heavily subsidized Soviet air transport system (Thompson 2003; Thompson 2008). Because this system no longer exists, some say that Russia must shrink its economic geography (Hill and Gaddy 2003). The need to resettle millions of northerners to save the cash-strapped Russian government money was realized early on, though there were precious few funds available for such a staggering undertaking ("Northern Lights-Out" 1993).

Under the Soviet system, since almost the entire economy was state owned and controlled, the various northern entitlements were supported by centrally planned budgetary transfers, state-owned enterprises and organizations and families. The state financed transportation of respective supplies to the northern territories with limited access. Prices were administratively fixed all over the country, and transfers allowed the regulation of living standards in the northern regions. With the economic transition, this system was no longer feasible and was replaced by a package of laws, the most notable of which was a "law on state guarantees and compensation for workers and residents of the North", which was passed on 19 February 1993, thus shifting much of the burden for special northern benefits from the federal government to local governments and enterprises. Other laws on pensions, children, the labour code and employment contained special provisions that provided benefits for northerners.

The legislation included a long list of benefits, such as for relocating to the North, which included lump-sum relocation grants, assistance with transport and free housing (World Bank 1998). There were various employment-related benefits including regional wage coefficients, tax breaks for the coefficient portion of wages, additional holidays, reduced work weeks, trips to the 'mainland' and additional severance pay. Another portion of the legislation included benefits for relocation from the North, such as free housing in the mainland, coverage of transport costs, partial funding of housing construction and free land. Additional northern benefits were early retirement for time worked in the North, credit towards early retirement for many of the occupations found primarily in the Far North, northern pension coefficients and transport for emergency medical service in the mainland. The problem is that many of the guaranteed benefits, privileges and wage increment programs have gone unfunded by the local governments that are supposed to support them or have been ignored by the newly private companies when they have been obliged to pay various "northern" benefits (Oleinik 2004; Crate and Nuttall 2003). In any case, the benefits are nowhere near sufficient to compensate for the huge increase in the cost of living in the North. The transition to a market economy has completely changed the fiscal, labour market and institutional environment to support northern privileges.

Northern labour policy is the combined responsibility of federal, legislative and regional authorities. Under Boris Yeltsin during the 1990s, a new State Committee for North Affairs, or Goskomsever, was created in June 1992 (Blakkisrud 2006). With the various reshuffles of government that took place during the decade, this committee and its portfolio went through various iterations and was not very effective in its mandate of implementing the government's northern policy. Goskomsever was the main government agency responsible for the implementation of the federal resettlement assistance schemes until its abolishment under Vladimir Putin in 2000. There are 'northern' committees in both the

Federation Council and the Duma. Issues and legislation regarding northern benefits, *rayonirovaniya* (fixing the boundaries of the Far North), northern migration measures and northern and arctic transport are in the portfolios of these committees.

The enormous costs of the northern development strategy pursued by the Soviet Union were seen as reasonable in that they helped to achieve various strategic goals, including allowing the country to become self-sufficient in strategic minerals and to increase export revenue. However, with shrinking government revenues during the period of steep economic decline in the 1990s, these costs became unsustainable. The main direct cost from the federal budget to the northern regions was the financing of what is called the "northern shipment" of food, fuel and other necessities. However, the value of these shipments decreased precipitously after the start of the economic transition from 1.58 percent of GDP in 1992 to just 0.12 percent in 1997 (World Bank 1998). According to World Bank estimates, the per-capita cost of housing and utilities in the Far North is four to five times higher than that in central Russia (World Bank 2007).

The World Bank and other international agencies have come to realize the inappropriateness of using the one-dollar-a-day poverty line in Russia because the cold climate requires additional expenditures on food, heat and winter clothing (World Bank 2005b). Nowhere is this more apparent than in the Far North. The current system of intergovernmental fiscal relations also includes transfers that are not officially targeted at the Far North but which in practice benefit the northern regions more than others. In 1997, when all the various extra costs of supporting the population of the sixteen regions of the Far North were totalled, this amounted to 3.16 percent of Russia's GDP (World Bank 1998). It would be impossible to completely move all the current population out of the Far North, but this does demonstrate that there is room for considerable cost reductions with a smaller northern population.

According to surveys, estimates and observations of the actions of people, there was a huge demand to migrate from the Far North that was not met with either the resources of individuals or government assistance. The previous budget-supported labour-rotation schemes in the North disintegrated under the new conditions, leaving many nonactive people in the Far North. According to a matrix of inter-regional migration demand compiled by Goskomsever in 1992, there were 1.3 million people on the application list who wished to leave the Far North

(Institute 1998). According to one survey of potential migrants in the Far North, the percentage of various social groups who expressed a desire to leave the North was sixty percent of pensioners, seventy percent of the disabled, fifty percent of the unemployed, fifty percent of recent college graduates and sixty-two percent of all respondents (World Bank 1998). Of those surveyed, twelve percent were born in the North and forty-seven percent had lived there thirty years or longer. Ninety-six percent indicated that they or their relatives were not able to finance resettlement and ninety-four percent indicated that they had no or insufficient savings (World Bank 1998).

In response to this demand for resettlement, a variety of migration assistance programs were devised by the federal and northern regional governments, northern enterprises and one based on a loan from the World Bank. The first federal law was government resolution No. 1141, passed on 4 November 1993. It entitles people leaving the North to compensation for housing equal to ten minimum wages for each year of service in the Far North. In most cases, it is the obligation of the employer to pay but most lack the resources to do so. There were a number of subsequent laws and decrees passed that aimed at northern migration assistance. The current federal program assisting with out-migration is federal law No. 125-FZ (on the housing subsidies for citizens migrating from the Far North regions and equated territories), which was passed on 25 October 2002 (World Bank 2007). However, based on the current levels of funding, in order to provide subsidies for all of the 690,000 applicants, it will take approximately 150 years. For the period of 2003 to 2005, 4,800 households (12,500 people) were rendered assistance at a cost of 90.7 million dollars. Other provisions of this and other related laws are not supported by necessary financial transfers.

Most of these laws relate to the construction of housing in the mainland (Institute 1998; Thompson 2004). Most are grossly underfunded as the state cannot meet all of its obligations to migrants (Maleva 1998). From 1998 to 2006, a total of sixty-six thousand people received housing certificates under the federal program (Committee for Problems of the North and Far East 2007). As of the beginning of 2007, there were 539,138 people on the waiting list to receive housing subsidies for migration. The five categories of people, in order of priority, are people in closed settlements (3,087); invalids (55,606); pensioners (297,986); the unemployed (1,009) and employed people with lengthy northern service (181,349).

Nearly all the northern regions devised a migration assistance program based upon housing construction in the mainland similar to the federal program. Regions were encouraged to develop a plan and submit it to Goskomsever (Institute 1998). An example is that of Murmansk Oblast, which started a program in 1996 and in the first two years was able to assist 1,500 families (five thousand people) with procuring flats in the south. The program looks for partially constructed flats and concludes contracts directly with construction companies. Local funds pay for the transport of people and goods, while federal funds from Goskomsever pay for housing. The program was targeted at pensioners, the unemployed, budget sector workers and invalids who had ten or more years in the Far North. As with the others, this program has run into financial problems, including racking up debts to construction companies in the south, and is now able to provide assistance to only a small portion of those wishing to migrate.

Many northern enterprises were classic one-company towns responsible for all of their social and public expenditures. With privatization and the economic transition, there was a desire on their part to shed many of these responsibilities and to have them taken over by local and municipal governments. For this reason, many wanted to reduce the size of both their workforces, and more significantly, the size of the nonworking populations they were obligated to support, so many devised their own migration assistance programs.

In order to assist with resettlement from the Far North and to test new migration assistance mechanisms, the Russian government borrowed US$ 80 million dollars from the World Bank for the "Northern Restructuring Project." The bulk of the funds are to assist twenty-five thousand people in voluntarily relocating from three northern regions—Vorkuta, Norilsk and the Susuman region of Magadan. The project was approved in June 2001. The payback period from the cost savings of downsizing the northern population in these regions was expected to be about five years. The loan was originally expected to be effective from 11 October 2001 until 30 September 2005, but because of delays in starting implementation, the closing date was delayed until June 2009.

From mid-2002, when the project came into effect, through to the end of 2005, 3,200 households (7,300 people) were relocated at a total cost of 25.1 million dollars. The aggregate annual savings from this relocation has been 8.2 million dollars, 2.3 million from the restructuring of housing and utilities and 5.9 million of budget savings from having less people in more expensive northern regions. In this case, the recoupable period was about 4.5 years, as planned. By the end of 2007, 10,579 people had received housing certificates and 8,431 had migrated from the three pilot regions.[10] The project seems to have stalled, even though the original intention was to expand the project to all of the northern regions, with the infusion of federal funds. This is due in part to Russia's changed relationship with the World Bank as it transitions to becoming a donor based upon its recent strong economic growth (ironically, most of this growth is based on the resource wealth of its northern regions).

There were a number of problems with many of these resettlement programs. The main one was that they were taking place during the period of steep economic decline of the 1990s and thus, most were greatly underfunded. Between 1993 and 1997, only 50.6 percent of the planned expenditures for the federal government's migration assistance program were made (Institute 1998; Thompson 2004). Most migrants from the Far North tended to move on their own, which is obvious when comparing the number of people assisted through all of the programs and the total flows from the Far North. According to one survey, only seven percent of migrants participated in an organized resettlement program (Institute 1998). People who participated in organized migration programs tended to be significantly older, less educated and more often female (Institute 1998). Many of these programs are greatly undersubscribed, even when properly funded (Thompson 2003). In addition, many of these programs were targeted towards less mobile nonworking segments of the northern population. There was significant resistance to migrating from a place that people were so familiar with, where they had built up significant place-specific social capital and where they had most of their social network (Round 2005; Thompson 2004).

Conclusion

With the slowdown in migration turnover and the seeming lack of support for any further migration assistance to northerners, it appears that the process of redistributing northerners to the market-determined counterfactual will be a protracted process. While laws continue to be proposed by the northern committees in the Duma and Federation Council, the period of state support for migration assistance from the Far North appears to be winding down, and the northern settlement structure has become market-driven (Fischer 2002). The costs of luring workers to northern enterprises have become the responsibility of private companies operating in the region. People will move to where the jobs are (World Bank 2005a). Through a conscious or unconscious decision, the responsibility for northern development and northern labour policy has devolved to the private sector, including some of Russia's wealthy oligarchs, with minimal government support. Though, in the opinion of some, the state should play a greater role in northern development because of national interests (Kotlyakov and Agranat 1994). With the abolishment of Goskomsever in 2000 and its functions dispersed to other agencies, it appears that the northern regions are not being treated any differently from other Russian regions (Blakkisrud and Hønneland 2006). Assistance to those left in the Far North seems to have fallen far down the government's list of priorities.

NOTES

1. The research presented in this chapter is part of a project of the European Science Foundation EUROCORES Program "Histories from the North—Environments, Movements, Narratives (BOREAS) and is titled "Moved by the State: Perspectives on Relocation and Resettlement in the Circumpolar North (MOVE)". The US portion of this project was funded by the National Science Foundation, Office of Polar Programs, Arctic Social Sciences Program. MOVE is an endorsed International Polar Year 2007–2008 project.

2. Sources for table 6.1:
   - 1989 Population Totals: Goskomstat Rossii, *Demograficheskiy yezhegodnik 2002*.
   - 1989–2006 Net Migration: Based on the residual method; data for 2002 implicitly include any census adjustments.
   - 1990; 1995; 2000–2002: Goskomstat Rossii, *Demographic Yearbook 2005* [http://www.gks.ru] [consulted 3 March 2006]).
   - 1990–1993 Births, Deaths and Natural Increase: Goskomstat Rossii, *Demograficheskiy yezhegodnik Rossiyskoy Federatsii 1993* (1994).
   - 1991–1994; 1996–1999: Goskomstat website [http://www.gks.ru] [consulted 12 May 2006]). These data have been revised based on corrections from the census.
   - 1994 Births, Deaths and Natural Increase: Goskomstat Rossii, *Sotsial'no-ekonomicheskoye polozheniye Rossii 1993–1994 gg.*
   - 1996 Births and Deaths: Goskomstat Rossii, *Sotsial'no-ekonomicheskoye polozheniye Rossii 1996 g.* (1997).

- 1997–1998 Births and Deaths: Goskomstat Rossii, *Regiony Rossii* (1999). Birth and death rates from this source are multiplied by mid-year population numbers. The published number of births and deaths are used for the national totals.
- 1999 Births and Deaths: Goskomstat Rossii, *Sotsial-no-ekonomicheskoye polozhenite Rossii v yanvarye 2001 g.*
- 2000–2001 Births and Deaths: Goskomstat Rossii, *Demograficheskiy yezhegodnik 2002.*
- 2002–2004 Births and Deaths: Goskomstat website [http://www.gks.ru] [consulted 15 February 2006]).
- 2005 Births and Deaths: Goskomstat website [http://www.gks.ru] [consulted 14 January 2007]).
- 2005 Population Totals: Goskomstat website [http://www.gks.ru] [consulted 14 January 2007]).
3. A more comprehensive measure of dispersion, the coefficient of variation (the standard deviation divided by the mean), showed the same trend going from 0.53 in 1990 to 0.71 in 2004.
4. Over this period, the coefficient of variation of gross regional product among Russian regions went from 0.43 to 0.72.
5. This is based strictly on the Soviet definitions of 'nationality' (*natsional'nost'*) and 'territorial-based ethnic homeland.' At the time of the breakup of the Soviet Union, there were fifty-three different ethnic homelands, and at the time of the 1989 USSR, 128 different nationalities were enumerated.
6. For analysis and case studies of population and economic change among regions and cities in the Russian North, see Tykkyläinen and Rautio (2008).
7. Compiled migration statistics are published annually by Goskomstat Rossii in two publications, *Demograficheskiy yezhegodnik Rossiyskoy Federatsii 20— g* (Demographic yearbook of the Russian Federation 20— g) and a small-tirazh publication titled, *Chislennost' i migratsiya naseleniya Rossiyskoy Federatsii v 20— g.* (Numbers and migration of the population of the Russian Federation in 20?).
8. This is the sum of all people registered as changing their place of residence and includes intraregional, inter-regional and foreign movements (Goskomstat Rossii [1991], *Demograficheskiy yezhegodnik Rossii*; Goskomstat Rossii [2005], *Chislennost' i migratsiya naseleniya Rossiyskoy Federatsii v 2005 godu, 2006*, 28).
9. See Khanty-Mansiy Okrug's website at [http://www.admhmao.ru/english/] accessed 20 February 2008)
10. The original name of the project was the "Northern Out-Migration Pilot Project" as it was created to test migration assistance schemes in three types of northern regions before being expanded to the entire Far North.

References

Armstrong, T. 1965. *Russian Settlement in the North*. Cambridge: Cambridge University Press.

Blakkisrud, H. 2006. "What Is to Be Done with the North?" In *Tackling Space: Federal Politics and the Russian North*, ed. Helge Blakkisrud and Geir Hønneland. Lanham, MD: University Press of America.

Blakkisrud, H., and G. Hønneland. 2006. "The Russian North? An Introduction." In *Tackling Space: Federal Politics and the Russian North*, ed. Helge Blakkisrud and Geir Hønneland. Lanham, MD: University Press of America.

Bond, A. R. 1985. "Northern Settlement Family-Style: Labor Planning and Population Policy in Norilsk." *Soviet Geography* 26: 26–47.

CIS Statistical Committee. 1996. *1989 USSR Census*. CD-ROM. EastView Publications.

Committee for Problems of the North and Far East, State Duma of the Russian Federation. 2007. *Migration from the Regions of the Far North and Equivalent Regions*. Moscow.

Crate, S., and M. Nuttall. 2003. "The Russian North in Circumpolar Context." *Polar Geography* 27: 85–96.

Dore, A. G. 1995. "Barents Sea Geology, Petroleum Resources and Commercial Potential." *Arctic* 48: 207–221.

Dyachenko, V. 2004. "Economic Development and Settlement of the Far East." In *International Symposium "The Russian in the Mirror of Statistics: The All-Russian Population Census 2002"*, ed. CIS Statistical Committee. Moscow: CIS Statistical Committee.

Fischer, P. A. 2002. "Migration and Development in Russia: Old and New Challenges and Lessons for Migration Policy." Paper presented at the conference *Migration Dialogue Seminar*, Santo Domingo, Dominican Republic.

Gerber, T. P. 2006. "Regional Economic Performance and Net Migration Rates in Russia, 1993–2002." *International Migration Review* 40: 661–697.

———. 2005a. "Individual and Contextual Determinants of Internal Migration in Russia, 1985–2001." Madison: University of Wisconsin.

———. 2005b. "Internal Migration Dynamics in Russia, 1985–2001: Determinants, Motivations, and Consequences." *Report Prepared for the National Council on Eurasian and East European Research*. Madison: University of Wisconsin.

Gray, P. A. 2005. *The Predicament of Chukotka's Indigenous Movement: Post-Soviet Activism in the Russian Far North*. Cambridge: Cambridge University Press.

Heleniak, T. 2008a. "Changing Settlement Patterns across the Russian North at the Turn of the Millennium." In *Russia's Northern Regions on the Edge:*

Communities, Industries and Populations from Murmansk to Magadan, ed. Markku Tykkyläinen and Vesa Rautio. Aleksanteri Institute, University of Helsinki: Kikimora Publications.

———. 2008b. "Migration and Population Change in the Russian Far North during the 1990s." In Migration in the Circumpolar North: New Concepts and Patterns, ed. Chris Southcott and Lee Huskey. Thunder Bay, ON: Lakehead University.

———. 2004. Internal Migration within the Countries of the ECA Region. Washington, DC: The World Bank.

Hill, F., and C. G. Gaddy. 2003. The Siberian Curse: How Communist Planners Left Russia Out in the Cold. Washington, DC: Brookings Institution Press.

Huskey, L. 2005. "Challenges to Economic Development Dimensions of 'Remoteness' in the North." Polar Geography 29: 119–125.

Huskey, L., and T. A. Morehouse. 1992. "Development in Remote Regions: What Do We Know?" Arctic 45: 128–137.

ICFMP Development. 2005. Overview of the Migration Systems in the CIS Countries. Vienna: ICMPD.

Institute, N. E. 1998. Migration from the Russian North: Profile, Mechanisms of Migration and Adjustment in Recipient Regions. Rotterdam, Moscow.

Ionstev, V., and I. Aleshkovski. 2006. "Determinants of Internal Migration in Contemporary Russia." Paper presented at the conference EAPC European Population Conference, Liverpool, UK.

Kotlyakov, V. M., and G. A. Agranat. 1994. "The Russian North: Problems and Prospects." Polar Geography and Geology 18: 285–295.

Luzin, G. P., M. Pretes and V. V. Vasiliev. 1994. "The Kola Peninsula: Geography, History and Resources." Arctic 47: 1–15.

Maleva, T. 1998. "Problems of Northern Migration: The Pechora Coal Basin." Occasional Papers. Moscow: The Carnegie Moscow Center, Carnegie Endowment for International Peace.

Mansoor, A., and B. Quillin, eds. 2007. Migration and Remittances: Eastern Europe and the Former Soviet Union. Washington, DC: The World Bank.

Mikhailova, T. 2005. Where Russians Should Live: A Counterfactual Alternative to Soviet Location Policy.

Moore, E. G., and D. L. McGuinness. 1999. "Geographic Dimensions of Aging." In Migration and Restructuring in the United States: A Geographic Perspective, ed. Kavita Pandit and Suzanne Davies Withers. Lanham, MD: Littlefield Publishers Inc.

"Northern Lights-Out." 1993. The Economist, March 6, 7801.

Oleinik, G. 2004. "Using the Census Results in Analysis of the Social and Economic Situation in Northern Areas of Russia." In *International Symposium "The Russian in the Mirror of Statistics: The All-Russian Population Census 2002"*, ed. CIS Statistical Committee. Moscow: CIS Statistical Committee.

Plane, D. A., and P. A. Rogerson. 1994. *The Geographical Analysis of Population: With Applications to Planning and Business*. New York: John Wiley and Sons, Inc.

Ribova, L. 2000. "Individual and Community Well-Being." *The Arctic. . . . is a web resource on human-environment relationships in the Arctic*. [http://www.thearctic.is] accessed 20 January 2008.

Rossii, G. 2005. *All-Russian Census of Population 2002*. Moscow: Goskomstat Rossii.

Round, J. 2005. "Rescaling Russia's Geography: The Challenges of Depopulating the Northern Periphery." *Europe-Asia Studies* 57: 705–727.

Smith, M. A., and K. Giles. 2007. "Russia and the Arctic: The 'Last Dash North.'" *Advanced Research and Assessment Group, Russian Series, 07/26*. Defense Academy of the United Kingdom.

Spies, M. 2007. "Potentials for Migration and Mobility among Oil Workers in the Russian North." Department of Geography, University of Joensuu.

——. 2006. "Distance between Home and Workplace as a Factor for Job Satisfaction in the North-West Russian Oil Industry." *Fennia* 2: 133–149.

Stammler-Gossmann, A. 2007. "Reshaping the North of Russia: Towards a Conception of Space." Rovaniemi, Finland; Arctic Centre, University of Lapland.

Thompson, N. 2008. *Settlers on the Edge: Identity and Modernization on Russia's Farthest Arctic Frontier*. Vancouver and Seattle: University of British Columbia Press and University of Washington Press, respectively.

——. 2004. "Migration and Resettlement in Chukotka: A Research Note." *Eurasian Geography and Economics* 45: 73–81.

——. 2003. "The Native Settler: Contesting Local Identities on Russia's Resource Frontier." *Polar Geography* 27: 136–158.

Tykkyläinen, Markku, and Vesa Rautio, eds. 2008. *Russia's Northern Regions on the Edge: Communities, Industries and Populations from Murmansk to Magadan*. Aleksanteri Institute, University of Helsinki: Kikimora Publications.

World Bank. 2007. *Summary of the Analytical Report on the Lessons and Expansion of the Northern Restructuring Pilot Project*. Washington, DC: The World Bank.

——. 2005a. *From Transition to Development: A Country Economic Memorandum for the Russian Federation. ECA PREM. Report No. 32308-RU*. Washington, DC: The World Bank.

———. 2005b. *Millennium Development Goals: Progress and Prospects in Europe and Central Asia*. Washington, DC: The World Bank.

———. 2005c. *Russian Federation: Reducing Poverty through Growth and Social Policy Reform*. *ECA PREM. Report No. 28923-RU*. Washington, DC: The World Bank.

———. 1998. *Policy Note on "Economic and Social Issues of Migration from the Russian North"*. Washington, DC: World Bank.

Chapter Seven

Indigenous Rights
in the Russian North

Indra Øverland

Introduction

T here are several reasons why it is of particular interest to include a chapter on the rights of Russia's northern indigenous peoples in this book. The interest these groups command in themselves is one reason: A total of thirty-nine northern ethnic groups are currently recognized as indigenous peoples in Russia.[1] These peoples represent diverse cultures and language groups, and have historically inhabited more than half the territory that now makes up the Russian Federation. They are an important part of the legacy of imperial expansion into the North and Siberia, and their status and rights today reflect on Russia's transition from a 19th-century empire to a 21st-century state, a transition that is particularly complex because of the intervening decades under Communist rule.

This chapter aims to answer the following question: What is the status of indigenous rights in the Russian North, and to what extent does Russia adhere to international standards on indigenous rights? A full examination of Russia's standards on indigenous rights in relation to the international situation would ideally entail the systematic comparison of practices in Russia and several other countries, for example the United States, Canada or Finland. However, that is beyond the scope of this chapter. Instead, it shall attempt to gauge the situation in Russia and relate it to the international legal instruments and norms that exist, only occasionally comparing it to the situation in other specific countries.

The Applicability of International Labour Organization Convention 169 in Russia

Before entering into a discussion of indigenous rights in Russia, it is necessary to briefly introduce the main indigenous rights instrument in international law: International Labour Organization (ILO) Convention 169.[2] This is a comprehensive legal instrument covering a range of issues pertaining to indigenous peoples, including land rights, access to natural resources, health, education, vocational training, conditions of employment and contacts across borders. Whereas the previous convention on indigenous rights, ILO Convention 107, assumed the gradual disappearance of indigenous and tribal populations as they were integrated into dominant societies, ILO Convention 169 adopts a general attitude of respect for the cultures and ways of life of indigenous and tribal peoples, emphasizing their right to continue to exist and to develop according to their own priorities. It sets minimum international standards, while leaving the door open for higher standards in countries that wish to go further. The convention is gradually being ratified by ILO member states and forms the basis for many national debates and policies on indigenous rights. As of 16 June 2008, it had been ratified by nineteen countries.

Russia has been under pressure from international bodies to ratify ILO Convention 169 and has occasionally seemed to be on the verge of doing so. Xanthaki (2004: 76) lists several events in this regard.[3] The 1996 issue of the ILO's newsletter on indigenous issues mentions that an ILO mission testified before the State Duma in 1994 on the desirability of ratifying ILO Convention 169, and that this was followed up with a meeting at the Ministry of Nationalities in September 1995 (ILO 1996: 2). The seven issues of the newsletter that have been published since, however, do not mention Russia one single time (ILO 1998–2005).

Official representatives of the former Soviet Union participated in all of the debates on the details of ILO Convention 169 as it was hammered out during the second half of the 1980s, and used their voting rights actively. They were also present at the official signing of the final document. In parliamentary hearings in the State Duma in 1994 it was decided to postpone the question of ratification until the requisite legislation on indigenous rights had been passed in Russia. Later, it was said that the convention could not be ratified because key issues concerning private ownership of land had not been resolved (Murashko 2002a: 9).

Now that there is both a relatively broad legal base for indigenous rights and the ownership of land in Russia and both arguments thus seem obsolete, ratification could, in principle, proceed.

A 2002 round table including representatives of key organs of the government agreed to establish an interministerial working group to work out the terminological differences between ILO Convention 169 and Russian law and maintain a dialogue with the ILO and identify the necessary adaptations of Russian laws, bearing in mind state ownership of land in Russia.[4] Once this work was completed successfully, the working group was to recommend that the president submit ILO Convention 169 to the State Duma for ratification (Murashko 2002a: 10). As of late 2005, however, there were still no clear signals that Russia intended to ratify the convention.

It is possible that Russia nonetheless can be held accountable to the standards set down in ILO Convention 169, although this is a complicated issue. On the one hand, several key texts on the rights of Russian indigenous peoples in an international legal perspective argue that ILO Convention 169 is partly applicable to Russia. Pavlov (2002: 39) points to the fact that Russia is a member of the ILO even though it has not signed ILO Convention 169. Xanthaki (2004: 76) argues that the interest the Russian Federation has shown in ILO Convention 169, along with the centrality of the convention, provide sufficient grounds for its application. The ILO itself recommends the use of the convention as a guideline in countries that have not ratified it, noting the example of Germany, which is a nonsignatory but has nonetheless based its development policy for cooperation with indigenous peoples in Latin America on the convention (Jensen, Rasmussen and Roy 2003: 72). The strongest argument for applying ILO Convention 169 to Russia is the fact that Russia "guarantees the rights of small indigenous peoples in accordance with the generally accepted principles and standards of international law" in Article 69 of the Constitution. On the other hand, the fact remains that Russia has until now decided not to ratify the convention and shows few signs of being posed to do so any time soon. This choice cannot simply be ignored, although it should not be given too much weight either.

The Definition of 'Indigenousness' in Russia

According to Russian law, the recognition of ethnic groups as indigenous peoples in Russia is based on their lifestyle, livelihoods, ethnic identity and population size. Of these criteria, only population size is relatively straightforward, whereas the others involve substantial subjectivity. In practice, historical administrative categories play an important role in determining which small groups are to be considered indigenous and which are not.

According to the restrictions on population size, only groups that number less than fifty thousand people can be considered numerically small indigenous peoples.[5] Hence, notwithstanding their claim to autochthony, larger non-Russian groups, such as the Sakha, Komi or Chechens, are not included in this concept because they count too many members (Osherenko et al. 1997: 33). This is not to say that they are not considered indigenous (*korennye*) in a broader sense, but rather that this indigenousness does not entail the type of rights bestowed on the smaller peoples in Russia or on indigenous peoples of all sizes internationally.

In 2005 the Congress of Karelians, in cooperation with the socioliberal party Yabloko, suggested raising the population ceiling for numerically small indigenous peoples from fifty thousand to seventy thousand. The stated purpose of this change was to make it possible for peoples such as the Karelians, who number around sixty-five thousand, to enjoy indigenous status and the associated rights (Glebov 2005: 2). However, Yabloko is one of the least popular parties in Russia, so little attention was paid to the proposal.

In contrast to Russia, the international understanding of 'indigenousness' usually places more emphasis on the history of conquest than on population size: In order to be considered indigenous, a people should have been in a given place before the arrival of a militarily, technologically or economically more dominant group. Thus, groups with several hundred thousand or even a million members are considered 'indigenous' in Latin America, because they were there before the Spanish conquistadors arrived. Unlike the situation in the Americas and Oceania, the Russian Empire did not arrive in the North and the Far East on boats at a clear point in history. Instead, it gradually moved in, expanding and entrenching its control over a time span of several hundred years. Thus, the distinction between old-timers and newcomers appears less cogent. Instead, there has been far greater focus on the small size of indigenous groups—both as a contrast to larger and more dominant groups, and because a group that is particularly small is more likely to be under the threat of extinction.

Another important limitation on the concept of indigenousness in Russia is that legislation on indigenous rights almost exclusively covers the northern groups among the numerically small indigenous peoples. As a result, the concept of indigenousness is almost identical with the concept of the "numerically small indigenous peoples of the North" (*korennye malochislennye narody Severa*), a term that was introduced by the Soviet authorities in the 1920s (Vakhtin 1994: 31; Kiselev and Kiseleva 1979: 20).[6] Through the trajectory of the Russian Empire and its successor states—the Soviet Union and the Russian Federation—both state and nonstate discourses on indigenousness and indigenous peoples came to be closely intertwined with various aspects of Arctic landscapes and cultures: taiga, tundra, reindeer herding, reindeer-drawn sledges, seal hunting, salmon fishing, shamanism and so on.

In addition, many of the numerically small peoples in the south are Muslim and thus have easily been lumped together with other Muslims in the southern parts of the country in the minds of administrators and the population at large. This indicates that the concept of indigenousness in the Russian Federation is still linked to the pattern of expansion of the Russian Empire. Although the small peoples of the southern Republic of Dagestan are occasionally referred to as indigenous (bringing the Russian concept more in line with international usage), most legislation and other attention has focused heavily on the indigenous peoples of the North.[7] This narrows down the number of peoples covered by most of Russia's legislation on indigenous rights, from '65' to '39.'[8]

However, in relation to the numerically small indigenous peoples of the North there has been a loosening up. During most of the Soviet period, there had been twenty-six officially recognized numerically small indigenous peoples of the North. After the collapse of the Soviet Union, several new groups began lobbying for this coveted status. The Russian authorities were initially unsure—should they stick to the well-established twenty-six or should they allow for the inclusion of almost twice as many groups? (Janhunen 1991: 111; Rybkin 1998: 3). The problem was compounded by the absence of clear criteria for what constituted an indigenous people apart from the fifty-thousand-population ceiling. In the end, the Russian authorities decided to allow for a wider range of groups, which are now included in the thirty-nine mentioned above.

In the context of this chapter, the critical question in relation to the classification of indigenous peoples in Russia is whether the population ceiling and northern geographical bias make it difficult to comply with international standards on indigenous rights. Some leeway must be allowed for the specific history, geography and differences between indigenous peoples and discourses on different continents. If that is granted, then the population ceiling is not so much a dent in Russian compliance with international indigenous rights standards as a challenge to the standards as such and the possibility of reaching a universal definition of indigenousness.

On the other hand, the geographical bias towards the Arctic and sub-Arctic areas is more difficult to reconcile with international norms. The fact that the Russian authorities have been unable to extend laws on indigenous rights to the southerly Republic of Dagestan, or even to determine which groups in Dagestan should be recognized as indigenous peoples, is certainly a lacuna in the state's indigenous rights record. Bearing in mind the patchwork ethnic landscape of Dagestan and volatility of interethnic relations in the region, it is not difficult to understand the hesitation with which the authorities approach indigenous issues in the republic, but it certainly does not strengthen the impression of a strong capacity for rights implementation.

On a more positive note, Russia does well in an international perspective in terms of the recognition of indigenous groups as peoples. Many states are reluctant to recognize indigenous groups as peoples, due to the implications of Article 1 of the Charter of the United Nations, which refers to the "equal rights and self-determination of peoples". In contrast, the formulation of Russian laws leaves little doubt that they are recognized as peoples, albeit numerically small ones (Xanthaki 2004: 95).

Russian Law

In the Constitution of the Russian Federation, adopted in 1993, the rights of indigenous peoples were established solidly with reference to international law. According to Article 69 of the Constitution, "the Russian Federation guarantees the rights of small indigenous peoples in accordance with the generally accepted principles and standards of international law and international treaties of the Russian Federation". This reflects the general principle laid down in Article 15.4, wherein it is stated that the Russian legal system shall be based on the generally recognized principles and norms of international law (compare the chapters by Hønneland and Jørgensen in this book; Pavlov 2003: 129). Article 15 emphasizes that in the case of contradiction between an international agreement and national law, the international agreement takes precedence (compare Kryazhkov 2004: 129). Article 72 gives state organs particular responsibility for the "protection of the original environment and traditional way of life of the numerically small ethnic communities" (Novikova 2004: 112).[9] In addition, high-level experts involved in writing Russian indigenous rights legislation have confirmed that Russia intends to follow up these parts of the constitution and treat its indigenous peoples in accordance with international standards (see Pavlov 2002: 36). Finally, Article 68 of the Constitution guarantees to all the peoples of the Russian Federation the right to keep and develop their native languages. This guarantee and other points on cultural rights in Russian law are in line with the standards of international legal instruments (Xanthaki 2004: 100–101).

At the level of the Constitution, international indigenous rights were thus incorporated at an early stage of the Russian Federation's legal evolution. It would, however, take several years after the adoption of the Constitution before laws specifically dedicated to indigenous rights were passed. Indigenous affairs in the Russian Federation are, at least in theory, regulated by a body of law established around the turn of the millennium, partly under Boris Yeltsin's presidency, partly under that of Vladimir Putin. Three laws constitute the main pillars of this body of law:

(1) On the Guarantees of the Rights of the Numerically Small Indigenous Peoples of the Russian Federation[10]

(2) On the General Principles of the Organization of the Communities of the Numerically Small Indigenous Peoples of the North, Siberia and the Far East of the Russian Federation;[1]

(3) On the Territories of Traditional Nature Use of the Numerically Small Indigenous Peoples of the North, Siberia and the Far East of the Russian Federation[12]

On the Guarantees of the Rights of Small Indigenous Peoples

The first law, on the guarantees of the rights of the small indigenous peoples, formally concerns all indigenous peoples in Russian but is primarily oriented towards the numerically small indigenous peoples of the North (Novikova 2004: 116). It enumerates a series of rights, indicating a benevolent policy towards indigenous peoples "in line with international standards". According to Pavlov (2003: 136), this is the most important of the three laws dedicated to indigenous rights. He sees it as playing a role for indigenous rights similar to the role that the Civil Codex plays for civil law or the Land Code plays for law relating to real estate in Russia, i.e., as the bedrock of indigenous rights in the Russian legal system.[13] As mentioned elsewhere in this book, the implementation of international legal standards requires both will and capacity, and the passing of the guarantees of rights law demonstrates that at least part of the state apparatus has the intention to uphold international indigenous rights. Yet, it is also worth underlining the fact that this will cannot be considered universal, as there was considerable resistance to the passing of the law (Pavlov 2003: 136).

The main weakness of the law is that besides listing a smorgasbord of formal rights, it lacks specific rules for matters of direct economic consequence for indigenous peoples (Blakkisrud and Øverland 2005: 175). Thus, the law is of little direct practical importance when it comes to improving the situation of indigenous peoples. The law generally conforms to the standards of the international legal instruments for indigenous and minority rights concerning natural resources (Xanthaki 2004: 97). There are, however, important differences between the formulations on the right to land in the Russian law and those in international instruments. Article 8 of the Russian law states that the small indigenous peoples of the North have the right to "own and use, free of charge, various categories of land required for supporting their traditional economic systems and crafts" (Pavlov 2002: 36, 39–40; Xanthaki 2004: 89). The emphasis here is on the right to continue to use land for traditional purposes, not the ownership of land and all of the associated resources on the basis of centuries of use and customary law.

This introduces a principle in the Russian approach to the protection of indigenous rights that is both contentious in Russia and differs fundamentally from the principles set out in international instruments on indigenous rights. For example, ILO Convention 169 emphasizes that

---

'land' is understood to include the "concept of territories, which covers the total environment of the areas which the peoples concerned occupy or otherwise use" (Article 13.2). This means that the concept of land "embraces the whole territory [indigenous peoples] use, including forests, rivers, mountains and sea, the surface as well as the sub-surface" (Jensen, Rasmussen and Roy 2003: 30).

Presumably referring to this point, Murashko (2002a: 10) writes that arguments from legal experts about the incompatibility of the terminology in ILO Convention 169 and Russian law were struck down at a Moscow round table on indigenous rights. According to Murashko, representatives of the ILO also pointed out that Convention 169 generally leaves it up to each state to choose how to realize the basic principles of the convention in accordance with national legislation. It is, however, difficult to see how the difference in the definition of 'land' can easily be resolved when Convention 169 is so clear on this point and there are such great subsoil and other values at stake in Russia (among them, oil, gas, gold, diamonds, bauxite, coal, uranium and hydroelectric power). On the other hand, Article 15 of Convention 169 recognizes the fact that many governments have reserved the rights to subsoil resources for themselves. In those cases, it requires that governments establish procedures through which they shall consult these peoples, with a view to ascertaining whether and to what degree their interests would be prejudiced, before undertaking or permitting any programs for the exploration or exploitation of such resources pertaining to their lands. The peoples concerned shall, wherever possible, participate in the benefits of such activities, and shall receive fair compensation for any damages they may sustain as a result of such activities.

Thus, whereas the Russian guarantees of rights law cannot be said to be the harbinger of international standards on indigenous rights to subsoil resources, it nonetheless stays within the limits set by ILO Convention 169. It should also be recognized that Russia is not the only state that has taken this path. For example, whereas the United States, on the basis of so-called Indian treaties, has frequently recognized the rights of indigenous peoples to land and natural resources in their totality (although often failing to uphold those rights in practice), Norway holds a view similar to the Russian one.

Another limitation of the guarantees of rights law is that it ascribes land rights to those who need it specifically in order to maintain their traditional activities (Article 8). According to Xanthaki (2004: 89–90), this contravenes international principles and has negative implications for those sections of indigenous populations who no longer follow traditional lifestyles. This leads to an issue that is being debated with increasing intensity today: the relationship between traditionalism and modernization (or conservation and change) in indigenous culture, and what impact these factors should have on indigenous rights. At the core of the matter is whether the members of indigenous peoples should be recognized as such and retain their rights, even if they no longer follow traditional lifestyles (Blakkisrud and Øverland 2005: 21). This question has also surfaced in connection with discussions about a proposal for a new version of the law on territories of traditional nature use, which is discussed later on in the chapter.

On Indigenous Communities

The second law—on the general principles of the organization of the communities of small indigenous peoples of the North, Siberia and the Far East—regulates the legal formation of local indigenous communities (*obshchiny*). It is more specific and has more practical ramifications than the guarantees of rights law, but it is still relatively general and economically insignificant. Land ownership and local self-government were central to the initial proposal for the indigenous communities law. An *obshchina* (indigenous community) was understood as being both an organ of local self-government and a legal entity that could own land. In the version of the law that was actually adopted, however, such notions were removed, fundamentally altering the spirit of the law (Novikova 2004: 116).

The main consequences of the indigenous communities law are the formal recognition of traditional local communities, and their classification as noncommercial entities, which makes them exempt from taxation. Not surprisingly, the law has been implemented relatively smoothly. During the first three years the law was in force, a total of 246 communities were registered across the country (Murashko and Bogoyavlenskiy 2004: 19). In terms of key indigenous rights, the law adds little. It is rather a mechanism that was necessary in the post-Soviet landscape of schizophrenic legal entities to fill the gap between the actual indigenous communities and attempts to enshrine their rights in formal law.

On Territories of Traditional Nature Use

The third law regulates the formation of territories of traditional nature use (*territorii traditsionnogo prirodopol'zovaniia*). A territory of traditional nature use is a particular type of protected area, within which indigenous peoples have special rights to the land. These rights are confined to usufruct: The law relates to subsistence activities and grants certain proprietary rights, especially connected to compensation for interference with traditional activities, and limited exclusionary rights. In some regards, territories of traditional nature use are similar to nature reserves or to North American Indian reservations.

The work towards the law on territories of traditional nature use had already started during the late Soviet period. A decree from the High Soviet from 1989 recommended the setting up of territories of traditional nature use for the numerically small indigenous peoples of the North and making them off limits for industrial development.[14] Although the Soviet Union collapsed before any territories of traditional nature use could be established, the idea was carried on in a presidential decree from 1992.[15]

Of the three laws specifically on indigenous rights, the law on territories of traditional nature use has by far the greatest potential direct impact on the lives of indigenous peoples, since it is envisaged as the main mechanism both for access to the land used by them for their traditional livelihoods and for ensuring the environmental protection of that land (Sulyandziga and Murashko 2003: 73). However, the law is surrounded by some confusion, as it contradicts the Land Code on the issue of land use. The latter, adopted shortly after the law on territories of traditional nature use, recognizes only two types of land use: ownership and rental. This leaves no room for the type of gratis (*bezvozmezdnyi*) usufruct right envisaged for indigenous peoples in the law on territories of traditional nature use. Moreover, a federal decree on the exact procedure for establishing territories of traditional nature use has yet to be adopted.

This ostensibly pivotal law has thus remained a paper tiger (Blakkisrud and Øverland 2005: 176). Despite several applications to set up territories of traditional nature use under federal law, so far not a single one has been registered (Murashko and Bogoyavlenskiy 2004: 19). The applications have instead gone to the courts, where appeals to revoke refusals have also been turned down (Kharyuchi 2004: 9). The most famous rejected case is that of the Tkhsanom Territory of Traditional Nature Use in the Koryak Autonomous Okrug (Infonor 2001: 20). In June 2003 it was submitted to the European Human Rights Court in Strasbourg by the legal NGO Rodnik on behalf of the Itelmen, a numerically small indigenous people. On 21 August 2004 the court announced that it would consider the case (Kharyuchi 2004: 9). The court requested additional evidence in January 2005, and as of the time of writing the case is still pending a decision (correspondence with Rodnik).

Although it has not been possible in practice to form territories of traditional nature use under the corresponding federal law, a presidential decree from 1991 allowed for the formation of such territories under regional legislation (Sirina 2004: 67).[16] Several indigenous peoples seized on this opportunity.[17] It is also possible that conflicts with the central authorities over resources make the regional authorities more positive towards initiatives to set up territories of traditional nature use.

The problem with many of these territories at the regional level, however, is that they are located on what is technically federally owned land. Attempts to transfer such territories of traditional nature use to the federal level have encountered the same problems as applications for the registration of new territories, and so far none have succeeded. The regional authorities, which are the most likely to establish territories of traditional nature use, insofar as they are closer and more accessible to indigenous peoples, have largely been eliminated from the equation (Murashko 2002b: 54–57; compare Kharyuchi 2004: 8). Until 2004 it seemed like there was still a possibility that the situation could improve and that some attempts might succeed. However, after 2004 the situation has only worsened.

Meanwhile, it has been suggested that the federal law is unworkable and that a new one should be passed instead (Sulyandziga and Murashko 2003). A governmental draft proposal for a new version of the law on territories of traditional nature use goes even further than the existing law and defines the "subjects of traditional nature use" as members of small northern indigenous peoples *or* as members of other ethnic groups who were born and live on the territories traditionally inhabited by indigenous peoples and who lead a subsistence lifestyle involving the traditional use of nature resources.

The draft proposal caused sharp reactions among indigenous activists (Sulyandziga and Murashko 2003: 75). Its emphasis on traditional livelihoods is contentious in two respects: because it excludes members of indigenous groups who do not follow a so-called traditional lifestyle, and because it includes individuals from other groups who do follow such a lifestyle (and were born and live on indigenous land). This means that the urbanized segment of indigenous peoples, which often constitutes the backbone of the indigenous organizations that promote indigenous rights, is excluded from those rights. The fact that members of other ethnic groups (e.g., rural ethnic Russians), who do follow the same lifestyle as indigenous peoples, are given the same rights makes this development particularly bitter for urbanized indigenous people. This tension is neither new in a Russian context nor unique to Russia in a global context (Murashko 2003: 115; Øverland 2000). It reflects the question of whether indigenous rights are about fending for specific ways of life, or the collective rights of specific ethnic groups or peoples, regardless of what lifestyle the members of those peoples choose to follow. This tension will be a key issue in the future development of indigenous policy in the Russian North.

In the absence of territories of traditional nature use, the use of indigenous lands would in principle have to be regulated by the Land Code. However, since indigenous peoples in Russia are mainly engaged in nonmonetary subsistence activities, they have no money to pay rent as required by the code, let alone to buy land. The numerically small northern indigenous peoples are thus caught in a situation where the legislation that could enable them to pursue their traditional lifestyle has not been implemented and other legislation makes it unfeasible for them to do so. For all practical purposes, they are barred from gaining legal control over the lands that have historically been theirs. This clearly contravenes both international and Russian law.

A Note on Regional Laws

The situation with regard to indigenous rights in Russia is particularly complex due to the federal nature of the Russian state, which entails law-making at several levels. Numerous articles in the Constitution open up for regional laws, including on indigenous issues (e.g., Articles 5, 66, 71–73 and 76; see Kryazhkov 2004: 130). For reasons of simplicity and because the federal level is more important in an international perspective, this chapter focuses on the establishment of indigenous rights at the federal level. Issues related to laws on indigenous rights at the regional level nonetheless deserve at least a short discussion.

Among the subjects of the Russian Federation, the Khanti-Mansi Autonomous Okrug, the Yamal-Nenets Autonomous Okrug and the Republic of Sakha lead the way on the formation of laws on indigenous rights. They are not only ahead of other subjects of the federation but also federal laws (Novikova 2004: 113). Nonetheless, Novikova (2004: 114–116) argues that the reasons for this are not objective but rather incidental, and that the autonomy of federation subjects is not necessarily advantageous for indigenous peoples. The only example she mentions of such an incidental reason is that the indigenous movement has been strong in some of the regions mentioned. This is not entirely convincing. Although there is no guarantee that ethnically based autonomy is advantageous for indigenous peoples, the fact that it has been so until now in several cases cannot be brushed aside so easily. The strength of the local indigenous movement also may not be an incidental factor. It is dependent on the approach of the local authorities and the atmosphere of civil society.

The Gap between De jure and De facto

On paper, the Russian Federation provides relatively good protection for its small northern indigenous peoples, compared to both rudimentary international rights standards and practices in other countries. The Russian state recognizes indigenous groups as peoples and makes extensive reference to international standards on a whole range of issues. In particular, the law on territories of traditional nature use provides relatively strong protection—de jure. In some respects, Russia is thus ahead of other states in relation to indigenous rights.

As in many fields of governance in Russia, the problem is not theory or principles but practice and implementation, as Sirina (this book) also points out in her examination of natural resource extraction and indigenous land use. Many indigenous peoples live in poverty. A handful of peoples are so small that their chances of survival are at best bleak—the Aliutors, Entsy, Kereks, Oroks and Taz all currently count less than five hundred members (Blakkisrud and Øverland 2005: 181; Bogoyavlenskiy 2004). Not a single territory of traditional nature use has been registered, and property rights, the linchpin of indigenous rights, remain in limbo.

There are two main reasons for the nonimplementation of the principles enshrined in the three key laws, the Constitution and other Russian legal texts. Firstly, there is a lack of funding. According to the Ministry of Economic Development and Trade, the two main federal target programs for economic and social development among the small northern indigenous peoples received only 11.5 percent of the planned funding between 1991 and 1996, and 6.6 percent between 1997 and 2001 (Matveeva 2003: 4; Blakkisrud and Øverland 2005: 185). The federal authorities have complained that the regions retain too many resources, making it difficult to do much at the federal level. There has been much discussion related to the possible redistribution of tax revenue from regions such as Tyumen Oblast and the Yamal-Nenets and Khanty-Mansi Autonomous okrugs—which would be the consequence of a proposed law on the redistribution of competencies between the federal and regional authorities.[18] One argument used to promote this law is the lack of financial resources at the federal level to finance the development programs for the numerically small indigenous peoples. At the same time, it would obviously weaken the ability of some of the well-endowed regions to support their indigenous peoples (Novikova 2004: 114).

The second reason for the nonimplementation of indigenous rights is the lack of coherence in Russian law in general and Russian law pertaining to indigenous rights in particular. Most analyses concur on this point: Pavlov (2003: 135) uses the formulation "unsystematised conglomerate of different normative-legal acts"; Xanthaki (2004: 88) writes of the "confusing and contradictory legislation". In addition to the above-mentioned example of legal incoherence involving the Land Code, it is worth mentioning another example involving fishing rights. In 1995 the law on fauna granted indigenous peoples privileged fishing rights over other citizens.[19] In 2001 the State Fishing Committee made rights to anadromous fish subject to open tenders (Xanthaki 2004: 94; International Work Group for Indigenous Affairs 2000: 36). As a result, many indigenous peoples who have had salmon and other river fish as their mainstay for centuries were effectively forced to catch their own fish illegally.

Another aspect of the incoherence of the legal system in Russia is the complex relationship between federal law and that of the subjects of

---

the federation. At a meeting with northern leaders, former president Putin stated that one of the main tasks ahead is the completion of the legal and normative base for the protection of indigenous peoples, including bringing federal and regional legislation into line ("Iz zaklyu-chitelnogo slova Prezidenta V. V. Putina na sobranii predstaviteley sev-ernykh territoriy Rossii" 2004: 4). Pavlov (2003: 141) notes that the pressure for reform comes not from indigenous peoples and their organizations but rather from governmental organs in the economic and financial sectors, and that this may result in the increased divergence of Russian law from international indigenous rights standards.

Conclusion

The Russian Federation has anchored indigenous rights in its legal system. Unlike some other states that have large indigenous populations within their territories, the Russian state recognizes indigenous groups as peoples and makes extensive reference to international standards on a whole range of indigenous issues. In particular, the law on territories of traditional land use provides relatively strong protection—de jure. In some respects, Russia could therefore be ahead of other states in upholding indigenous rights. On the other hand, there are serious problems with the implementation of the indigenous rights enshrined in Russian law, and many of the country's indigenous peoples have been left destitute. Specifically, the right to land, perhaps the most important of all to northern indigenous peoples, is not implemented properly. Two important reasons for the lack of implementation are the incoherence of the legal system and lack of funding.

The implementation of indigenous rights in Russia is not only a question of Russia complying with international standards but also participating in the formation of those standards. It would be impossible for as globally important a country as Russia, with so many indigenous peoples among its population, to disconnect itself entirely from emergent international standards. This applies regardless of what Russia chooses to do, for example, concerning ratification of ILO Convention 169. If Russia does not ratify the convention, not only will the rights of Russia's own northern indigenous peoples be less secure but the convention will also be weaker at the international level. On the other hand, if Russia were to ratify the convention, indigenous rights activists in countries such as Finland or Australia could argue that if a country such as Russia can ratify the convention, then their own states should also be capable of doing so.

One possibility that cannot be ignored is that Russian compliance, to the degree that it exists, may be partly incidental. The survival of northern indigenous peoples in the post-Soviet period may partly be due to out-migration from the North and de-industrialization as the Soviet industrial complex collapsed. The current economic revival and increasing interest in the energy resources of the North—such as the natural gas fields of the Yamal Peninsula—may reverse this trend and bring renewed industrialization, in-migration and threats to the rights of northern indigenous peoples. The implementation of indigenous rights depends on both the will and the ability or capacity to govern of the state in question. Clearly, central state actors in Russia have made an effort to bring the Russian legal system into line with central international indigenous rights standards and have made significant advances in terms of law-making. De facto, however, the final leg of rights implementation—the actual rule of law—has been poorly upheld. In principle, this could be due to a lack of either will or capability. In Russia's case, it is probably a result of both. Since 'ability'-related issues, such as the contradictions between different parts of the legal system, are obviously involved, the full extent of 'will' cannot be known until these problems have been solved.

Notes

1. This number is based on the report from the Russian Federation under the Framework Convention on the Protection of National Minorities, ACFC/SR(1999)015. For a detailed discussion of the definition of 'northern indigenous peoples,' see Blakkisrud and Øverland (2005: 171–175).
2. A United Nations (UN) Declaration on Indigenous Rights was adopted in 2007. Although it was a big step forwards for the indigenous movement, it is more declarative in nature and involves fewer obligations than ILO Convention 169.
.3 The UN Committee on Economic, Social and Cultural Rights has queried why the Russian Federation has not signed the convention (Question 21 in *Replies by the Government of the Russian Federation to the List of Issues to Be Taken Up in Connection with the Consideration of the Fourth Periodic Reports of the Russian Federation concerning the Rights Referred to in Articles 1-15 of the International Covenant on Economic, Social and Cultural Rights*, UN Doc HR/CESCR/NONE/2003/5). The International Committee

on the Elimination of Racial Discrimination (CERD) has also asked the Russian authorities why ILO Convention 169 has not been signed (*Summary of 1134th Meeting*, UN Doc. CERD/C/SR/1134, 1996).

4. The round table included representatives of the Federation Council, State Duma, Constitutional Court and various regional authorities and nongovernmental organizations (NGOs), including the Russian Association of Indigenous Peoples of the North (Murashko 2002a: 9).

5. This criterion is set out in Article 1, On the Guarantees of the Rights of Small Indigenous Peoples of the Russian Federation.

6. Various terms were used to refer to the small northern indigenous peoples during the Soviet period. See Slezkine (1994: 1) and Schindler (1992: 53). The word *malochislennye* is translated more accurately as "numerically small", but "small" is often used for simplicity. Terminological issues are discussed in greater detail later on in the chapter.

7. For example, the three major laws on indigenous issues adopted around the turn of the millennium (to be discussed later in the chapter) all make reference to the small northern indigenous peoples in their titles and throughout their texts—but not the southern ones.

8.. The number '65' is from the *Report from the Russian Federation* under the *Framework Convention on the Protection of National Minorities*, ACFC/SR(1999)015. The smaller number is from Postanovlenie Pravitel'stva Rossiiskoy Federatsii, *O edinom perechne korennykh malochislennykh narodov Rossiiskoy Federatsii*, 24 March 2000. The latter document mentions a total of forty-five numerically small indigenous peoples outside Dagestan, thirty-nine of which are northern (Blakkisrud and Øverland 2005: 172).

9. In Russian: *Zashita iskonnoy sredy obitaniya i traditsionnogo obraza zhizni malochislennykh etnicheskikh obshchnostei.*

10. In Russian: *O garantiakh prav korennykh malochislennykh narodov Rossiyskoy Federatsii* (1999).

11. In Russian: *Ob obshchikh printsipakh organizatsii obshchin korennykh malochislennykh narodov Severa, Sibiri i Dal'nego Vostoka Rossiyskiy Federatsii* (2000).

12. In Russian: *O territoriakh traditsionnogo prirodopol'zovaniya korennykh malochislennykh narodov Severa, Sibiri i Dal'nego Vostoka Rossiyskoy Federatsii* (2001).

13. *Grazhdanskiy kodeks Rossiyskoy Federatsii* (2 October 1994); *Zemelnyy kodeks Rossiyskoy Federatsii* (25 October 2001).

14. Postanovlenie Verkhovnogo Soveta SSSR, 27 November 1989, *O neotlozhnykh merakh ekologicheskogo ozdorovleniya strany*, point 11. This is another example of the connection frequently made between indigenous issues and environmental protection, as mentioned previously in the chapter (compare Pavlov 2003: 137–138).

15. Ukaz prezidenta Rossiyskoy Federatsii, 22 April 1992, No. 397, *O neotlozhnykh merakh po zashchite mest prozhivaniya i khozyaystennoy deyatel'nosti malochislennykh narodov Severa.*

16. *O territoriakh traditsionnogo prirodopolzovaniya*, presidential decree, 1991.

17. For more information on the formation of territories of traditional nature use at the regional level, see Murashko and Bogoyavlenskiy (2004: 19).

18. In Russian: *Ob obshchikh printsipakh organizatsii zakonodatelnykh i ispolnitelnykh organov gosudarstvennoy vlasti subektov Rossiyskoy Federatsii.*

19. *O faune*, 24 April 1995.

References

Blakkisrud, Helge, and Indra Øverland. 2005. "The Evolution of Federal Indigenous Policy in the Post-Soviet North." In *Tackling Space: Federal Politics and the Russian North*, ed. Helge Blakkisrud and Geir Flikke. Lanham, MD: University Press of America, 175–192.

Bogoyavlenskiy, Dmitriy. 2004. "Vymirayut li narody Severa?" *Demoskop Weekly*, 165–166.

Glebov, Pavel. 2005. "Beregite karelov! Karelov podderzhala fraktsiya Yabloko-NPSR." *Karelskaya Guberniya* 33: 480: 2.

Henson, Eric, and Jonathan Taylor. 2001. *Native America at the New Millennium.* Harvard: John F. Kennedy School of Government.

ILO (International Labour Organization). 1998–2005. *Recent Developments in the ILO Concerning Indigenous and Tribal Peoples.* Geneva: ILO.

——. 1996. *Recent Developments in the ILO Concerning Indigenous and Tribal Peoples.* Geneva: ILO.

International Work Group for Indigenous Affairs (IWGIA). 2000. *The Indigenous World 1999–2000.* Copenhagen: IWGIA

"Iz zaklyuchitelnogo slova Prezidenta V. V. Putina na sobranii predstaviteley severnykh territoriy Rossii." 2004. *Zhivaya Arktika*, 15: 4.

Janhunen, Juha. 1991. "Ethnic Death and Survival in the Soviet North."*Journal de la Société Finno-Ougrienne* 83: 111–122.

Jensen, Marianne, Henriette Rasmussen and Chandra Roy. 2003. *ILO Convention on Indigenous and Tribal Peoples: A Manual.* New York: ILO.

"Kamtjatka-guvernør begår overgreb mot itelmenerne." 2001. *Ifonor: Nyhedsbrev om oprindelige folk i Russland* 2: 1: 20.

Kharyuchi, S. N. 2004. "Prezidentu Rossiyskoy Federatsii V. V. Putinu." In *Sovremennoye polozheniye i perspektivy razvitiya malochislennykh narodov*

Severa, Sibiri i Dalnego Vostoka', ed. V. A. Tishkov. Moscow: Institute of Ethnology and Anthropology, Russian Academy of Science, 8–9.

Kiselev, A. A., and T. A. Kiseleva. 1979. *Sovetskie saamy: istoriia, ekonomika, kul'-tura*. Murmansk: Murmanskoe knizhnoe izdatel'stvo.

Kryazhkov, V. A. 2004. "Pravovye osnovy razvitiya narodov Severa i Sibiri." In *Sovremennoye polozheniye i perspektivy razvitiya malochislennykh narodov Severa, Sibiri i Dalnego Vostoka'*, ed. V. A. Tishkov. Moscow: Institute of Ethnology and Anthropology, Russian Academy of Science, 124–132.

Matveeva, Klavdiya. 2003. "Korennye malochislennye narody i federal'nye tselovye programmy." *Ekonomika korennykh narodov* 1: 1: 4–5.

Murashko, Olga. 2002a. "Perspektivy ratifikatsii Rossiyskoy Federatsiey Konventsii MOT No 169." *Zhivaya Arktika—Mir korennykh narodov* 11–12: 9–10.

———. 2002b. "Pochemu ne rabotaet fedralnyy zakon o territoriakh traditsionnogo prirodopolzovaniya." *Zhivaya Arktika—Mir korennykh narodov* 11–12: 54–57.

Murashko, O., and D. Bogoyavlenskiy. 2004. "Korennye narody Severa: itogi perepisi 2002 g. i politicheskaya situatsiya. Interpretatsiya itogov perepisi 2002 g." *Zhivaya Arktika— Mir korennykh narodov* 15: 16–21.

Novikova, N. I. 2004. "Gosodarstvenno-edministrativnoe ustroystvo i samoupravlenie." In *Sovremennoye polozheniye i perspektivy razvitiya malochislennykh narodov Severa, Sibiri i Dalnego Vostoka'*, ed. V. A. Tishkov. Moscow: Institute of Ethnology and Anthropology, Russian Academy of Science, 111–123.

Osherenko, Gail et al. 1997. "The Northern Sea Route and Native Peoples: Lessons from the 20th Century for the 21st." *INSROP Working Paper* No. 93. Lysaker, Norway: Fridtjof Nansen Institute.

Pavlov, P. N. 2003. "Mezhdunarodnoe pravo i reformirovanie zakonodatel'stva Rossiyskoy Federatsii o korennykh malochislennykh narodakh." In *Uchastie korennykh narodov v politicheskoy zhizni stran tsirkumpolyarnogo regiona: rossiyskaya realnost' zarubezhnyy opyt*, ed. Russian Association of Indigenous Peoples of the North (RAIPON) and IWGIA. Moskva: RAIPON, 129–142.

———. 2002. "Osobennosti pravovogo regulirovaniya ispolzovaniya i okhrany zemel kak ocnovy zhizni i deyatelnosti korennykh narodov severa v mezhdunarodnykh dogovorakh, v zakonodatelstve Rossiyskoy Imperii i v zakonodatelstve zarubezhnykh stran." *Zhivaya Arktika—Mir korennykh narodov* 11–12: 35–53.

Risse, Thomas, Stephen C. Ropp and Kathryn Sikkink, eds. 1999. *The Power of Human Rights: International Norms and Domestic Change.* Cambridge: Cambridge University Press.

Rybkin, Artom. 1998. *Indigenous Peoples of Russia: Modern Structure of Self-Organisation and Interactions with State Bodies.* Moscow: World Association of Reindeer Herders.

Schindler, Debra. 1992. "Russian Hegemony and Indigenous Rights in Chukotka." *Études/Inuit/Studies* 16: 1–2: 51–74.

Sirina, A. A. 2004. "Khozyastvo i sotsialnaya sfera." In *Sovremennoye polozheniye i perspektivy razvitiya malochislennykh narodov Severa, Sibiri i Dalnego Vostoka'*, ed. V. A. Tishkov. Moscow: Institute of Ethnology and Anthropology, Russian Academy of Science, 54–76.

Slezkine, Yuri. 1994. *Arctic Mirrors: Russia and the Small Peoples of the North.* Ithaca, NY: Cornell University Press.

Sulyandziga, Pavel, and Olga Murashko. 2003. "Diskussiya ob izmeneniyakh v federalnom zakonodatelstve prodolzhaetsya." *Zhivaya arktika—Mir korennykh narodov* 13: 73–78.

Xanthaki, Alexandra. 2004. "Indigenous Rights in the Russian Federation: The Case of Numerically Small Peoples of the Russian North, Siberia and Far East." *Human Rights Quarterly* 26: 74–105.

Chapter Eight

Oil and Gas Development in Russia and Northern Indigenous Peoples

Anna A. Sirina

Introduction

Oil and gas extraction has become a top priority of the Russian economy. The revenues from exporting oil and gas make up about sixty percent of the federal budget (for more detail, see Moe and Wilson Rowe, this book). However, this rapid development of oil and gas has already produced a new reality marked by numerous internal problems—among them, growing access to formerly remote regions and communities, increased migration and changing population and settlement structures and increased ecological risks and catastrophes. Their socio-cultural influence is cumulative and difficult to predict. Considerable deposits of oil and gas, as well as gold, coal, lead and nickel, are located in Siberia, the North and the Far East of the Russian Federation, making these vast territories of great importance from a geopolitical, strategic and resource perspective, as other chapters in this book attest.

The socio-economic and cultural development of northern indigenous peoples is a declared national priority of the Russian Federation (Tishkov 2004). However, as yet their interests have not been given proper weight in connection with the development of large industrial projects, although scholars and activists have begun to pay greater attention to this issue (Stepanov 1999; Murashko 2002; Markhinin and Udalova 2002; Zakluchenie 2002; Messhtyb and Kankapaa 2005; Murashko 2004; Sirina and Fondahl 2006; Roon 2006; Sirina, Yarlykapov and Funk 2008; Stammler and Forbes 2006; Stammler and Wilson 2006). Western European countries are the main consumers of Russian oil and gas resources. Their governments have also expressed interest in study-ing the environmental and social situation in the regions of oil and gas extraction, feeling a responsibility for minimizing the negative impacts on the local environment and communities (ENSINOR 2007; Stammler and Wilson 2006; Nuttall and Wessendorf 2006). With globalization, this research has assumed a truly international character. This chapter dis-cusses some of the current problems in the relationships between the northern indigenous peoples of Russia, oil and gas developers and gov-ernmental structures. These relationships, and how they play out in practice, are examined in detail through a case study of the Eastern Siberia-Pacific Ocean (ESPO) pipeline assessment process.

Indigenous Peoples of the Northern Areas

Russian legislation defines the indigenous minorities of the Russian Federation as "peoples living on the traditional lands of their ancestors, preserving a traditional way of life, livelihoods and trades, numbering in the Russian Federation less than 50,000 people and considering them-selves to be autonomous ethnic communities" (On Guaranteeing the Rights of Indigenous Minorities of the Russian Federation, Article 1).

According to the All-Russian Census (2002), the total number of northern indigenous peoples in the Russian Federation is 252,222 (Sokolova and Stepanov 2007: 76). In 2000 the Russian government adopted an updated official list of indigenous minorities. Since 1925, when the original list was adopted, the number of officially recognized nations/ethnic groups has increased from twenty-six to forty. The revised list of indigenous peoples of the North, with information on the areas where they live and conduct their subsistence economies, was adopted in order to protect their common rights as indigenous minori-ties, according to federal legislation.

Russia's northern indigenous peoples live in groups dispersed across the North, Siberia and the Far East. They comprise between 0.2 and 12 percent of the whole population in these regions, although in so-called compact residence areas the figure may exceed 30 percent. The social structures within these communities have undergone major changes, especially during the 20th century. They are structured into three different though interconnected groups according to place of residence: (i) the urban population; (ii) the rural population and

---

(iii) those who live outside permanent settlements in the taiga and the tundra. The rural population of northern indigenous peoples numbers 173,559 (68.8 percent); the urban population, 78,663 (31.2 percent) (Sokolova and Stepanov 2007:76). According to federal legislation, only groups involved in the traditional subsistence economy and maintaining traditional modes of life are entitled to official status as northern indigenous peoples and may enjoy a range of privileges stipulated in federal and regional laws. The rest of the northern minorities live in accordance with the laws regulating the lives of all citizens of the Russian Federation.

It is estimated that between ten and fifteen percent of the northern indigenous population is nomadic. In some regions, like the Yamal Peninsula, nomads make up to forty percent of the northern indigenous population. Over half of the indigenous rural population is involved in seasonal activities like fur hunting, fishing, gathering and, to a lesser degree, reindeer herding (Sirina 2004: 56). Most of the indigenous minorities of the North, Siberia and the Far East combine formal and informal economic activities, as in other northern indigenous communities throughout the world. Experts, activists and scholars speak about today's discrepancy between the rigidly determined status of indigenous peoples and their real economic and cultural practices, which presuppose a broader scale of interests than the 'traditional way of life' assigned to them (Novikova and Yakel' 2006). To provide further nuance to this picture, one must note that in Siberia and elsewhere in the North, there are many settlements with populations of mixed ethnicity, due to the many mixed marriages that are a product of more than three hundred years of Russian expansion into, and presence in, Siberia.

The Soviet Legacy

The paternalistic policy of the Soviet Union made a dual impact on the peoples of the North. On the one hand, their way of life and culture changed dramatically as a result of forced settlement, collectivization and industrialization. On the other hand, the federal government subsidized the traditional (formal) economy, providing indigenous and local peoples with free education and supporting transport and communications. The patchy industrial exploration of Soviet Siberia soothed the sharpness of ecological problems by spreading development over vast scattered areas. Moreover, the Communist Party required that mining ventures participate in the social and economic development of communities and regions. Ivan P. Apoka from Magadan Oblast (who died in middle age) expressed the nostalgia shared by many reindeer herders on the eve of the millennium: "There were times when reindeer herders got connected on the radio and shouted that they were out of batteries. A helicopter would fly to deliver them a box of batteries. Those were the days!" Such feelings of nostalgia were caused by the abrupt transition of the 1990s, with its social and economic crisis, as well as memories of some of the real Soviet achievements, albeit somewhat romanticized.

And indeed, the changes have been many. The population of Magadan Oblast, which at that time included Chukotka, has been halved since 1989, as its residents returned to the Russian 'mainland' after their jobs with state agencies and enterprises disappeared (see Heleniak, this book, for a detailed discussion of post-Soviet population changes in the Russian North). The economy of northern indigenous peoples was heavily dependent on the industrial development of the region. The collapse of the gold and silver industry had dramatic consequences for northern indigenous peoples, as the consumers of reindeer meat left and state subsidies were cancelled (Sirina 2004: 57).

New Russian Government Policy

Official policy towards northern indigenous peoples has been evolving rapidly. While during the era of perestroika the economic situation was worsening, political activity increased dramatically, producing a number of indigenous organizations, of which RAIPON has remained the most active. Along with activists, anthropologists, lawyers and federal and regional authorities, RAIPON has played an important role in forcing the implementation of legislation aimed at benefiting northern indigenous minorities. The state national policy has been changing, shifting its focus from individual ethnic groups to a territorial unit or region. The intention has been to shift from the former paternalistic policy towards one of protectionism. The concept of "culturally oriented modernization" has been suggested.

The issue of self-determination, understood as the right to participate in the process of governance and self-governance, has arisen as well, and new consideration has been given to the concept of autonomous okrug/districts as special administrative and territorial units. For example, the total indigenous population of Khanty-Mansiisk Autonomous Okrug (KMAO) is twenty-nine thousand (two percent of the whole regional population), and the territory is incredibly rich in oil and gas. In the body of legislation of this autonomous district, there are forty-one pieces of effective legislation and eleven nominal laws devoted solely to indigenous minorities. By 2001 recognition had been granted to 477 indigenous minority lands (now known as territories of traditional nature use), with a total area of 13,825 hectares. Some two thousand people (approximately seven percent of the indigenous minorities) have such territories and live there all year round; some three thousand people live seasonally on the granted land.

Half the territories of traditional nature use have been alienated, following agreement with indigenous peoples: 673 extraction licences have been issued to sixty-one companies (Stammler and Forbes 2006). However, according to Tishkov, the new oil and gas 'regional' elite has used the ethno-territorial bodies to achieve its own political goals, which have nothing in common with the initial goals of self-determination for northern indigenous peoples (Tishkov 2004: 12). Whether the situation has changed since KMAO joined the Tyumen Oblast is a question in need of further study.

Northern indigenous minority rights are protected by the 1993 Constitution of the Russian Federation (Kostitutsia 1993, Articles 69, 71) and by a number of federal laws. Especially important here are the laws "O garantiach prav korennych malochislennych narodov Rossiskoi Federatsii" (O garantiach, 1999) On Guaranteeing the Rights of Indigenous Minorities of the Russian Federation"]; "Ob obschich printsi-pakh organizatsii obshchin korennukh malochislennuch narodov Severa, Sibiri i Dal'nego Vostoka Rossiskoi Federatsii" (Ob obshchich, 2000) ["On General Principles of Organizing Communities of Indigenous Minorities of the North, Siberia and the Far East of the Russian Federation"] and "O Territoriaych traditsionnogo prirodopol'zovaniya korennuch mal-ochislennuch narodov Severa, Sibiri i Dal'nego Vostoka Rossiskoi Federatsii." (O territoriac, 2001) ["On the Territories of Traditional Nature Use of Indigenous Peoples of the North, Siberia and the Far East of the Russian Federation"]. The peculiarity and perhaps the strength of Russian laws regarding indigenous rights (contrary to analogous laws in other countries like Canada, the United States and Australia) is that they focus less on ancestry and more on the protection of traditional activities and the land bases that enable their continuation (Sirina and Fondahl 2008; see also Øverland, this book). Russian legislation extends the rights of indigenous minorities to representatives of other peoples, as well, if they are involved in traditional nature management and are acknowledged by the indigenous community. This has been characterized as the "Russian style" in the land claim process (Fondahl et al. 2001), and to some degree reflects the multinational character of the population and the peculiarities of nature use in the Russian North.

Indigenous peoples have obtained the right to claim the territories where they continue to hunt, herd reindeer and fish. Territories of traditional nature use have been established, aimed at "the protection of the age-old places of inhabitance and traditional way of life of the indigenous peoples, the maintenance and development of the unique cultures of the indigenous peoples, and the protection . . . of biological diversity" (Article 4 of the Law "On territories of traditional nature use"). According to legislation, territories of traditional nature use may be established on three levels: federal, regional and local (Article 5). Territories of traditional nature use have the status of "specially protected natural areas" (Article 1) and are handed over free of charge. Territory subjects are communities and other associations. In the case of industrial development, a part of a territory of traditional nature use may be withdrawn, on the condition that it is replaced with some other territory. The peoples of the North are entitled to reimbursement for losses caused by damage done to their original habitats (Article 12).

However, when the Law "On territories of traditional nature use" use was adopted, no such federal territories had been established. At the same time, there is an urgent need to legalize them. To date, three indigenous communities have jointly sued the federal government for not providing them with such territories, and these claims are being tried in court. These claims come from the communities that first encountered oil and gas development—the Evenki, the Yakut and the local Russians of the Katanga Region in Irkutsk Oblast. In November 2007 regional territories of traditional nature use were provided for them by the Irkutsk regional government, but the issue had not been solved on the federal level.

Regional-level territories of traditional nature use make up twenty-five percent of KMAO (Stammler and Forbes 2006). In line with the law of the Yakutian republic on territories of traditional nature use, the process of creating regional territories is underway along the oil pipeline

---

route in southern Yakutia. However, the legal status of these regional territories of traditional nature use is questionable, as all the existing such territories have been established on federal land, so these territories are entitled to federal status. Because of this uncertain situation, developers very often take possession of the land from the householders without agreements (Mis'kova 2005: 131–133; Zen'ko 2001: 24). Nevertheless, the right to the territory, even if not quite legal, gives the householders the possibility for indemnity in exchange for signing economic agreements (contracts) with industrial companies. The households receive equipment and compensation, as well as broader economic assistance. On the other hand, individual agreements can be, and have been, controversial, as the extent of compensation is not defined in federal legislation. Very often it is not correlated with the actual damage incurred.

On its own, the concept of territories of traditional nature use is not above criticism. One crucial point is that common land ownership is being replaced by private property. The organization of strictly defined territories for conducting subsistence economies destroys the principles of common land use still practiced in many regions of the North, Siberia and the Far East. Moreover, difficulties may arise in changing the land borders in complex and unpredictable circumstances, such as harvest failure (Rumyantsev 1998). The concept of territories of traditional nature use is probably not capable of fully accommodating the needs of large-scale reindeer herders, as on the Yamal Peninsula, where vast expanses of land are a precondition for conducting reindeer breeding. And finally, there is the concern that the identity and social relations of the indigenous peoples are undergoing serious changes due to this new system of land tenure.

The reindeer herders of the Yamal Peninsula have put forward the problem of the "illegal" status of the land being traditionally occupied.[1] The same problem is faced by most northern indigenous communities involved in the formal economy. Scholars and experts agree that the federal authorities have not yet been prepared to follow the adopted indigenous rights laws consistently and purposefully. In the meantime, this has enabled developers to move ahead with asserting their own land claims (Novikova and Yakel' 2006).

The regions have been more active than the federal government in regulating the relationships between indigenous minorities and developers. Territories of traditional nature use are most extensive in the areas where the peoples of the North directly encounter industrial exploration, or where they live within national administrative borders, as in Yakutia. Practical agreements often precede laws, demonstrating that a legislative base is not essential for starting up dialogue. On the regional level, we may note a diversity of relationship-building approaches, ranging from close cooperation between the regional government, indigenous households and oil and gas companies in western Siberia and Yakutia, to partnership between indigenous peoples and Western companies on Sakhalin and in Nenets Autonomous District. The role of the regional government is crucially important in such relationships (Stammler and Wilson 2006).

Apart from the procedural problems of implementing existing laws, there are real gaps in the legislation. According to the 1995 Law on Ecological Expert Review, all industrial projects have to be ecologically assessed by a government agency. The same law also includes a short chapter on socio-economic impact assessment (Spiridonov 2006). Additionally, project impact has to be examined under the 2002 Law on Objects (Monuments of History and Culture) of Cultural Heritage, which concerns historical and cultural assessment reviews in connection with exposing landmarks. A company has no legal right to start a project without conducting such an assessment. However, existing legislation does not provide the legal tools for conducting full-scale impact assessments of the indigenous and local communities. The federal law draft, "On Protecting the Habitat, Environment, Livelihood and Nature Use of Indigenous Minorities of the Russian Federation" (formerly known as "The Federal Law on Ethnological Expert Review") is now under review in the State Duma of the Russian Federation. The intention is to close some gaps in the legislation, not least on conducting impact assessments.

Case Study: The Eastern Siberia-Pacific Ocean Pipeline Assessment

The ESPO pipeline is likely to be the world's longest pipeline (4,188 km in total), crossing six major political-administrative regions of the Russian Federation. The Russian oil transport company Transneft' will move oil from Siberia to the Chinese border and to the Pacific coast, where it can be transported to markets throughout Asia. On 31 December 2004, the Russian prime minister signed the order for its construction. Although given approval to proceed with preparatory work on the route eighty to one hundred kilometres from Lake Baikal, Transneft' changed its mind and in 2005 chose to pursue a third route running less than one kilometre from the lake along the Baikal-Amur railway line.[2] This area is seismically highly unstable. Its montane rivers feed into the northern end of Lake Baikal, the deepest freshwater lake in the world. Since 1996 this territory has been included on the UNESCO World Natural Heritage List.

Some seven hundred Evenkis are living in the mixed communities north of Lake Baikal; about sixty percent of them are involved in traditional activities like fishing, hunting, gathering and reindeer herding. Their informal economy also includes truck farming, cattle farming and ecological tourism. With the collapse of local economic enterprises, unemployment officially stands at forty to sixty percent in the villages; a more accurate figure is probably between seventy and eighty percent. The people are highly dependent on social subsidies. Two Evenki settlements, Kholodnoe and Uoyan, would be in the direct impact zone of the pipeline route, and pipeline construction would imperil their subsistence activity and way of life. A survey of three villages carried out in July/August 2005 by the author and Canadian geographer Gail Fondahl[3] indicated that forty-eight percent of the local population oppose construction of the pipeline, while thirty-five percent support it "on condition that ecological requirements are adhered to". Seven percent of the population support it outright (Fondahl and Sirina 2006b).[4]

Russian law requires that citizens be provided with a chance to participate, and make their views known, in environmental impact assessments (EIAs). Transneft' was slow to provide information and host public hearings. In fact, the Evenki were not aware of the plans for the pipeline until the first influx of workers arrived: "They've already been living here two times, those who want to build a pipeline. Last year and now. The surveyors, the construction workers... We don't know the details. I haven't talked with them, I just heard that they are living here".[5] Then, during July/August 2005, Transneft' organized a series of public hearings along the pipeline route. EIA documents were made accessible for review in the regional centre, which is located at some distance from the Evenki communities. Many Evenki found this approach problematic, given their stark poverty:

> Recently this Moscovite came to ask these guys [about their opinions of the pipeline]. He said, "Come to see me in Severobaikal'sk". They said

to him, "How are we to get there?" To get to Severobaikal'sk you need ninety rubles. There and back. And for ninety rubles, how many loaves of bread can you buy? Ten loaves. You either buy the bread or go there.[6]

The author, along with Fondahl, attended the public hearing in the village of Kholodnaya on 13 July 2005. The people were asking questions about issues that worried them and expressing their fears, but they were interrupted and told to ask "specific" questions. The hearings showed that the company was manipulating the information and exhibiting no respect for indigenous minorities. Such attitudes are unfortunately deeply rooted in Russian governmental authorities and business administration, as well as in society at large.

Three main points of concern became obvious. First, the Evenki wanted assurances that the potential for environmental degradation would be minimal. They were worried about the ecological situation, especially in connection with the possibility of maintaining their traditional use of nature. Second, the local Evenki wished to benefit directly from the construction through the provision of new jobs. Third, they demanded that any compensation and rents from the pipeline transecting their homelands be shared with them.

Transneft' replied that forty people from the Severobaikal'sk region would be hired and trained. The population of the region (including the city of Severobaikal'sk) is approximately forty-one thousand (only 1.7 percent of whom are Evenki). Thus, forty positions would amount to 0.1 percent of the population. There was no guarantee that any of those would be local villagers or Evenki.

The local people also hoped that, however the pipeline was routed, payments for its rental could invigorate the local economy. How would these payments be shared between republic, regional and local municipal (village) governments? A few Evenki families have petitioned for, and received, extensive landholdings on which to re-establish and pursue reindeer herding. They do not own this land but have usage rights for twenty-five years. Would these families have a right to compensation were the pipeline to transect their land? At the hearings, some argued that the benefits should be paid not to individuals or to specific households but to the whole community. The Evenkis' concerns have remained unanswered. Any benefits they could receive are still poorly defined and not at all guaranteed, and the question of compensation is very much open to legal interpretation, which in turn is subject to political manipulation (Fondahl and Sirina 2006b: 58–59).

In the area, we identified a landmark called the Memory Trail (fourteen kilometres long and four hundred metres to one kilometre wide) that was included in the list of regionally protected landmarks. Following our study, our recommendations were, among others: (i) search for alternative routes for the oil pipeline; (ii) involve the public in the planning process; (iii) arrange early and permanent consultations; (iv) involve the indigenous and local people in the negotiating process; (v) follow the laws and conduct a just social policy and (vi) conduct monitoring of the project impact on the indigenous and local population (Sirina and Fondahl 2006).

The original project had been approved by the State Ecological Expert Commission, which proves that it is possible to lobby for industrial interests and manipulate expert opinion and the public at the topmost level. However, on 26 April 2006, in Tomsk, at the meeting with the heads of administration of the federal subjects in the Siberian federal district, then President Vladimir Putin demanded that the project route be changed and the pipeline moved at least forty kilometres northward: "This example shows how sensitive the EIA process in Russia can be to political decisions" (Spiridonov 2006: 51). This section of the pipeline route, known as "East Siberia-Pacific Ocean Expanded", is now close to the largest oil fields in the north of Irkutsk Oblast' and Yakutia, a solution that is ecologically safer and economically more feasible.

Here, it should be noted that the Sakha Republic (Yakutia) has been actively building its statehood within the framework of the Russian Federation and supporting the rights of its peoples, including its indigenous peoples of the North. On 30 October 2006, parliamentary hearings, initiated by the Sakha Republic (Yakutia) Association of Indigenous Peoples of the North, took place in Yakutsk. They resulted in a series of recommendations, adopted in close collaboration between the government of the republic, the association and nongovernmental environmental organizations. These recommendations consider the problems of industrial exploration of indigenous minorities' traditional habitats and present specific requirements for governmental authorities and commercial enterprises aimed at identifying and mitigating the negative consequences of industrial exploration. This is a positive example of the developing interaction between governmental authorities, indigenous minorities of the North and industrial ventures (Yakutia trebuet 2007).

Concluding Thoughts

The extraction and export of nonrenewable resources were not approved by about half of our survey respondents. How can this attitude be explained? The reasons include ecological/environmental problems; unresolved legal questions concerning northern indigenous minorities and their rights to the land they use for traditional activities; discontent among the local communities and authorities as to the current principles of revenue distribution and negative attitudes towards the oligarchic and raw-material model of the present Russian economy. All these issues were brought up at the public hearing in Kholodnaya village (Sirina and Fondahl 2006). These attitudes also reflect the broader ongoing discussions on oil and gas development in Russia. For example, "Russia loses a dozen billion dollars a year due to surplus energy consumption and the selling of the underprocessed crude oil and raw materials and low surplus. Is it really necessary to extract considerably more energy resources in this situation?" (Bobylev 2006).[7]

Foreign companies carrying out oil and gas business in Russia have noted the gaps in existing legislation, for example, concerning the indigenous peoples who live in villages and towns (Bradshaw 2005)—which is partly true. However, nothing was said about the exclusive rights of northern indigenous minorities at the public hearing we attended in Kholodnoe. The local people, including the indigenous population, did not capitalize on the national aspect of the problem but acted locally as the citizens of one village and one state.

In conclusion, the question remains: Are the nature-use practices of traditional subsistence economies compatible with industrial exploration? There is no simple answer. Some think these activities can be quite compatible if the oligarchic model of the Russian economy is changed; others say it is possible to minimize negative impacts through preventive measures to protect the environment and the equitable allocation of profits within the local communities. The proposed ESPO pipeline project along the northern shore of Lake Baikal trained the spotlight on a whole range of problems, not only the legal rights of northern indigenous peoples. This project has also shown how flexible Russian legislation can be under the influence of powerful administrative resources (Sirina and Fondahl 2006; Spiridonov 2006).

Today, considerable experience has been accumulated when it comes to interaction between the indigenous peoples of the North, industrial ventures, the federal government, ethnologists and non-governmental organizations. The most recent initiative of the oil company TNK-BP to conduct an independent expert assessment of the pipeline corridors with Kovykta Gas Condensate Deposit shows that companies have become seriously concerned about their image and the ecological component of their activities in Russia.[8] Why did TNK-BP put forward this unprecedented initiative? An independent expert assessment that had been done in 2007 (Sirina et al. 2008)[9] was not necessarily needed in those times of industrial project development. The initiative was taken because of problems with a licence on the Kovykta gas deposit, which was finally sold by TNK-BP to Gasprom (Mironova 2007).

One can not but see that ecological and socio-cultural issues, including issues of northern indigenous peoples, are quite often used as the means of solving internal company problems or political goals. However, this situation has created an interesting experience of conducting preliminary independent expert assessment. The lessons from this experience should be used to promote more harmonic relations between industrial companies, indigenous peoples of the northern regions of Russia and the Russian Federation.

NOTES

1. See Arktinen Keskus Artic Centre, [http://www.arcticcentre.org/?deptid=25427] [consulted 9 February 2009].

2. The new, third 'northern' pipeline route is called "the expanded ESPO pipeline route". Construction was started in 2006 from Ust'-Kut in Irkutsk province to Skovorodino in Amur province through a territory of the Yakutia republic. The length of this new line would be 2,757 km. Up to 2015, the pipeline would move forty million tons of crude oil per year.

3. The results have been published in Russian and in English (Sirina and Fonahl 2 006; Fondahl and Sirina 2006; Fondahl and Sirina 2006a).

4. The surveys were conducted among 127 people (twenty-four percent of the adult population) in the villages of Kholodnaya, Dushkachan and Uoyan. The respondents included mostly Evenkis but other nationalities as well.

5. Comment made by an Evenki woman in her forties at Kholodnaya village, July 2005.

6. Comment made by an Evenki male in his forties at Kholodnaya village, July 2005.

7. See also [http://www.council.gov.ru/files/journalsf/item/20070201092953.pdf] [consulted 9 February 2009].

8. See [http://www.tnk-bp.com] [consulted 9 February 2009].

9. The expert assessment is devoted to ethno-cultural issues. The rest of the report, concerning ecological and geopolitical issues, can be found on the TNK-BP website.

REFERENCES

Bobylev, S. N. July 2006. "Energeticheskaya bezopasnost' i ecologicheskaya ustoichivost." *Economicheskoe obozrenie* 4: 57–60.

Bradshaw, M. 2005. "Kompaniya zashchitnikov okryzhayushchei sredy protiv proekta Sakhalin-2." *Otchet po neftegazovym rasrabotkam Tikhookeanskogo poberezh'ya Rossii*, 3.

ENSINOR. 2007. *Environmental and Social Impacts of Industrialization in Northern Russia*. Project website. [http://www.arcticcentre.org/?deptid=25427].

Fondahl G. et al. 2001. "Native 'Land Claims,' Russian Style." *The Canadian Geographer* 45: 4: 545–561.

Fondahl, G., and A. Sirina. 2006a. "Oil Pipeline Development and Indigenous Rights in Eastern Siberia." *Indigenous Affairs*, 2–3: 58–67.

———. 2006. "Rights and Risks: Evenki Concerns Regarding the Proposed Eastern Siberia-Pacific Ocean Pipeline." *Sibirica. Interdisciplinary Journal of Siberian Studies* 5: 2: 115–138.

Konstitutsia. 12 December 1993. Konstitutsia Rossiskoi Federatsii.

Kryazhkov, V. A. 2005. "Status korennukh malochislennukh narodov Rossii." *Pravovye akty*, 3.

Marchinin V. V. and I. V. Udalova. 2002. Traditsionnoe khozyastvo narodov severa i neftegazovyi kompleks. Sotsiologicheskoe issledovanie v Khanty-Mansiiskom avtonomnom okruge. Novosibirsk:Nauka

Messhtyb, N., and P. Kankapaa. 2005. "Social Impact Assessment of the Oil Marine Transportation in Nenets Autonomous District." Environmental Protection and Management System for the Arctic. Social Impact. Arctic Center, University of Lapland. GROWTH Project GRD2-2000-30112 "ARCOP" D4.1.4.1–3.

Mironova, Yu. 25 June 2007. "Britantsy otdali sibirskii gas. Kovyktinskoe mestorozhdenie snova prinadlezhit Rossii." *Izvestia*, 8.

Mis'kova, Ö. V. 2005. "Fol'klor i kino. Problema posrednichestva v etnografich-eskom dialoge // V poiskakh sebya. Narody Severa i Sibiri v postsovets-kich transformatsiaykh." M.: Nauka, 108–154.

Murashko, O. A. 2004. "Zashchita iskonnoi sredy obitaniya i traditsionnogo obraza zhizni korennych malochislennuch narodov Severa, Sibiri i Dal'nego Vostoka Rossiskoi Federatsii: vozmozhnosti regional'nogo zakon-odatel'stva." M.: AKMNSSiDV.

Murashko, O. A., ed. 2002. "Opyt provedeniya etnologicheskoi ekspertizy. Otsenka potentsial'nogo vozdeistviya programmy OAO 'Gazprom' poiskovo-razvedochnych rabot v akvatoriach Obskoi i Tazovskoi gub na komponenty ustoichivogo razvitia etnicheskich grupp malochislennych narodov Severa." M.: Radynitsa.

Novikova, N. I., and Yu A. Yakel'. 2006. "Sudebnaya zaschita prava na traditsionnoe prirodopol'zovanie: antropologo-pravovye aspecty" M.: IEA RAS (Issledovania po prikladnoi i neotlozhnoi etnologii. No. 189).

Nuttall, M., and K. Wessendorf, eds. 2006. "Arctic Oil and Gas Development." *Indigenous Affairs*, 2–3.

Ob ob'ektach. 25 June 2002. "Ob ob'ektach kul'turnogo naslediya (pamyatnikach istorii i kul'tury) narodov Rossiskoi Federatsii." *Federal'nyi zakon*, No. 73-FZ.

Ob obshchich. 20 July 2000. "Ob obshchich printsipakh organizatsii obshchin korennukh malochislennuch narodov Severa, Sibiri i Dal'nego Vostoka Rossiskoi Federatsii." *Federal'nyi zakon*, No. 104-FZ.

O garantiach. 30 April 1999. "O garantiach prav korennych malochislennych narodov Rossiskoi Federatsii". *Federal'nyi zakon*, No. 82-FZ.

O territoriach. 7 May 2001 "O Territoriaych traditsionnogo prirodopol'zovaniya korennuch malochislennuch narodov Severa, Sibiri i Dal'nego Vostoka Rossiskoi Federatsii." *Federal'nyi zakon*, No. 49-FZ.

Roon, T. 2006. "Globalization of Sakhalin's Oil Industry: Partnership or Conflict? A Reflection on the *Etnologicheskaia Ekspertiza*." *Sibirica* 5: 2: 95–114.

Rumyantsev, N. A. 1998. "Khozyastvo evenkov Yuzhnoi Yakutii: sostoyanie, problemy // Narody Severa: puti, problemy razvitiya." Neryungri, 47–51.

Sila nefti I gaza // Pro et Contra. 2006. 2–3: 6–104.

Sirina, A. A. 2004. "Khozyastvo i sotsial'naya sfera // Sovremennoe polozhenie i perspectivy razvitiya malochislennych narodov Severa, Sibiri i Dal'nego Vostoka." Nezavisimyi exspertnyi doklad. M.: IEA RAN, 54–76.

Sirina, A. A. et al. 2008. "Gaz na export: etnokul'turnye problemy transportirovki." M.: IEA RAS (Issledovaniya po prikladnoi I neotlozhnoi etnologii. No. 205).

Sirina, A. A., and G. Fondahl. 2008. "Prizrak nefteprovoda na severe Baikala." *Etnograficheskoe Obozrenie*, 3: 60–70.

———. 2006. "Evenki Severnogo Pribaikal'ya i proekt stroitel'stva nefteprovoda Vostochnaya Sibir'—Tikhii okean." M.: IEA RAS. (Issledovaniya po prikladnoi i neotlozhnoi etnologii. No. 186).

Sirina, A. A., A. A. Yarlykapov and D. A. Funk. 2008. "Antropologia doby-vayushchei promushlennosti." *Etnograficheskoe Obozrenie*, Special Issue "Ecologiya, neft', kul'tura," 3: 3–5.

Sokolova, Z. P., and V. V. Stepanov. 2007. "Korennye malochislennye narody Severa. Dinamika chislennosti po dannym perepisei naseleniya." *Etnograficheskoe Obozrenie* 5: 75–95.

Spiridonov, V. 2006. "Large-Scale Hydrocarbon-Related Industrial Projects in Russia's Coastal Regions: The Risks Arising from the Absence of Strategic Environmental Assessment." *Sibirica* 5: 2: 43–76.

Stammler, F., and B. Forbes. 2006. "Oil and Gas Development in Western Siberia and Timan-Pechora." *Indigenous Affairs* 2–3: 48–57.

Stammler, F., and E. Wilson. Autumn 2006. "Dialogue for Development: An Exploration of Relations between Oil and Gas Companies, Communities, and the State." *Sibirica*, 5: 2: 1–42.

Stepanov, V., ed. 1999. *Metody etnologicheskoi ekspertizy*. M.: IEA RAN.

Tishkov, V. A. 2004. "Vvedenie // Sovremennoe polozhenie i perspectivy razvitiya malochislennych narodov Severa, Sibiri i Dal'nego Vostoka." Nezavisimyi exspertnyi doklad. M.: Izd-vo SO RAN, 5–12.

Trushkin, V. V., and S. G. Shapkhaev. 2003. *Metodicheskoe posobie po otsenke obshchestvennoi effectivnosti investitsionnych proektov*. Ulan-Ude: Respublikanskaya tipografiya.

Wilson, E., and K. Swiderska. 2008. "Gornodobuvayuschaya promushlennost' i korennye narody v Rossii: regulirovanie, uchastie i rol' antropologov." *Etnograficheskoe Obozrenie*, 3: 17–28.

Yakutia trebuet. 2007. "Yakutia trebuet soblyudenia zakonnosti pri realizatsii proekta truboprovodnoi sistemy "Vostochnaia Sibir'-Tikhii okean" na ee territorii"// Mir korennych narodov. *Zhivaya Arctica* 20: 95–100

Zakluchenie. February 2002. "Zakluchenie expertnoi komissii obshchestvennoi ecologicheskoi ekspertizy materialov proekta 'Obosnovanie investitsii stroitel'stva nefteprovoda Rossiya-Kitai OAO 'NK YuKOS' Orlinga. Informatsionnyi vestnik, No. 3.

Zen'ko, M. A. 2001. "Sovremennyi Yamal: etnoecologicheskie i etnosocial'nye problemy." M.: IEA RAS (Issledovaniya po prikladnoi i neotlozhnoi etnologii. No. 139).

Afterword

The Intersection of Northern and National Policies

Elana Wilson Rowe

T his brief afterword aims to pull together some of the key trends identified in the preceding chapters and link them with overall features of Russian domestic and foreign policy. In particular, impacts from the policies and political directions forwarded under the presidencies of Vladmir Putin (2000–2004; 2004–2008) are examined. The extent to which the Russian North can be understood as 'opened' or 'closed' is then taken up. The afterword then concludes by speculating on how increased geopolitical attention on the North—its resources, its unresolved maritime claims, its military history and its changing physical environment—may shape Russian policy in the medium term.

There have been a plethora of political and economic changes in the transition from a Yeltsin to a Putin presidency.[1] Today, we see an overall continuation of established policies under President Dmitry Medvedev, with Putin playing an equally important role in Russian politics as prime minister. There are a few key ideas and changes that have been implemented in the past eight years that have had a bearing on Russia's northern politics, ideas that previous chapters in this book have taken up, directly and indirectly.[2] These include (i) pragmatism and assertively pursuing Russia's interests in foreign policy; (ii) economic modernization and (iii) recentralization of authority from the regions to the federal centre.

When it comes to foreign policy, Putin's presidencies were marked initially by a 'pragmatic turn' and later by an increasing assertiveness supported by rising revenues from oil and gas (see Baev in this book for how such a policy has played out in the North; Sakwa 2004; Lo 2003;

Trenin and Lo 2005). In part, this meant the pronounced marginaliza-
tion of a debate about ideological orientation that preoccupied the post-
Soviet leadership under Boris Yeltsin—the question of whether Russia
'belongs' in the West, the East or somewhere in between. Russia's foreign policy today should not be understood as either pro-Western or
anti-Western—in many ways, Russian foreign policy has been de-ideol-
ogized in relationship to the traditional East/West dichotomy (Trenin
and Lo 2005; Secrieru 2006).

While Putin certainly shared the aim of his predecessors of restoring
Russia's great-power status, his first presidential term suggested that this
pursuit was not to be at the expense of key relationships with the West
(Tysgankov 2006). His second term, however, has indicated a growing
realization that Russia can afford to be more assertive and less clearly
aligned at the international level without any immediate repercussions.
This trend has been marked by a growing emphasis (especially in
2004–2007) on the idea of Russia as a 'sovereign democracy,' not to be
judged by foreign standards, and as an 'energy superpower,' particularly in relationship to a Europe largely dependent on Russian gas exports.[3]
However, in relationship to the North, as Baev notes in this book,
Russian leaders and civil servants have remained diplomatic and legally
minded in practice when it comes to important questions, like the delin-
eation of the northern continental shelf. This is despite the symbolic
actions and nationalistic political rhetoric corresponding to the more
assertive turn, mentioned above and examined in detail in Chapter Two.

In the absence of an ideological agenda in favour of, or opposing,
the 'West,' Putin has attempted to reset the agenda in positive terms,
arguing about Russia's interests rather than casting its foreign-policy
stances as efforts to thwart Western plans or influence (Lo 2003: 74–75).
This focus on interests has mixed consequences for northern politics.
Hønneland's chapter on international cooperation in the North illustrates that increased attention within the Russian political establishment
towards 'interests' overall and the absence of more overarching or prin-
cipled commitments to international cooperation has evoked suspicion
about the motivations of other Arctic states. For example, through this
lens, efforts like the Barents cooperation can be seen simply as vehicles
through which other Western states are seeking to achieve their own
interests, at the expense of Russia.

The emphasis on Russia's immediate interests may also deflect
Russian political attention from pressing northern issues that do not top

the federal agenda overall. In their chapters, Øverland, Sirina and Heleniak point to the socio-economic problems facing the indigenous and nonindigenous residents of the Russian North, in large part linked to the collapse of the Soviet planned economy. In terms of indigenous peoples' rights, while existing legislation provides a good point of departure for addressing some of these problems, the protection of indigenous peoples' rights and livelihoods is hampered by an absence of political will and perhaps the capacity to ensure proper domestic implementation. Øverland argues that it is important for Russia to be involved in the development of standards and regimes relating to indigenous peoples at the international level, in part because Russian definitions of indigenousness differ to an extent from the dominant paradigm drawn from a North American context.[4] If the primary emphasis in foreign policy is on seeking advantage according to the geopolitical interests of the day, one can imagine that such long-term regime development is unlikely to garner much political commitment.

Putin's pursuit of restoring Russia's great-power status also differed from his post-Soviet predecessor in his acknowledgement that such status would have to be regained through deeds—not simply asserted. Putin, particularly in his first presidential term, emphasized the task of economic modernization and often referred to the economic nature of power in the contemporary world. Likewise, the first years of his second presidential term were marked by accelerated efforts to build a strong federal centre with the presidential administration at its core and seek ways to build and exercise Russia's economic soft power (Tysgankov 2005). In light of this focus on economic modernization, ZumBrunnen (this book), as well as many other scholars examining Russia's participation in the Kyoto Protocol regime, have emphasized the importance of linking climate compliance to Russia's desire to modernize, in particular the effort to become more energy efficient on the domestic front. The desire to achieve profits—even if only in the short term—was also behind Moscow's push towards nationalizing the oil industry and ensuring that the gas industry remained primarily in state hands (see Moe and Wilson Rowe, this book). Given the weakly institutionalized tax structure and corrupt and nontransparent business environment in Russia, direct state ownership was seen as the most foolproof way of ensuring the state profited from Russia's natural resource wealth, much of which lies in the North.

In thinking about policy change in the North, it is also essential to take into consideration the effects of Putin's recentralization of power in northern regions. The early days of the post-Soviet period were marked by a pronounced decentralization, with many former centrally held competencies being devolved to regional governments. Decentralization was replaced with recentralization after the change of presidency in 1999–2000. Putin's goal was to strengthen the executive vertical and ensure that regional profits flowed into federal coffers and that federal policy was implemented. The reduction of regional power introduced difficulties into existing forms of cross-border cooperation (see Hønneland's contribution to the book on the Barents and other forms of bilateral cooperation) that often involved regional, rather than solely central, governments and actors.

This recentralization necessitated reorganizing the bureaucracy overall and introduced waves of attempted bureaucratic reform that continue today.[5] Such reorganization has disrupted established connections for cross-border cooperation on environmental issues, as Hønneland asserts and, as Jørgensen argues in relation to the fisheries sector, has repeatedly swallowed time and administrative resources that could have been usefully applied to other challenges. It also remains unclear whether such reforms have resulted in a governmental structure capable of handling the challenges facing Russia, not least in the North. Jørgensen, in her chapter on fisheries, notes that the sector is widely considered "inefficient, criminalized and unreformable" and that there are continued struggles to establish a stable legal and institutional framework for the sector, primarily because of a lack of consensus between key players on basic management principles. Moe and Wilson Rowe, in looking at Russian strategy towards offshore petroleum development, raise the question of whether identifying oil and gas as a strategic geopolitically important sector actually is resulting in strategic long-term policy-thinking.

This package of changing political orientations described above, among others, has shaped northern policy in a number of ways. One way of describing Russia's evolving relationship with the North, both within and outside of its borders in light of these changes, is as a tension between the securitization of northern space and the nationalization of northern resources and more international and market-driven orientations. While the social and environmental challenges inherited from the Soviet Union have necessitated the involvement of foreign actors and financial contributions, the strategic significance of natural resources and the more assertive foreign policy built upon these energy resources seem to be pulling in the direction of an increasingly closed and securitized North.

One vivid example of this 'closing' of the Russian North comes from the Arctic Military Environmental Cooperation (AMEC), established by the military authorities of Norway, Russia and the United States in 1996. AMEC focused on spent nuclear fuel containment and remediation of radioactive pollution in the North, with particular attention paid to the Northern Fleet in northwest Russia and enhancing Russian capacities for handling radioactive waste. In February 2007 a Norwegian representative within the AMEC project, Ingjerd Kroken, was denied entry to Russia on a routine work visit. The Russian Ministry of Foreign Affairs later stated that Kroken had been engaged in illegal information-gathering, even though all of AMEC's work had been carried out either on request from or in agreement with the Russian Northern Fleet and other relevant authorities.[6] This rejection of the AMEC representative sent a signal of changing attitudes in Russian political and security circles towards both being a recipient of 'aid' via capacity-building projects and the extent to which the Russian North (the military North in particular) is to be open to other actors and multilateral activities. Hønneland's chapter illustrates other examples of the ways in which environmental cooperation has been problematized along these lines.

As Baev suggests in his chapter, the securitization of a complex agenda of northern problems that would be best tackled through international cooperation and involvement of civil society and local populations does not bode well for the development and implementation of appropriate policy measures. On the other hand, that northern politics are increasingly geopoliticized—due to the increasing geopolitical attention paid to the North, as well as the clear economic importance of the region—can be seen to have a bright side for international interaction. That the North is clearly established as intertwined with Russia's international political and economic interests may serve to keep northern issues on the Russian federal agenda, where political interest and involvement have been lacking (see Wilson Rowe 2009). As Oldfield, Kouzmina and Shaw (2003) note, there is an overall low priority assigned by Russian decision-makers to environmental issues, particularly when environmental concerns would interfere with other pressing political-economic interests. Much of the northern cooperation thus far

has been structured around such environmental and scientific cooperation and that the North now has also been assigned a 'high political' significance may serve to attract and sustain Russian political interest and
involvement.

NOTES

1. It is also important to note that referring to policies as 'Putin policies' is not meant to
   imply that Putin himself has been the sole decision-maker. In fact, much of Putin's
   authority is best understood as resulting from a skill in balancing and coordinating
   the opinions and positions of the political elite.
2. See the Introduction to this book and Blakkisrud (2006) for a discussion of changes
   made within northern policy.
3. It seems that these particular notions invoked to signal Russia's increasing assertiveness did not achieve the desired results, in that both the 'sovereign democracy' and
   'energy superpower' discourses have nearly disappeared from the political discourse
   of the Putin-Medvedev political tandem.
4. For more on these differing definitions, see Wilson (2007).
5. The need for reducing the size and complexity and increasing the efficiency of the
   bureaucracy is frequently mentioned by President Medvedev, most recently in his
   5 November 2008 Address to the Federal Assembly, [http://www.kremlin.ru/eng/
   speeches/2008/11/05/2144_type70029type82917type127286_208836.shtml] [consult-
   ed 2 December 2008].
6. See Digges (2007) for an overview of this incident and Rowe (2007) for an analysis (in
   Norwegian).

REFERENCES

Blakkisrud, Helge. 2006. "What's to Be Done with the North?" In *Tackling Space:
Federal Politics and the Russian North*, ed. Helge Blakkisrud and Geir
Hønneland. Lanham, MD: University Press of America.

Digges, Charles. 18 April 2007. "Norwegian AMEC Advisor's Expulsion from
Russia Gets Murky as Local Media Hint at Espionage." [http://www
.bellona.com/articles/articles_2007/kroken_spy] [consulted 1 July 2008].

Lo, Bobo. 2003. *Vladimir Putin and the Evolution of Russian Foreign Policy*. London:
Wiley-Blackwell.

Oldfield, Jonathan D., Anna Kouzmina and Denis J. B. Shaw. 2003. "Russia's
Involvement in the International Environmental Process: A Research
Report." *Eurasian Geography and Economics* 44: 2: 157–168.

Rowe, Lars. 14 May 2007. "Den russiske pendelen svinger" (The Russian pendulum swings). *Dagbladet*. [http://www.dagbladet.no/kultur/2007/05/14/500566.html].

Sakwa, Richard. 2004. *Putin: Russia's Choice*. London: Routledge.

Secrieru, Stanislav. November 2006. *Russia's Quest for Strategic Identity*. NATO Defence College Occasional Paper.

Trenin, Dmitry, and Bobo Lo. 2005. *The Landscape of Russian Foreign Policy Decision-Making*. Moscow: Carnegie Moscow Centre. [http://www.carnegie.ru].

Tysgankov, Andrei. 2006. *Russia's Foreign Policy: Change and Continuity in National Identity*. Lanham, MD: Rowman & Littlefield.

——. 2005. "Vladimir Putin's Vision of Russia as a Normal Great Power." *Post-Soviet Affairs* 21: 2: 132–158.

Wilson, Elana. 2007. "Indigenousness and the Mobility of Knowledge: Promoting Canadian Governance Practices in the Russian North." *Sibirica* 6: 2: 26–50.

Wilson Rowe, E. 2009. "Russian Regional Multilateralism: The Case of the Arctic Council." In *The Multilateral Dimension of Russian Foreign Policy*, ed. Elana Wilson Rowe and Stina Torjesen. London: Routledge.

Index

A

Afghanistan, 19
Agranat, G.A., 158
Aleksandrov, S., 24
Aleshkovski, I., 140, 144
Aliutors (indigenous people), 178
Anderson, L.G., 51n7
Andres, R.J., 57, 62
Anisimov, O.A., 66, 68
Apoka, I.P., 190
Arbatov, A., 29n4
Arctic Council, 6
Arctic Military Environmental
    Cooperation (AMEC), 43–44, 207
Arctic Monitoring and Assessment
    Programme (AMAP), 9
Arkhangel'sk Oblast, 132, 136, 137
Armstrong, T., 151–152
Australia, 10, 29n10, 72, 191
Avdeeva, T.G., 72, 73, 76

B

Baev, P., 2, 7, 8, 9, 10, 17–30, 36, 203,
    207
Ball, J., 118
ballistic missile submarines (SSBNs),
    23, 24
Balzer, H., 109
Barabanov, M., 30n20
Barents Euro-Arctic Council (BEAC),
    36
Barents Euro-Arctic Region (BEAR), 6,
    35–51

- development and objectives,
    36–38
- environmental protection, 42–44
- fisheries management, 38–42
- Russian developments and priori-
    ties, 44–48
Barents Health Program, 37–38
Barents Initiative, 17
Barents Sea, 20, 23, 26, 35, 36, 38–39,
    40–41, 42, 44, 46, 47, 48, 49, 56, 88,
    112, 117, 119. *See also* Barents Euro-
    Arctic Region (BEAR)
Belarus, 145, 146
Bellona Foundation, 30n23
Belolutskaia, M.A., 68
bilateral cooperation, 35–52
Bitz, C.M., 65
Blakkisrud, H., 2, 3, 4, 149, 153, 158,
    172, 174, 175, 178, 179, 180n1,
    181n8, 208n2
Bobylev, S.N., 198
Boden, T.A., 57, 62
Bogdanchikov, S., 26, 30n22, 122
Bogoyavlenskiy, D., 174, 175, 178,
    183n17
Bohn, T.J., 69
Bond, A.R., 151
Bondarenko, A., 29n15
Borgerson, S., 7, 30n24
Bradshaw, M., 111, 198
Bravo, M., 10
British RAF (Royal Air Force), 22
Buryatia (Buryat Republic), 3, 151

Bush, G.W., 71, 72

C

Canada, 2, 18, 36, 66–67, 134, 165, 191
carbon credits, 8, 75–76, 78, 79. *See also* greenhouse gases (GHGs)
carbon dioxide, 58–59, 62, 67–68
Chilingarov, A., 6, 10
China, 75, 118, 122, 123
Chugunov, D., 114
Chukotka Autonomous Okrug, 2, 3, 129, 132, 136, 137, 140, 143, 145, 147, 151, 190
Clean Development Mechanism (CDM), 72, 75
climate change, 5, 7, 8, 17, 53–80
climate contrarians, 70–71
- empirical assessment of, 54–58
- future climate policy, 79–80
- IPCC A1B 'business as usual' assumptions, 63–65
- Kyoto Protocol, 8, 11, 54, 58, 62, 70–80, 205
- ocean-atmosphere CO_2 exchange in the Arctic, 68
- permafrost melting, 63, 68–70, 74
- Russian GHG emission trends, 58–62
ClimateScienceWatch, 71
Cold War, 1, 5, 18, 35, 37, 46, 50
Congress of Karelians, 168
Constitution of 1993, 4, 170–171, 178, 191–192
Conventional Forces in Europe (CFE), 20
Council of Baltic Sea States, 6
Crate, S., 153
Crimean War, 18
cross-border cooperation, 35–52
Czech Republic, 19

D

Dagestan, Republic of, 169, 170, 182n8
Davydov, D., 100
Denisov, A., 5
Denmark, 36, 42
Digges, C., 30n23, 208n6

domestic policy, 2–5, 76, 151–157, 203–208
Dore, A.G., 130
Dyachenko, V., 150

E

Eastern Siberian-Pacific Ocean (ESPO) pipeline project, 12, 188, 194–197, 198
Elder, M., 77, 79, 80, 117
Entsy (indigenous people), 178
Environmental and Social Impacts of Industrialization in Northern Russia (ENSINOR), 188
environmental impact assessments (EIAs), 195, 197
environmental protection, 42–44
European Human Rights Court, 176
Evenki Autonomous Okrug, 3, 132, 136, 137, 192
Evenki (indigenous people), 192, 195–197
ExxonMobil, 71, 123

F

Farizova, S., 25
Federal Border Service, 97
Federal Fisheries Agency, 92–93, 97, 101
Federal Service for Ecological, Technological and Nuclear Surveillance (Rostekhnadzor), 45
Federal Service for Hydrometeorology and Environmental Monitoring (Rosgidromet), 45–46
Federal Service for Veterinary and Phytosanitary Control, 93, 96, 97, 104n10
Federal Service of Surveillance in Ecology and Resource Use (Rosprirodnadzor), 45
Feifer, G., 69
Ferrero-Waldner, 17
Field, C.B., 69
Finland, 20, 35, 36, 44, 165
Fischer, P.A., 158
Fisheries Agency, 95

Fisheries Committee, 92
fisheries management, 87–104
 - bilateral cooperation with
   Norway, 38–42
 - developments in 2007-2008,
   94–101
 - quota auctions, 93, 98, 103n4
 - Soviet legacy, 88–89
 - total allowable catches (TAC),
   40–41, 42
Fondahl, G., 187, 192, 195, 196, 197,
   198, 199n3
Forbes, B., 187, 191, 192
foreign direct investment (FDI), 76, 77
foreign policy, 26, 44, 113, 203–208
Former Soviet Union (FSU), 2–3, 18,
   45, 108, 131
 - bilateral cooperation with
   Norway on fisheries management,
   39–41
 - indigenous peoples and, 175,
   189–190
 - labour policy, 151–153, 154
 - maritime claims, 9–10
 - Navy, 18, 19, 23, 24
 - population migration and settlement patterns, 129, 131–134
Fradkov, Mikhail, 95
France, 36
Frauenfeld, O.W., 68
Funk, D.A., 187

G
Gaddy, C.G., 141, 152
Gazprom, 9, 26, 108, 109, 110, 111,
   112, 116, 117, 118–119, 120–123, 199
gender ratios, 147–148
General Circulation Models (GCMs),
   55–57, 63–65, 66
Gerber, T.P., 134, 136, 137, 139, 144, 147
Germany, 36
Giles, K., 129
Glebov, P., 168
Global Partnership against the Spread
   of Weapons and Materials of Mass
   Destruction, 43
global warming. See climate change

Goble, P., 4
Golts, A., 22, 30n23
Gorbachev, Mikhail, 42–43
Gordeev, Aleksey, 95, 96
Gorodnitsky, A., 30n21
Goskomsever, 3, 153, 154, 156, 158
Gray, P.A., 140, 143, 147
Greeland ice sheet, 55, 66
Green Investment Schemes, 74
greenhouse gases (GHGs), 54, 73. See
   also climate change; Kyoto Protocol
 - carbon credits, 8, 75–76, 78, 79
 - IPCC A1B 'business as usual'
   assumptions, 63–65
 - IPCC guidelines, 76, 77–78
 - permafrost melting, 69
 - Russian emission trends, 57–62
Grigor'ev, M., 115
Grubb, M., 70, 72, 73, 76
Gulag system, 151

H
Hansen, J., 71
Harper, T., 71
Harrington, C., 29n9
Hassner, P., 29n4
Heartland Institute, 71
Heleniak, T., 3, 11, 18, 129–159, 205
Henry, L.A., 73
Hill, F., 141, 152
Holdsworth, N., 29n7
Holland, M.M., 65
Hønneland, G., 4, 5, 6, 10, 28n1, 35–51,
   88, 93, 94, 97, 103n3, 104n8, 149,
   158, 171
Huskey, L., 150
hydrocarbons, 2, 3, 8, 9, 10, 11, 17,
   25–28, 109, 110, 111, 115, 119

I
Iceland, 36
Ilyasov, Stanislav, 95
India, 75
indigenous peoples/indigenous
   rights, 5, 37, 165–185
 - Constitution of 1993, 170–171,
   191–192

- ESPO pipeline assessment, 194–197
- guarantees of rights, 172–174, 191
- 'indigenousness' defined, 168–170, 188

International Labour Organization (ILO) Convention 169, 166–167
- oil and gas development and, 187–202
- organization of indigenous communities, 174
- policies toward, 177–180, 190–194
- Soviet impact on, 189–190
- statistics, 188–189
- territories of traditional nature use, 175–177, 191, 192–194

Instanes, A., 68
Institute, N.E., 144, 147, 155, 157
Intergovernmental Panel on Climate Change (IPCC), 55, 69, 72, 78
- A1B 'business as usual' assumptions, 63–65
- GHG guidelines, 76, 77
International Committee on the Elimination of Racial Discrimination (CERD), 182n3
International Council for the Exploration of the Sea (ICES), 39, 40, 41, 42, 46–47, 48, 49
international emissions trading (IET), 72, 75, 79
International Labour Organization (ILO) Convention 169, 166–167, 172–174, 180, 180n2
International Polar Year (IPY), 6
Ionstev, V., 140, 144
Irkutsk Oblast, 3, 192, 197
Italy, 36
Ivanov, S., 26
Ivanova, M., 88–89, 103n3, 104n8
Izrael, Yuri, 70

J

Janhunen, J., 169
Japan, 36, 89
Jensen, M., 167, 173
Joint Implementation (JI) projects, 73, 75, 76, 77

Joint Norwegian-Russian Commission for Nuclear Safety, 49
Joint Norwegian-(Soviet)/Russian Commission on Environmental Protection, 42, 44, 46, 49, 171
Joint Norwegian-(Soviet/)Russian Fisheries Commission, 39–40, 41, 46, 48
Jørgensen, A.K., 11, 87–104, 112, 171
Joughin, I., 66

K

Kamchatka Oblast, 118, 132, 136, 137, 140, 143
Kanagaratnam, P., 66
Kane, I., 53
Kankapaa, P., 187
Kara Sea, 43, 111, 117, 119, 120
Karaganov, S., 29n5
Karas, J., 70, 72, 73, 76
Karelian Republic, 36, 88, 132, 136, 137, 147, 168
Kazakhstan, 21
Kereks (indigenous people), 178
Keskitalo, E.C.H., 5, 50n3
Khanty-Mansi Autonomous Okrug, 3, 4, 129, 132, 136, 137, 138, 140, 142, 143, 145, 146, 178, 179, 191, 192
Kharyuchi, S.N., 175, 176
Khrushchev, Nikita, 30n17
Khrustalev, L.N., 68
Kirillov, D., 119
Kirkenes Declaration (1993), 36
Kiselev, A.A., 169
Kiseleva, T.A., 169
Kola Peninsula, 18, 27, 35–51
Kolesnikov, A., 29n11
Koltunova, O., 104n7
Komi Republic, 3, 36, 132, 136, 137, 143, 151, 168
Korea, 89
Korean National Oil Company, 125n6
Korppoo, A., 70, 72, 73, 76
Koryak Autonomous Okrug, 132, 136, 137, 147, 176
Kotlyakov, V.M., 158
Kouzmina, A., 207

Kovykta Gas Condensate Deposit, 199
Kramnik, I., 8
Krayniy, Andrey, 95, 97–99, 100,
    101–102, 103
Kristensen, H., 24
Kroken, I., 207
Kryazhkov, V.A., 177
Kryukov, V., 3, 4
Kyoto Protocol, 8, 11, 54, 58, 62,
    70–80, 205

L

labour policy, 151–157
    - evolution of northern labour poli-
      cy, 151–157
    - International Labour Organization
      (ILO) Convention 169, 166–167,
      172–174, 180, 180n2
    - regions in recession and resur-
      gence, 149–151
Land Code, 172, 175, 177, 179
Lavrov, C.A., 68
Lavrov, Sergei, 10
Law on Ecological Expert Review
    (1995), 194
Law on Objects (Monuments of
    History and Culture) of Cultural
    Heritage (2002), 194
Ledeneva, L., 97
Lefebvre, S., 29n8
Leningrad Military District, 20
Lesikhina, N., 30n23
Letkova, V., 53
Levanevsky, S., 23
liquified natural gas (LNG), 112, 118,
    120
Litovkin, V., 20, 21
Lizun, V., 29n11
Lo, B., 12n6, 203, 204
Lomonosov Ridge, 10, 25
Long-Range Aviation, 19, 21–23
Lukin, M., 30n20
Lukoil, 110
Luzin, G.P., 151

M

Magadan Oblast, 132, 136, 137, 140,
    143, 145, 151, 190

Makhlin, M., 115
Maleva, T., 155
Manning, M., 55
Mansoor, A., 133, 136, 138
maritime claims, 9–10, 18, 203
Markhinin, V.V., 187
Marland, G., 57, 62
Masshtyb, N., 187
Matveeva, K., 179
McCannon, J., 29n16
McDonald, G.M., 69
McGuinness, D.L., 148
Medetsky, A., 116
Medvedev, Dmitry, 19, 25, 96, 121,
    123, 124, 203, 208
Medvedev, S., 29n5
Melnikov, Vladimir, 70
Mendeleev Ridge, 10, 25
Mentyukova, S., 90, 98, 100, 104n14
methane hydrates, 69
migration, 129–159
    - characteristics of northern
      migrants and their impact on the
      Far North, 146–148
    - by destination, 137–144
    - migration/resettlement assistance
      programs, 155–157
    - mobility of northern populations
      and place-specific social capital,
      144–146
    - regional patterns, 134–137
Mikhailova, T., 129, 134
military, Russian, 7–8, 17–30
    - Arctic hydrocarbons, 25–28
    - Long-Range Aviation, 21–23
    - Northern Fleet, 23–25, 27, 35, 207
    - northern geopolitics, 19–21
Milov, V., 30n21
Ministry of Agriculture, 92, 95–96
Ministry of Economic Development
    and Trade, 3, 115, 179
Ministry of Energy and Industry, 115
Ministry of Finance, 5, 115
Ministry of Natural Resources, 45, 46,
    76, 111, 112, 115, 116, 121
Ministry of Trade and Economic
    Development, 91, 93

Mironova, J., 96
Mironova, Y., 199
Mirovitskaya, N., 51n7
Mis'kova, Ö.V., 193
Moe, A., 3, 4, 5, 9, 11, 27, 72, 73,
    107–125, 187, 206
Moore, E.G., 148
Morehouse, T.A., 150
Moshkin, M., 26
Multilateral Nuclear Environmental
    Program in the Russian Federation,
    43
Murashko, O., 166, 167, 173, 174, 175,
    176, 177, 181n4, 183n17, 187
Murmansk Fish Combinate, 88, 90
Murmansk Oblast, 27, 36, 48, 88, 132,
    136, 137
Murmansk Trawl Fleet, 88
Murray, I., 121

N
Nakken, O., 51n7
Naumov, S., 112, 115
Naval Doctrine, 24
Nenets Autonomous Okrug, 3, 36,
    132, 137, 151, 194
Netherlands, 22, 36, 42
Neumann, I., 50n3
Nikel, N., 44
nonviable settlements, 150–151
Nordstream pipeline, 120
Norris, R., 24
North Atlantic Treaty Organization
    (NATO), 18, 19–20
North Caucasus Military District, 20
North Pole, 9, 17, 21, 29n17, 130
Northeast Atlantic Fisheries
    Commission, 39
Northern Fleet, 23–25, 27, 35, 207
northern labour policy, 151–157
Norway, 1, 2, 20, 27, 35–51, 89, 207
Norwegian Directorate of Fisheries,
    42
Norwegian-Russian Commission on
    Nuclear Safety, 43
Novikova, N.I., 171, 172, 174, 178, 179,
    189, 193

nuclear technology and safety, 10, 18,
    22, 23, 24, 27, 36, 43–44, 45, 49,
    50n2, 207
Nuttall, M., 153, 188

O
oil, gas, and minerals industries, 5, 7,
    8–9, 80, 107–127, 129
  - Gazprom and Rosneft's offshore
    strategies and interaction, 117–123
  - geopolitical significance, 108–111
  - indigenous peoples and, 187–202
  - Russian offshore strategy, 111–116
Oldfield, J., 51n10, 207
Oleinik, G., 149, 153
Oleynik, G., 4
Oroks (indigenous people), 178
Orrtung, R., 9
Osherenko, G., 168
Ovchinnikov, A., 92
Øverland, I., 7, 11–12, 165–183, 192,
    205

P
Pacific Fleet, 23, 24, 25
Parker, R., 58
Pautzke, C.G., 88
Pavlov, P.N., 167, 171, 172, 179, 180,
    182n14
Pearce, F., 69
Pechora Sea, 118, 119
permafrost melting, 63, 68–70, 74
Perovic, J., 9
Plane, D.A., 142, 144
Poland, 19, 36
pollution, 5, 43, 44, 45, 207
Portugal, 42
Pretes, M., 151
production-sharing agreements
    (PSA), 110, 114, 115, 123
Putin, Vladimir, 3, 10, 18, 19, 20, 21,
    22, 24, 26, 74, 76, 94, 95, 101–102,
    108–109, 121, 153, 171, 180, 197, 203,
    204, 205, 206

Q
Quillin, B., 133, 136, 138

R

Rasmussen, H., 167, 173
Raupach, M.R., 69
Rautio, V., 159n6
Red Cross, 3
Redman, J., 80
Rees, W.G., 68
renewable energy, 77
Ribova, L., 150
Rignot, E., 66
Rodin, I., 26
Rodnik (NGO), 176
Rogerson, P.A., 142, 144
Roon, T., 187
Rosenergo, 115
Rosgidromet, 45–46
Rosneft, 9, 26, 108, 109, 110, 116,
    117–119, 120–123
Rosprirodnadzor, 45
Rosprom, 115
Rossii, G., 151
Rostekhnadzor, 45
Round, J., 140, 150, 157
Rowe, L., 50n6, 51n8
Roy, C., 167, 173
Rumyantsev, N.A., 193
Russian Academy of Sciences'
    Institute of Climatology and
    Ecology, 70
Russian Association of Indigenous
    Peoples of the North (RAIPON),
    181n4, 190
Russian Exclusive Economic Zone
    (EEZ), 89, 97, 99, 100
Russian Federal Research Institute of
    Fisheries and Oceanography
    (VNIRO), 47–48
Russia's Institute of the Earth's
    Cryosphere, 70
Rybkin, A., 169

S

Saami (indigenous people), 37
Sakha (Yakutia) Republic, 3, 68, 132,
    136, 137, 178, 192, 193, 194, 197,
    199n2
Sakhalin Oblast, 132, 137, 194

Sakhalin projects, 27, 110, 111, 112,
    117, 118, 122, 123, 124
Sakwa, R., 203
Sample, I., 69
Schindler, D., 181n5
Schmid, R.E., 66
sea ice, 7, 55, 63, 65, 66–67, 130
Sea of Okhotsk, 117, 122
Sechin, I., 121
Secrieru, S., 204
Sergeev, O., 30n19
Sever, M., 69
Sevryba (Northfish), 88–89
Shaw, D.J.B., 207
Shirshov Institute of Oceanography,
    30n21
Shschedrunova, E., 99
Shtokman, 27, 119, 120, 121
Siberia
    - climate change, 63, 66, 68, 69
    - indigenous peoples, 146, 171, 174,
        188, 189–190, 191
    - non-renewable resources, 12, 114,
        122, 123, 187, 188, 194–197, 198
    - population patterns and migration,
        129, 134, 135, 137, 146, 147, 148
Simmons, D., 121
Sirina, A., 12, 178, 187–200, 205
Skorlygina, N., 26
Slezkine, Y., 181n5
Smith, L.C., 69, 70
Smith, M.A., 129
Sokolova, Z.P., 188, 189
Solava, 17
Sörlin, S., 10
sovereignty rights, 2, 7, 9–10, 18, 39
Soviet Ministry of the Fishing
    Industry, 47, 88
Soviet Navy, 18, 19, 23, 24
Sovkomflot, 118
Spain, 42
Spies, M., 140, 150
Spiridonov, V., 194, 197, 198
Stalin, Joseph, 18, 21, 23, 151
Stammler, F., 187, 188, 191, 192, 194
Stammler-Gossmann, A., 130, 151

State Committee for Environmental Protection, 45
State Committee for Fisheries, 47, 92, 93, 95–97, 101, 179
State Committee for North Affairs (Goskomsever), 3, 153, 154, 156, 158
State Duma's International Affairs Committee, 75
State Ecological Expert Commission, 197
Statoil, 27, 125n9, 133
Stepanov, V.V., 187, 188, 189
Stokke, O., 5, 28n1, 50n1, 50n3, 50n6, 51n7
Stoltenberg, T., 36
Strategic Aviation, 21–23
Strel'tov, Y., 1, 12n3
submarines, 23, 24, 27, 43, 44
Sulyandziga, P., 175, 176
Sundstrom, L.M., 73
Sweden, 10, 35, 36

T
Tangen, K., 73
Taylor, J.M., 70
Taymyr Autonomous Okrug, 132, 136, 137, 143
Taz (indigenous people), 178
Tennberg, M., 5, 50n3
territories of traditional nature use, 175–177, 191, 192–194
Thompson, D.W.J., 55
Thompson, N., 140, 150, 151, 152, 155, 157
Tishkov, V.A., 187, 191
Tkhsanom Territory of Traditional Nature Use, 176
TNK-BP, 110, 199
Tomsk Oblast, 3
Torjesen, S., 7
Total, 27
total allowable catches (TAC), 40–41, 42
Transneft', 118, 194, 195, 196
Tremblay, B., 65
Trenin, D., 12n6, 29n2, 204
Trutnev, Y., 112, 114
Tsyganok, A., 29n9

Tunander, O., 28n1, 50n1
Tutubalina, O.V., 68
Tuva Republic, 132, 136, 137, 140
Tykkyläinen, M., 159n6
Tysgankov, A., 204, 205
Tyumen Oblast, 179, 191

U
Udalova, I.V., 187
Ukraine, 19, 21, 145, 146
Union of Concerned Scientists, 71
United Kingdom, 22, 36, 42, 43–44
United Nations (UN)
  - Charter, 170
  - Commission on the Limits of the Continental Shelf, 9–10, 20
  - Committee on Economic, Social and Cultural Rights, 180n3
  - Convention on the Law of the Sea (UNCLOS), 7, 9–10, 20, 30, 38–39
  - Declaration on Indigenous Rights, 180n2
  - Educational, Scientific and Cultural Organization (UNESCO), 195
  - Framework Convention on Climate Change (UNFCCC), 8, 71–72, 76, 78. See also Kyoto Protocol
United Stated Geological Survey, 9
United States, 1, 9, 17–18, 19, 27, 36, 44, 69, 71, 72, 73, 75–76, 165, 191, 207

V
Vakhtin, N., 169
Varlamov, D., 111, 125n2
Varlamov, S.P., 68
Vasiliev, V.V., 151
Veletminskiy, I., 115, 125n2
Veterinary Service, 93, 96, 97, 104n10
Vinocour, J., 29n13
Vylegazhnin, A.N., 88
Vysotsky, Vladimir, 25, 30n18

W
Walter, K.M., 69
Wessendorf, K., 188
White, G., 118

Wilson Rowe, E., 1–13, 27, 107–125, 187, 188, 194, 203–208
World Climate Change Conference (2003), 70
World Trade Organization (WTO), 73, 75, 76
World Wildlife Federation, 75
Wrangel Island, 18

X

Xanthaki, A., 166, 170, 171, 172, 173–174, 179

Y

Yakel', Y.A., 189, 193
Yakut, 192
Yakutia. *See* Sakha (Yakutia) Republic

Yamal-Nenets Autonomous Okrug, 3, 27, 129, 132, 136, 137, 138, 140, 143, 145, 146, 178, 179
Yamal Peninsula, 69, 181, 193, 198
Yarlykapov, A.A., 187
Yeltsin, Boris, 3, 4, 153, 203
Young, O., 5
Yuganskneftegaz, 121
Yukos, 120, 122

Z

Zarubezhneft, 116, 125n3
Zen'ko, M.A., 193
Zhang, T., 68
Zilanov, V.K, 88
ZumBrunnen, C., 8, 11, 53–80

Composed by Lynne Mackay in Palatino 10/13

The paper used in this publication is Rolland HiTec 50 White 50 lb.

PRINTED AND BOUNDED IN CANADA